ELIE WIESEL:
MESSENGER TO ALL HUMANITY

Elie Wiesel:
Messenger to All Humanity

Robert McAfee Brown

UNIVERSITY OF NOTRE DAME PRESS
Notre Dame   London

Grateful acknowledgment is made to: Random House, Inc., for permission to quote from the following works by Elie Wiesel: *A Beggar in Jerusalem*, translated by Lily Edelman and the author, 1970. *One Generation After*, translated by Lily Edelman and the author, 1970. *Souls on Fire*, translated by Marion Wiesel, 1972. *Ani Maamin: A Song Lost and Found Again*, translated by Marion Wiesel, 1973. *The Oath*, translated by Marion Wiesel, 1973. *Zalmen, or The Madness of God*, translated by Nathan Edelman, 1974. *Messengers of God*, translated by Marion Wiesel, 1976. *A Jew Today*, translated by Marion Wiesel, 1978. *The Trial of God*, translated by Marion Wiesel, 1979.

Hill and Wang, a division of Farrar, Straus, and Giroux, Inc., for permission to quote from the following works by Elie Wiesel: *Night*, translated from the French by Stella Rodway. © Les Editions de Minuit, 1958. English translation © MacGibbon & Kee, 1960. *Dawn*, translated from the French by Frances Frenaye. © Editions du Seuil, 1960. English translation © Elie Wiesel, 1961. *The Accident*, translated from the French by Anne Borchardt. © Editions du Seuil, 1961. English translation © Elie Wiesel, 1962.

Holt, Rinehart and Winston, Publishers, for permission to quote from the following works by Elie Wiesel: *The Town Beyond the Wall*, translated by Stephen Becker. © 1964 by Elie Wiesel. *The Gates of the Forest*, translated by Frances Frenaye. © 1966 by Holt, Rinehart and Winston. *Legends of our Time*. © 1968 by Elie Wiesel. *The Jews of Silence*, translated from the Hebrew by Neal Kozodoy.

Summit Books, for permission to quote from the *The Testament* by Elie Wiesel, 1981.

Paulist Press, for permission to quote from *Harry James Cargas in Conversation with Elie Wiesel*. © 1976 by Harry James Cargas.

KTAV Publishing House, for permission to quote from *Auschwitz: Beginning of a New Era?*, edited by Eva Fleischner, 1977.

Indiana University Press, for Permission to quote from *Confronting the Holocaust*, edited by Rosenfeld and Greenberg, 1978.

Library of Congress Cataloging in Publication Data

Brown, Robert McAfee, 1920–
    Elie Wiesel, messenger to all humanity.

    Bibliography: p.
    Includes index.
    1. Wiesel, Elie, 1928–   —Criticism and interpretation.   2. Holocaust, Jewish (1939–1945), in literature.
3. Wiesel, Elie, 1928–   —Religion and ethics.
4. Holocaust (Jewish theology)   I. Title.
PQ2683.I32Z59   1983   813'.54   82–40383
ISBN 0–268–00908–2

TO ELIE WIESEL

I tried very hard, my friend, not to write this book. At every stage it seemed a tampering with things I had no right to touch. But because each exposure to your work moves me more deeply, I feel compelled to share a portion of what you have given me. To receive and not to share—that would be a denial of all that I have learned from you.

You have said that to be a Jew means to testify; such must also be the obligation of a Christian. And you have taught us all—Jews, Christians, and all humanity—that before testifying ourselves, we must listen to the testimony of others. I have tried to listen to your testimony. And now I feel obligated . . . to testify.

Since gifts mean most when they come from the givers themselves, rather than through intermediaries, I hope most of all that those who read my pages will be moved to read yours.

Contents

List of Abbreviations

Accident	*The Accident*
Beggar	*A Beggar in Jerusalem*
Conversation	*Harry James Cargas in Conversation with Elie Wiesel*
Dimensions	*Dimensions of the Holocaust*
Gates	*The Gates of the Forest*
Generation	*One Generation After*
Legends	*Legends of our Time*
Masters	*Four Hasidic Masters and their Struggle Against Melancholy*
Messengers	*Messengers of God*
Portraits	*Five Biblical Portraits*
Responses	*Responses to Elie Wiesel*
Silence	*The Jews of Silence*
Souls	*Souls on Fire*
Testament	*The Testament*
Town	*The Town Beyond the Wall*
Trial	*The Trial of God*
Victory	*A Small Measure of Victory*
Zalman	*Zalman, or The Madness of God*

Acknowledgments

Because of an embarrassment of riches I cannot possibly thank all those who have contributed so substantially to whatever merit this volume possesses.

My debt to Elie Wiesel is indicated elsewhere. His friendship, encouragement, and availability during the writing remain a source of wonder and gratitude to me.

I have benefited immensely from the reactions of my companions in the classrooms of Stanford University, Union Theological Seminary, and Pacific School of Religion, as we have struggled together to confront the implications of Wiesel's writings for our own lives—an initially harsh blessing that finally heals. I am grateful for special assistance from Barbara Pescan and Annie Sultan.

Some of the material in Chapter 6 was originally given as a lecture at Mercy College, Detroit, Michigan, in a Holocaust series under the leadership of Dr. Carol Rittner, R.S.M., and materials in Chapters 2 and 3 were the basis for lectures given at Southwestern University, Georgetown, Texas, under the leadership of Dr. Farley Snell, and at the Chautauqua Institution, under the leadership of Dr. Ralph Loew. On all these occasions I received substantial help in discussion sessions.

I am particularly grateful to the Jewish members of the U.S. Holocaust Memorial Council, on which we serve under Elie Wiesel's leadership, for their openness to my attempts to enter, at however far remove, into experiences many of them have known at first hand. They could have resented my presence or ignored me. But they did neither thing. Instead they embraced me. The warmth of that embrace persuades me that

there are no barriers too high or too wide for human beings
to overcome.

For material help during two periods of uninterrupted writing I am indebted to Dr. Robert Lynn and the Lilly Endow-
ment, Inc., and to Dr. Jerry Hochbaum and the Memorial
Foundation for Jewish Culture.

Portions of the material have appeared in the following
journals: *Christianity and Crisis, Christian Century, Commonweal,
Face to Face, Theology Today,* and the *NICM Journal;* and in the
following books: Weisel et al, *Dimensions of the Holocaust,* Northwestern University Press, 1978; Brown, *Creative Dislocation—
The Movement of Grace,* Abingdon, 1980; and Ryan, ed., *Human
Responses to the Holocaust,* Edwin Mellin Press, 1981.

Two matters of logistics. First, as an aid to the reader, I have
kept page references to Wiesel's own writings within the text
itself. Other quotations or references are footnoted. Second,
readers who are bothered by references to "man" and "mankind" should remember (a) that most of Wiesel's novels were
written before sexist language was an issue, so that he cannot
be held retrospectively culpable for language that now dis-
turbs many people; (b) that he writes in French, in which
l'homme is a stronger word than *personne;* and (c) that in the face
of the enormity of the issues with which he is dealing, his own
affirmation that he means the French word to be understood
inclusively should enable all readers to find themselves addressed by his words.

This is not a "critical" appraisal of Wiesel, and I make no
apologies for the fact. My concern has been to expound him
clearly enough and sympathetically enough so that readers can
go on to confront him at first hand. Then they can, if they wish,
engage in critique. The critique, for me, has been the other
way around. Elie Wiesel has forced me to reevaluate a whole
lifetime of assumptions.

Let the pupil be content to acknowledge a debt to his rebbe.

Robert McAfee Brown
Heath, Massachusetts
Palo Alto, California
1979–1981

Introduction

Make the introduction concise and the conclusion abrupt—with nothing in between.
—Rebbe Naphtali, as cited in Wiesel's
Four Hasidic Masters, p. 108

Rebbe Naphtali's advice is admirable. We direct it at others while ignoring it ourselves. Fortunately, Rebbe Naphtali himself wrote many words, so he too is guilty of selective application.

If the present introduction honors the rebbe's injunction more in the breach than in the observance, it is with admirable intent—to explain enough so that what comes "in between" can be kept within more reasonable bounds.

The original working title for this book was *Elie Wiesel: Messenger to Jews and Christians.* From the beginning it was clear to me that Wiesel was a *messenger to Jews,* helping them deal with the devastation we call the Holocaust. I considered myself eavesdropper to an important conversation, an outsider who was nevertheless permitted and even encouraged to listen.

I soon discovered that I too was being addressed. It was not a comfortable discovery. For if Jews are plagued by their identity with the victims of the Holocaust, Wiesel reminded me that Christians must be plagued by their identity with the executioners. I discovered that when Wiesel spoke out of his Jewish stance, he forced me to confront my Christian stance—a matter to be explored in due course. A *messenger to Christians* as well.

As I shared my discovery of Wiesel with university under-

1

graduates, many of whom were neither Jews nor Christians, I discovered that he spoke more widely yet to North American humanists, South American radicals; Danes, Germans; theists, atheists; technicians, poets; liberals, traditionalists; theologians, empiricists. His themes touch us all. He is a *messenger to all humanity*. So it is to "all humanity" that these pages are addressed, to all who are willing, even at personal jeopardy, to wrestle with the deep moral dilemmas he has identified with fearful accuracy. Let us not discount personal jeopardy—a price is paid by those who confront haunting questions and realize there is no retreat once confrontation has begun with the writings of this tormented and yet (the term is mine) grace-filled man. If at the beginning they seem like a stiletto designed to wound, at the end they will be a scalpel, designed to heal. The only thing that can dull the keen edge of the blade is indifference.

Elie Wiesel has experienced all of the depths, and some of the heights, of the human venture. He does not evade ghastly revelations of human depravity, nor will he let us do so. But he does not engage in his exercise of dreadful memory to torment or taunt, but to warn and exhort—reminding us that human beings, confronted with the worst of the past, must structure their futures so that the worst will never again find embodiment. The hope is vulnerable; indeed, it is challenged daily, but on the day it is extinguished, the human venture will also have been extinguished.

With what moral dilemmas does Wiesel confront us? These, at least:

1. How could a decent people, recipients of the best of western culture, corporately engage in the murder of six million people for no other reason than that the people were Jews?

2. How could the rest of the world remain silent in the face of such outrage, thus becoming complicit in the deed itself?

3. How can we remain indifferent today, when potential repetition of such activity looms on the horizon and threatens to define the future?

4. How can we continue to believe in a force for goodness, or a pattern of meaning, or a God, when there exist such cancellations of our moral endeavor?

5. How, out of the ashes of past destructiveness, can we rebuild a world that is safe against such assaults in the future?

Most of us prefer to avoid such questions. Life is tidier without them. I have experienced the seductiveness of such evasion, and I do not believe I am unique. But I have to keep confronting such questions because Elie Wiesel's writings force me to do so. He issues challenges to which I am obligated to respond. He offers ways of coping with the challenges to which I am also obligated to respond.

So a dialogue is proposed.

How can the non-Jew speak?

Before the dialogue begins, there is a problem to confront: by what right does someone like the present author—non-Jew and noninhabitant of the death camps—participate in the dialogue at all?

All survivors attest that it is impossible to communicate the reality of their experience. And if Jewish survivors of the camps cannot communicate their experience, how can non-Jews who were never in the camps even approach the subject? What possible credentials could authenticate our right to do so? If, as Wiesel has said, "those who know do not speak," is it not also the case that "those who speak do not know"?

The experience they endured is not an experience the rest of us can share. We live in a different time, a different place, a different world. *We live in a different universe.* Ours is a universe in which Auschwitz has never entered; theirs is a universe from which it is never absent. Stephen Spender, reviewing the writings of Nelly Sachs, a survivor, reflects, "Most writers gaze at the furnace through a fire-proofed window in a thick wall."[1] And the insulation of that wall is too efficient for us to feel the heat.

I press the point in personal terms: I wrote much of this book in a place of great beauty—where nature wears a beneficent garb and people are caring—all the while trying to deal with a world where fire destroyed brutally rather than warming gently and where human nature was destructive rather than supportive.

During these months *night* was not the scene of burning babies but an encircling arm of protection and rest; *dawn* was not a moment when bullets killed innocent hostages, but a moment fresh and clean and full of promise; *day* [2] was not a time when life was passively surrendered to oncoming vehicles, but an occasion of energy and hope. While I was reading about prisoners standing at attention for hours on end in subzero weather, I was sitting in a well-heated house. Any time I was learning that hunger pangs lead starving people to steal moldy turnips from each other, I could (if I chose) go to the kitchen for a snack. While absorbing descriptions of nightly invasions by *kapos* arbitrarily selecting victims from the bunks of the camps and making sport of them with lashes or dogs, I could lie comfortably in bed, assured that the lock on my front door was secure. . . .

So it is, in varying degrees, for all of us. We have not been citizens of *l'univers concentrationnaire*.[3] We never can be. It is the cheapest sentimentality, and the most expensive betrayal, to assume that we can enter the world of Auschwitz, however remotely.

Let Wiesel press the case:

> Accept the idea that you will never see what they have seen— and go on seeing now, that you will never know the faces that haunt their nights, that you will never hear the cries that rent their sleep. Accept the idea that you will never penetrate the cursed and spellbound universe they carry within themselves with unfailing loyalty.
>
> And so I tell you: You who have not experienced their anguish, you who do not speak their language, you who do not mourn their dead, think before you offend them, before you betray them. Think before you substitute your memory for theirs. (*A Jew Today*, pp. 207–208)

The line is clearly drawn: "Whoever has not lived through the event can never know it. And whoever has lived through it can never fully reveal it" (p. 198). A universal bind.

Those who write at second hand betray the dead, or misrepresent the truth, or impose premature understanding upon awesome complexity, or worst of all, trivialize. Concern about the Holocaust becomes fashionable. Wiesel's sternest indictment: "Yesterday people said, 'Auschwitz, never heard of it.' Now they say, 'Oh yes, we know all about it' " (pp. 202–203).

Some writers have enough sensitivity to keep their distance, surrounding the Holocaust with "sacred awe":

> The greatest novelists of the time—Malraux and Mauriac, Faulkner and Silone and Thomas Mann and Camus—chose to stay away from it. It was their way of showing respect toward the dead—and the survivors as well. Also, it was their way of admitting their inability to cope with themes where imagination weighed less than experience. They were honest enough to realize that they may not penetrate into a domain haunted by so many dead and buried under so many ashes. They chose not to describe something they could not fathom. ("Art and Culture after the Holocaust," p. 412)

Conclusion? "There is no such thing as Holocaust literature—there cannot be. Auschwitz negates all literature. . . . Holocaust literature? The very term is a contradiction" (*A Jew Today*, p. 197).

And yet, and yet . . . there *is* a holocaust literature. Elie Wiesel himself has helped create it. So have other survivors: Primo Levi, Nelly Sachs, Robert Donat, Paul Celan, Ernst Weichert, Vladka Meed, Pierre Gascar, Tadeusz Borowski. How they speak of the unspeakable is a problem we will later face; at least they have earned the right to try. But, to press our question, how can we?

The unavoidable question, How can we dare to speak?, has an unavoidable answer, *Simply because we cannot dare not to speak.* While a certain kind of silence acknowledges inadequacy, another kind of silence exemplifies betrayal, choosing to ignore reality because reality has become unpalatable. Such ignoring kills the dead a second time; it obliterates them from human memory as well.

So even we must write about it. With all the dangers of misrepresentation, trivialization, and blasphemy, the Holocaust must be studied, reflected upon, written about, recalled. Wiesel himself finally agrees, though he adds a warning: "But it must be approached with fear and trembling. And above all, with humility. Some writers have shown that this is possible" (*A Jew Today*, p. 202). A ray of hope, Terence Des Pres, an outsider, sets his sights realistically: "Not to betray is as much as I can hope for."[4]

The basic rule: never attempt to speak *for* survivors, never attempt to speak *instead of* survivors (see *A Jew Today,* p. 203). Positively: speak only to provide one more place where survivors can speak *for themselves.*

That is what this book attempts: to provide a place where one survivor can speak for himself. Although we cannot enter Elie Wiesel's world, we can let him enter ours. A chronicle at second hand is justified if it forces confrontation with the chronicler at first hand—a confrontation we would prefer to avoid, and no longer have the luxury of avoiding, even though he leads us to the outer precincts of a void whose center he has had the unsought opportunity of exploring, encountering depths of evil we have never imagined, let alone acknowledged.

In listening to him we may be shattered. The risk is always present. But there is another possibility—the discovery that, *in spite of everything,* it is still possible to sing and shout defiance, to fling down a challenge to despair, and even, in powerful and incomprehensible ways, to initiate and respond to occasions for rejoicing. If we truly hear descriptions that would validate despair, perhaps, just perhaps, we can be guided to the edge of affirmations that go beyond despair.

But until we have taken both journeys, we have not really taken either one.

How do we respond to stories?

How is contact made between Elie Wiesel's world, *l'univers concentrationnaire,* and our world?

The connecting link is story.

Elie Wiesel is not a historian (though he deals with the stuff of history), nor is he a collector of data (though every line he writes provides data for a new geography of the soul and of hell), nor a systematician (though systematic reflection can follow from his words). No, he is a teller of tales. You want to know about the kingdom of night? There is no way to describe the kingdom of night. But let me tell you a story. . . . You want to know about the condition of the human heart? There is no way to describe the condition of the human heart. But let me tell you a story . . . You want a description of the indescribable? There is no way to describe the indescribable. But let me tell you a story. . . .

If we are to learn from Elie Wiesel, we must listen to stories. His stories. They challenge our stories. They open horizons we had never seen before. They smash barriers we had thought were impregnable. They leave us desolate. They also bind us in new and deeper relationships.

And almost immediately, we lay violent hands upon them. We wrench them from their teller. They are meant to be shared—but not preempted. And we preempt them. We classify them. We codify them. We deduce lessons from them. *We interpret them.* Instead of letting them stand on their own, we rush in and say, "Here is what the story means. This is what the teller of tales is *really* trying to say." Instead of letting the stories write themselves upon our hearts, we write books about the stories.

Surely if the tales needed commentary, if interpretation were necessary, the teller himself would have provided commentary and interpretation. We can be faithful to the teller of tales only by hearing his tales and repeating them, or—another possibility—telling other tales that point us back to his.

But chapters, paragraphs, footnotes?

It would be an act of fidelity to respond to Elie Wiesel, "Your story weaves a spell that leaves me speechless. I cannot yet reply. Tell the same story again . . . Differently." And it would be an act of equal fidelity to hear his story and respond with a story of our own: "Ah yes! That reminds me of the time they were preparing for a great festival at Lodz. Three merchants came all the way from Vilna. Hidden under the merchandise in their carts. . . ." And when the second story was finished, the hearers would understand the first story better. There is such an episode in *The Town Beyond the Wall,* located in a bar in Tangiers. The process works.

Most of us lack the sensitivity for either creative silence or story-response. We have only the pedestrian tools of reflection, analysis, systematization, even footnotes. We must respond with what we presently possess, hoping that such response will place new possessions at our disposal.

But we can take heart. All such procedures are validated *if they lead back to the story*, which in the process will have become a different story, telling us ever new things. Analysis, comparison, interpretation, classification are all legitimate, if they finally confront us once more with the story and the storyteller.

And then, it can begin to transform our lives. For the story, initially so strange, has become a story that involves us.

On denying the story: a necessary digression

There is a way to avoid involvement. It is an ugly way, but it is too widespread to be ignored. It denies the truth of the story.

The Holocaust? Jewish propaganda created to arouse sympathy for the State of Israel. Gas chambers? Disinfectant shower baths, just as the Nazis said. Treblinka? Auschwitz? Work centers, not death camps. Crematoria? Well, there were a few crematoria, but only to dispose of the bodies of Jews who had died of natural causes in the work camps. Six million Jewish deaths? An exaggeration. There were at most only a million, and they died from epidemics or the aforesaid natural causes. ("Only a million . . ." The mind boggles.)

This is revisionist history with a vengeance. It would not be worth dignifying with comment, save that it is widespread enough to be frightening. The library at the Holocaust memorial in Jerusalem, Yad Vashem, contains over ninety books, in many languages, all claiming that the Holocaust never happened. It is the fear of every survivor, not least Elie Wiesel, that when the voice of the last survivor has been silenced by death, the next generation will be taught that the Holocaust was, in a favorite phrase of the crypto-revisionists, "the hoax of the twentieth century."

Wiesel's play, *Zalmen, or The Madness of God,* offers a miniature parallel to this phenomenon. During a time of Jewish oppression in Russia, a timid rabbi is persuaded by his beadle, Zalmen, to tell foreigners visiting his synagogue that "the

Torah here is in peril and the spirit of a whole people is being crushed. . . . If you, our brothers, forsake us, we will be the last of the Jews in this land, the last witnesses" (pp. 82–83).

Scandal. The Commissar of Jewish Affairs must get to the bottom of the matter: Who instigated it? How many Jews were in on the conspiracy? What other plans are afoot? All the usual questions. And with things threatening to get out of hand, the Commissar does a very clever thing. He decides to treat the whole episode as a nonepisode. The official line: it never happened. The case is closed for there is no case. The inspector addresses the rabbi:

> As far as we're concerned—as far as the outside world is concerned—you have done nothing. Your dream was the dream of a madman. Why should we make you into a martyr? Turn you into an example? Your revolt . . . quite simply *did not take place!* (p.170)

There are few parallels between Wiesel and the rabbi (the one is courageous and forthright, the other timid and bumbling), but there are awesome parallels between the situations of the two—to speak and be ignored, to cry out in pain and not even hear an echo, to be told that the events one has lived through "quite simply did not take place."

Since the message is threatening, it will be denied that there even was a message. We only thought there was.

This is no fanciful scenario. It happened in Russia, and it is happening in the United States and dozens of other countries.

One of the most detailed of these denials of the Holocaust (which we will not dignify by naming) is by an "academician" whose scholarly qualification for assessing the most complex historical event of the twentieth century is a doctoral degree in electrical engineering. All the apparatus—main text, "documentation," appendices, footnotes, bibliography, index—is designed to prove that there never was a Holocaust. The procedure is simple: call any data that supports your case "self-evident," discount any data that challenges your case by calling it biased, opportunistic, propagandistic, or false. Herewith:

The "legend" of gassed Jews is a "hoax." Figures from "Jewish or Communist" sources must be discounted; Nazi statistics, on the other hand, can be accepted as accurate. Auschwitz is an "alleged" extermination center; we have only Jewish evidence that it was. Anne Frank's diary is a fake. Distinctions between crimes against Germans and crimes against non-Germans (i.e., Jews) are "merely a bit of sophistry." Corpse-laden trains must be seen "in context." "Diverse recreational activities" such as "concerts, cabaret performers, movies, and athletic contests" were a regular feature of life in Auschwitz. Jews did not suffer at Theriesenstadt. "Zionists" initiated the "legend" that exterminations were taking place in the camps. Trials of Auschwitz leaders are a "frame-up" based on "a pack of lies." The notion that Zyklon B was used to gas prisoners is "idiotic," "nonsensical," and "incomparably ludicrous." Reports of beatings of prisoners by guards can be dismissed as propaganda because "it is known that this was not the case." It is a "certainty" that the massive export of Hungarian Jews to Germany and Poland "did not occur." Claims that the extermination program had priority over military transport are "absolutely ridiculous." The accepted story of what happened in Auschwitz is "a fabrication constructed of perjury, forgery, distortion of fact, and misrepresentation of documents." Evidence that the *Einsatzgrüppen* engaged in massive exterminations in Poland and Russia is "simply funny." The people who "suffered most" in the war were not the Jews but the Germans. The gas chamber theory is "garbage." Claims of Nazi brutality are a "myth."

Adolf Hitler did not lack skilled apologists in his lifetime; in death he has found one to surpass them all.

To those wishing them so, such claims assume authority. A "scholar" says there was no Holocaust? He must be right. A "professor" says the gas chambers are a hoax and there were no beatings in the camps? How like the Jews to have tricked us. There was no attempt to exterminate Jews? Thank God. Now we can all relax again.

There is no greater indignity than to say to a suffering person, "Your suffering is a fake. . . . You invented it to gain sympathy. . . . You are an impostor." One hesitates to explore the motives of those who can say that accounts of the mass murders of Jews in Poland and Russia are "simply funny." But one must never hesitate to explore why many people would

like to believe them: it would be such a blessing not to have
to believe the Holocaust happened. We would be relieved of
fears that people are guilty of deep evil; we would be absolved
of guilt for possible complicity; we could continue to believe
that basically all is well, and that the human story is an attrac-
tive one of which we can be proud, rather than an ugly one of
which we must be ashamed.

There is a price paid for following such a path, however:
attempts to deny a past Holocaust almost ensure that there will
be a future one.

Standing before an audience at Northwestern University,
telling about his time as a boy in the kingdom of night, and his
hope that by telling the tale he could forestall its repetition,
Elie Wiesel continued:

> What that boy could not have imagined then, and nobody has
> imagined since, was that one day the story would be denied
> altogether. That one day he would have to stand here before
> you and simply tell you, "Yes, it was true."(*Dimensions*, p.5)

Those who deny, Wiesel continued, "speak obscenely." And
how does one confront obscenity?

> I confess I do not know how to handle this situation. Are we
> really to debate these ideas or charges? Is it not beneath our
> dignity and the dignity of the dead even to refute these lies? But
> then, is silence the answer? It never was. And that is why we try
> to tell the tale. But what are the messengers of the dead to do
> with their memories? They would much rather speak about
> other things. But who then would protest against the recent
> attempts to kill the victims again? . . . I do not know how you
> react to all this. I can only tell you what one survivor feels. More
> than sadness, he feels dismay, and more than dismay he feels
> despair, and even more than despair he feels disgust. (*Dimen-*
> *sions*, p. 19; see also *A Jew Today*, pp. 43–46)

The story of the storyteller

In the face of those who "speak obscenely" by attempting
to deny the story, we too must register disgust. And having

done so, turn our backs on those who disgust us and listen no longer, listening instead to Elie Wiesel telling the story once more, a story that supplies its own credentials.

The story of Elie Wiesel is the story of his characters, and the story of his characters is the story of Elie Wiesel. His denials are theirs, their denials are his. The affirmations, when they begin to come, are likewise common property. Wiesel the man and Wiesel the author are one.[5] To learn more about the story of the storyteller is to know more about both story and storyteller.

Where do we begin? A long way back.

Nestled fourth in a series of *Five Biblical Portraits* is Wiesel's treatment of the prophet Jeremiah. Neither first nor last, this inauspiciously placed essay may be our best clue to the life and mission of its author. Critics usually compare Wiesel with Job, the one who challenged God with the forever unanswered question "Why?", and Wiesel himself ends an earlier book, *Messengers of God,* with a chapter on Job, whom he describes as "our contemporary." Wiesel has high praise for Job . . . until near the end. For Job finally capitulates and withdraws his complaint against God. One whirlwind and he is on his knees, mouthing orthodox platitudes. "The fighter has turned into a lamb" (p. 233).

Wiesel would have preferred another ending in which Job remained a fighter. And he salvages the biblical text only by ingeniously suggesting that Job's pious assertions at the end were spoken in a mocking tone, their very orthodoxy suggesting—on the lips of one like Job—that their content is spurious, and that "in spite or perhaps because of appearances, Job continued to interrogate God" (p. 235).

A man who capitulates quickly under divine pressure and subsequently mocks God rather than engaging in ongoing contestation is not a sufficient prophetic counterpart for Elie Wiesel. A minority report must be entered: our best understanding of Wiesel comes from comparison with Jeremiah rather than with Job—Jeremiah, who never accepted answers from God but kept hurling back new questions and challenges, who was neither awed by whirlwinds nor intimidated by their creator, who never saw prosperity as a sign of divine favor, whose ongoing question was always, Why do the wicked prosper? Why do the righteous suffer?

Already we are describing Elie Wiesel. Without constructing artificial parallels between the two, let us note some ways in which Wiesel, writing about Jeremiah, is writing about himself.

"Jeremiah was a victim of injustice by virtue of his origin" (pp. 102–103).

Elie Wiesel was a victim of injustice by virtue of his origin. Many people who lived in Sighet, a town situated in the Carpathian mountains, were inconvenienced by the Nazi occupation in April 1944. Some suffered loss. A few were killed. All Jews, however, were deported to Auschwitz, where most of them were sent to the gas chambers. Why? By virtue of their origins. To be a Jew was enough to be marked for death.

Before becoming "a victim of injustice by virtue of his origin," Elie Wiesel, born on September 30, 1928, lived fourteen years steeped in the traditions of Hasidic Judaism, studying Torah, midrash, and kabbala. When the cattlecars disgorged their passengers at Birkenau, Elie Wiesel lost his mother and little sister at the first "selection," and his father later on in Buchenwald. When liberation occurred, Wiesel almost died from food poisoning.

"[Jeremiah is] a survivor, a witness . . . [who] after being singed by its flames went on to retell it to any who would listen" (pp. 100–101).

Elie Wiesel was a survivor, sent to Paris after liberation and food poisoning, at age fifteen. He learned a new language, studied, pondered, worked, and starved. His faith was more rudely challenged after the ordeal than during it. Humanity and God? Enemies of one another. Both together? Enemies of the Jewish people. The Germans? Executioners. The Poles, Hungarians, French? Accomplices. Pius XII? Spectator.

Perhaps there were answers in the East. There was a search for solace in Hindu mysticism, a retreat into meditation that was shattered by the inescapable reality of Indians dying on the streets as others walked, uncaring, over the corpses.

The only apparent resolution: insulate oneself against feeling and caring. No laughter, no tears. Only silence.

But there was a need to express that could not be stifled. To be a survivor was not enough; one must also be a witness. Eight hundred pages about the camps were written in Yiddish. But nothing was to be shared for ten years, the self-imposed limitation Wiesel placed on speaking. And when he finally spoke, it was about silence, the silence of the world in the face of the enormity. Title of the Yiddish manuscript: *And the World Has Remained Silent.* Much condensed, it later appeared in French. *La Nuit* it was called: *Night.* The survivor had become a witness. Singed by the flames, he started retelling the catastrophe to anyone who would listen.

". . . *he shatters serenity. . . . he forces us to look at what we refuse to see"* (p. 109).

Those who listen are not reassured. He displays a world no one wants to see, a world where values are destroyed by being reversed: the wicked prosper, the good suffer. Jeremiah's age-old complaint is contemporary. The scars endure in the survivors described in *Dawn* and *The Accident*—"spiritual amputees" outwardly walking the streets of Jerusalem or Times Square but inwardly unable to dwell anywhere save Sobibor or Treblinka.

And in every character who escaped the burning dwells the charred soul of Elie Wiesel.

"[Jeremiah wanted] to teach his contemporaries and their descendants a lesson: there comes a time when one must look away from death and turn away from the dead; one must cling to life. . . . One must not wait for the tragedy to end before building or rebuilding life" (pp. 120–121).

After three books and the better part of a fourth, in which the journey of Elie Wiesel is mirrored, light begins to penetrate a darkness that until then has eclipsed light. People begin to look at one another without mistrust. The horror is still there, but something else is there. Life is beginning to be reaffirmed.

Elie Wiesel moved to the United States, worked as a correspondent for Jewish journals, and continued to write novels in which, out of ongoing desolation, something beyond desolation began to be visible.

Personal affirmation became possible. Shortly after the

publication of *A Beggar in Jerusalem,* dedicated to "Marion," Elie Wiesel married Marion Erster Rose, herself a survivor. They have a son—Shlomo Elisha, named after Wiesel's father —and Marion's daughter, Jennifer, from an earlier marriage.

"No one is as alone as the man who must speak and is not heard" (p. 123).

A dozen books were written, in which the Holocaust was an omnipresent backdrop and undergirding—books written to alert, to bring about change, to create a climate in which a Holocaust could never be repeated. But nothing seemed to change.

It appeared once again that "the world has remained silent." Another book, *The Oath,* explored the destructive solitude of one "who must speak and is not heard." People preferred not to hear, but to forget.

"It is up to the prophet to stop the process [of forgetting] by forcing them to remember: the covenant, the Law, the promise of the beginning, the moral thrust of Israel's adventure" (p. 112).

Having entertained the notion of ceasing to speak, Wiesel reaffirmed the necessity of continuing to speak. In 1972 he became Distinguished Professor of Jewish Studies at City College in New York, where he taught until 1978, when he was appointed Andrew Mellon Distinguished Professor of Humanities at Boston University. Jewish Studies, Humanities, not Holocaust Studies; the Holocaust permeates all that he says or does, but there are other ways to force people to remember. He writes and teaches and lectures about Hasidic tales, Hasidic masters, biblical tales, biblical characters (Jeremiah is a case in point), midrashic materials. The venture into the depths of the present requires a venture into the depths of the past, to remind people of "the covenant, the Law, the promise of the beginning, the moral thrust of Israel's adventure."

"Jeremiah tried to convince them that God too is suffering—that He too is in exile. . . . There was something else: he reminded them of their own responsibility for their fate" (p. 110).

Retelling the ancient story of humanity is also a retelling of the ancient story of God. Increasingly the two are intertwined. Time: November 11, 1973. Place: Carnegie Music Hall, New York City. Occasion: premiere of a cantata, words by Elie Wiesel, music by Darius Milhaud, entitled *Ani Maamin,* which means *I Believe.* It sings of a God who finally chooses to suffer with the children of earth, and it sings of the way in which the children of earth must take responsibility for their own fate— because of God, despite God.

"The prophet of Israel has become the prophet to all nations. He now understands—and makes others understand—that Israel's destiny affects everyone else's. What happens to Judah will eventually happen to Babylon, then Rome, and ultimately to the entire world. And so the most Jewish of the Jewish prophets becomes the most universal among them" (pp. 122–123).

In 1978 President Carter appointed Elie Wiesel chairman of what is now the United States Holocaust Memorial Council, charged with proposing a memorial that will remember the past and honor the dead, but also educate for the future, so that no holocaust can ever again threaten any individual or any people. The particularity of Jewish suffering can never be remembered only as an end in itself; it is a foretaste of what can happen to any person, any people. If Jews can be burned, so can others. To start with a concern for his own people—as Wiesel always does—is never to end there; it becomes, in turn, a starting place for concern for all peoples.

This most Jewish of writers becomes the most universal among them.

"Testimony. . . . He has no choice: he must do something with his life. If he survives, it must be for a reason; he must do something with every minute—for every minute is a minute of grace" (p. 124).

To be called to bear testimony is an awesome responsibility. To have been spared to do so when six million were not is even more awesome. To have been spared a second time—as Wiesel felt after surviving an accident in Times Square in 1956—is a responsibility so awesome that every minute counts.

The literary outpouring since then can be explained only by Wiesel's belief that he, too, "must do something with every minute—for every minute is a minute of grace"—a gift for the use of which he is held accountable.

There is an exacting regimen in order to render account-ability: 6:00 to 10:00 A.M. every day is set aside solely for writing, an almost inviolable preserve. Three kinds of writing proceed simultaneously—a novel in a contemporary setting, lectures on Hasidic materials (with an extension to the Talmud promised in the near future), and lectures on biblical charac-ters, an area of literary creation that is increasingly central to Wiesel. In addition are the classroom preparations, the essays, articles, and plays—all written in French. "One style," he says, "is all I can master in a lifetime."

Style.

"His simplicity is deceptive" (p. 101).

Wiesel's one book dealing directly with the Holocaust has 116 pages of text. His "most intimate form of writing," dia-logues published in the collections of essays, have not an extra word. Everything is simplicity itself—sparse, taut, lean. And deceptive. For every word points to things that can never be seen, to complexities beyond our ability to grasp. The simpler the sentence, the more complex the idea.

"As with every genuine work of art, [the] opening statement contains all that is to follow" (p. 101).

Each opening sentence provides the key to the book. The subsequent plot can almost be unraveled from the first page. We shall see.

"Jeremiah's ultimate lesson for all tellers of tales: to rewrite is more difficult and more important than to write; to transmit is more vital than to invent" (p. 126).

Wiesel, supreme exemplar of "tellers of tales," does not need to invent. He is content to transmit, to tell tales be-queathed to him by his Hasidic grandfather, or by Hitler's storm troopers . . . or by Jeremiah.

He had often wondered what Jeremiah meant when he wrote, "I look at the mountains and they are quaking. . . . All the birds have fled."

Quaking mountains? Elie Wiesel visits Babi Yar, site of the

massacre of 80,000 Jews between Rosh Hashanah and Yom Kippur, and learns that after the mass burial, "the ground was shaking for weeks on end. The mountains of corpses made the earth quake. . . . And I understood Jeremiah" (p. 126).

A place from which birds have fled?

> I understood the prophet's imagery only when I returned to Auschwitz and Birkenau in the summer of 1979. Then and only then did I remember that, during the tempest of fire and silence, there were no birds to be seen on the horizon: they had fled the skies above all the death-camps. I stood in Birkenau and remembered Jeremiah. (p. 126)

"[His is] the story of a solitary prophet who would have given anything, including his life, to be able to tell another kind of tale, one filled with joy and fervor rather than sorrow and anguish" (pp. 126–127).

"He wanted to speak of other things; he wanted to be a normal person, dealing with customary human problems and not with eternity and death, but he had no choice" (p. 103).

A price is paid by the "solitary prophet," be he Jeremiah or Elie Wiesel. "Sorrow and anguish" are the content of the message, but, despite and because of that, there are sometimes "joy and fervor" as well. But never one without the other.

The combination of the two is represented in the eyes and the handshake. Elie Wiesel is slight of build, with sharp features, black hair, and intensely piercing eyes. They are eyes that have seen sorrow and anguish beyond what most who look into them can imagine. They could communicate sorrow and anguish, and they do. They could communicate anger, and they do not. Anger, anger deep within the soul, is expressed through the hand that guides the pen, rather than through the eyes that seek another. The handshake, for one so frail, is surprisingly and affirmatively warm and powerful. Together, the eyes and the handshake do not pass judgment; they establish rapport and invite response.

Victim of unparalleled disasters, Elie Wiesel refuses to let their memory destroy him, and he refuses to employ his memories to destroy others. Either reaction we could understand. That neither reaction is undertaken is a secret we must seek to learn from him.

CHAPTER 1

Becoming a Messenger:
An Impossible Necessity
(a journey of the self)

I am obsessed with the messenger aspect of man. The greatest tragedy of all, though, could be when the messenger is deprived of his message. Imagine a messenger waiting for a message he must pass on—but does not receive.
—Wiesel, *A Small Measure of Victory*, p. 24

The issue is memory. And memory is double-edged. In one of Wiesel's short stories, "The Scrolls, Too, Are Mortal," Issachar comments in a burst of insight and despair: "Memory is not only a kingdom, it is also a graveyard" (*A Jew Today*, p. 81).

Memory is a *kingdom*. It enables Wiesel to conjure up beautiful images from his childhood in Sighet—of his grandfather and the stories old Dodye Feig told him; of Shabbat, anticipated in wonder, celebrated in tremulous hope ("Will the Messiah come this time?"), remembered in awe, and then once again anticipated in wonder; of a world in which God still dwelt and prayer was as natural, and as necessary, as breathing.

But memory is also a *graveyard*. The kingdom became a graveyard for Wiesel, which is to say that it became another kind of kingdom—a kingdom of night, a kingdom of darkness where no light was found, where death, rather than being the daily exception, became the daily expectation. And all that

memory could deliver for many years were the all-too cor-
poreal phantoms of the graveyard. One may "survive" while
living in a graveyard, and discover that survival is a curse
rather than a blessing. For Eliezer in *The Accident,* it was a curse.
He knew himself as "a grave for the unburied dead" (p. 53),
and was companion of the dead to the exclusion of those living
alongside him in Times Square and Carnegie Music Hall.
Every venture into the past became another stick of wood on
the funeral pyre of his ongoing death in the present. Not until
well into Wiesel's fourth book, *The Town Beyond the Wall,* does
a character begin to transcend the verdict of the graveyard and
begin to rebuild the foundations of a kingdom in which memory could release rather than destroy.

No wonder, then, that Wiesel, on a visit to Kiev, site of a
massive slaughter of Jews at Babi Yar in 1943, felt constrained
to say to the mayor, "Mr. Mayor, the problem for all of us—for
you as for us—is: what do we do with our memories? We must
deal with them or they will crush us." Confronting memories
not only involves acknowledging their reality and honoring
those victimized, but determining to appropriate the memories in the present for the sake of the future: "Those who have
died in anonymity," Wiesel continued, "must not be remembered in anonymity. Our collective remembrance must save
future generations from anonymity."[1]

How does one deal with memory? One becomes a messenger, a transmitter, both of the kingdom and of the graveyard.
To be a messenger does not guarantee a new kingdom, but to
fail to be a messenger guarantees a new graveyard.

We can discern five steps in becoming a messenger of an
event, in this case, the Event of the Holocaust:

1. The Event took place: one must speak.
2. The Event defies description: one cannot speak.
3. The Event suggests an alternative: one could choose silence.
4. The Event precludes silence: one must become a messenger.
5. The Event suggests a certain kind of message: one can be
   a teller of tales.

The Event took place: one must speak

The Event, for so it must be identified, is the Holocaust, a time, etymologically and existentially, of "burnt offerings."[2] Burnings there had been before, of witches and infidels, saints and martyrs, heretics and schismatics, young and old. But the new burnings were burnings with a difference. Not only were there victims who were military, political, ideological opponents of the Nazis, there were also victims whose only "crime" was being Jewish. Having the wrong grandparents was sufficient reason for incineration; the murder of children—Jewish children—is the quintessential expression of Holocaust logic. The Nazi intention eludes us unless we recognize that destruction of the Jews was finally more important than winning the war. Example: when the tide was turning and the war was all but lost, German military commandants had difficulty getting trains to transport troops to the battle front, while Eichmann, in charge of "Jewish Affairs for the Third Reich," always got trains to transport Jews to extermination centers.

At this point in our study, conventional wisdom would dictate the inclusion of a description of the Holocaust, an array of facts to describe what happened, so that Wiesel's writings could be seen in context. There are books that provide such information, information to which we always need exposure.[3] But our approach will be different. For not all have spoken of the Event through analysis of documents, discernment of historical trends, examination of the motives of political and military leaders. A few have spoken of the Event through its impact on single human lives or groups of lives. Sifting through the ashes of memory, they have told stories, drawn portraits, composed laments, morally committed to telling their story so that the future for others will not recapitulate their own past. They communicate less by analytic description than by human recital.

Elie Wiesel is preeminent among such messengers. While he has written essays, cited statistics, done documentary research, he has nevertheless approached the Holocaust chiefly as a teller of tales, his own and others. Tales of that time and that place are interspersed with tales of other times and other places, all of them circling around the Event, uncovering this or that truth, exposing this or that falsehood, celebrating this or that momentary triumph, mourning this or that permanent defeat.

The impact is cumulative, the result all-encompassing. When he is not writing about the Holocaust, he is writing about nothing else—the story of Abraham and Isaac is the prefigured story of Elie Wiesel's father and Elie Wiesel. When he is writing only about the Holocaust, he is writing about everything else—the story of Elie Wiesel's father and Elie Wiesel is the reenacted story of Abraham and Isaac. At the end of the storytelling we will know more than we knew at the beginning, which means that we will know less. But when the subject matter is the Holocaust, to know that we will know less at the end than we knew at the beginning is already to have begun to know more.

If that seems a defiance of ordinary logic, it is only an example of Auschwitz logic.

A curse goes with it:

> As for me, I too like to attend a good concert or smile back at a pretty girl. I bless bread and sanctify the wine, and no one is happier than I when, under my pen, words fall into place, fit into a design and create the illusion that they are leading somewhere.
>
> In truth, I know where they lead. To where there are no words. To the mysterious forests where fathers and sons, Jews already marked by the executioner, always the same, tell each other a story, always the same. To where women with dark dilated pupils, violated and drunk with pain, escort their children to the altar and beyond.
>
> Then there arises from the very depths of my being an irresistible desire to let everything go. To throw away the pen, burn all bridges and start to run and curse and leave the present far behind. To seek the moment that gave birth to these images, and never again to hear the laughter, and the moaning of the wind whipped by the shadows, always the same shadows. (*Generation*, p. 51)

An awesome sequence:

The words always lead back to the story.

The story always leads back to the horror—the mysterious forest, the executioner, the violated women.

The horror always leads back to the desire to negate, to deny.

But the storyteller does not have to privilege of such a resolution. He is under orders: orders to tell the story. Again and again. And again.

In telling of tales about the kingdom of night, there is a privilege of place reserved for the survivor, the one who was *there*. The rest of us cannot get close to the Event itself, but with the survivor's help we can slightly decrease the distance. And in ways we cannot yet understand, the survivor's story back then becomes an integral part of our story right now. If that seems unlikely, let us reserve judgment until we have heard the survivor's testimony.

The different approaches—analytical description and human recital—need each other, and they concur on the essential starting point: the Event took place, one must speak.

The Event defies description: one cannot speak

Those who have spoken record a second perception as well: having tried to speak, they discover that attempts to speak of this Event are doomed. One cannot speak of the Holocaust. Theodore Adorno puts the case most strongly: "To write poetry after Auschwitz is barbaric." George Steiner feels that language is stretched beyond endurance when Auschwitz is the subject, or when language is used in a world in which Auschwitz occurred.

So, on frequent occasions, does Elie Wiesel.

There is a double bind here. On the one hand, there is a bind for *the messenger:* the Event is so awesomely different from all other events that the messenger searches in vain for tools of language to do it justice. On the other hand, there is a bind for *the listener:* both an inability to hear because of the awesome difference, and an unwillingness to hear, since the consequences of the message are too devastating.

All of which places the messenger in a double bind: his own attempts to speak are foredoomed to self-acknowledged failure, and even if what he says is heard, the listener is foredoomed to misunderstand or evade.

We must examine these binds in more detail.

The basic reason that attempts to speak about the Holocaust are foredoomed to failure is simply *the uniqueness of the Event* itself. Although the adjective "unique" is not ordinarily subject to comparison, yet in a post-Auschwitz world we can paraphrase George Orwell: all events are unique but some are more unique than others. The Holocaust is not one in a series of examples of human depravity. It is *sui generis.* Wiesel insists on this:

> What happened twenty-five years ago was so unique; even within the framework of our own history, it is unique. It never happened before. It can be compared to no other event. The victim was another victim, and the executioner another executioner. It was a mutation on a cosmic scale. (*Responses,* p. 151)

Descriptions are made by means of comparisons. Analogies are embedded in all attempts to communicate: *this* event, of which we do not know, is like *that* one of which we know at least a little. But what if there is nothing with which to make a comparison, no analogy that will hold? Then we begin to understand the bind of the messenger: "By its uniqueness," Wiesel writes, "the Holocaust defies literature." He continues:

> Therein lies the dilemma of the storyteller who sees himself essentially as a witness, the drama of the messenger unable to deliver his message: how is one to speak of it, how is one not to speak of it? Certainly there can be no other theme for him: all situations, all conflicts, all obsessions will, by comparison, seem pallid and futile. (*Generation,* p. 10)

So the messenger appears doomed from the start: "What he hopes to transmit can never be transmitted. All he can possibly hope to achieve is to communicate the impossibility of communication" (*Dimensions,* p. 8).

Consequence: the one who must speak will feel guilty of betrayal. Discussing the matter with other Jewish writers, Wiesel acknowledges, "Yes, we are concerned. We do try to put the experience into words. But can we? Language is poor and inadequate. *The moment it is told, the experience turns to betrayal"* ("Jewish Values in the Post-Holocaust Future," p. 284, italics added).

That is bad enough: to transmit is to betray. But Wiesel is

forced to concede that the polar opposite is true also: not to transmit is also to betray: "I believed that, having survived by chance, I was duty-bound to give meaning to my survival, to justify each moment of my life. I knew the story had to be told. *Not to transmit an experience is to betray it*"("Why I Write," p.201).

Who can grasp the pathos of this situation: to speak is to betray, not to speak is to betray. There is no way not to betray. Why not? Because none of the interpretive categories work any more. We cannot draw lines that connect *l'univers concentrationnaire* and our own universe. No common experiences link them. No language drawn from one world can communicate to the other. Words become obstacles, not enablers, to understanding.

> The language of night was not human; it was primitive, almost animal—hoarse shouting, screams, muffled moaning, savage howling, the sound of beating . . . This is the concentration camp language. It negated all other language and took its place. Rather than link, it became wall. Could it be surmounted? Could the reader be brought to the other side? I knew the answer to be negative, and yet I also knew that "no" had to become "yes." ("Why I Write," p. 201).

In the world of scholars, philosophers, theologians, people of letters, a vocabulary of considerable sophistication is used, built up over centuries of use. And yet Wiesel insists that "Auschwitz, by definition, is beyond their vocabulary." Terence Des Pres offers an exegesis of the insistence:

> Wiesel means that in this special case, our traditional categories of value and interpretation have been demolished by the very event they would seek to explain. The negativity of the Holocaust was so total, the event so massive and complete in itself, that concepts drawn from tradition and civilized experience—in short the key terms of *our* world—become, if not useless, then extremely problematic . . . Think of any key concept in the vocabulary of civilized discourse and immediately, if its sounding board is the Holocaust, you are in trouble.[4]

Surely non-Auschwitz vocabulary contains at least one "key concept" that can help us describe Auschwitz. That is the concept of *hell*. If there is one realm with which Auschwitz can be compared, "hell" is surely that realm. George Steiner, the one most reticent about the possibility of speech in relation to the Holocaust, writes:

> The camp embodies often down to minutiae, the images and chronicles of Hell in European art and thought from the twelfth to the eighteenth centuries. It is these representations which gave to the deranged horrors of Belsen a kind of "expected logic." . . . The concentration and death camps of the twentieth century, wherever they exist, under whatever regime, are *Hell made immanent.* They are the transference of Hell from below the earth to its surface.[5]

But does that finally help us understand the horror of the camps? All that we know of hell (from poets and artists, let alone theologians) suggests that there is a perverse *rightness* about it, a grim justice: evil ones are punished, malefactors receive their just desserts, criminals pay the price of their criminality. But that does not describe Auschwitz, where evil ones are punishers, not the punished; malefactors mete out unjust deserts to innocents; criminals force others to pay the ultimate price for not being criminals. Hell has no "innocents," whereas Auschwitz is peopled with "innocents" who are punished for no reason, no crime, no sin, that could conceivably demand such penalty. The hell of Dante and Milton has form and symmetry and structure, governed by a logic that, once accepted, is inexorable. Auschwitz, too, had its logic —Jews are to be exterminated—but it was a "logic" riddled with chance and caprice, the whim of a *kapo* or a Dr. Mengele who decides by a flick of the wrist who will work and who will burn.

Berish, in *The Oath,* finds the analogy of hell insufficient even for a pogrom. Pogroms are worse, he tells his daughter:

> You don't know what a pogrom is, you cannot know. Insanity unleashed, demons at liberty. The basest instincts, the most vile laughter. Hell's flames frighten me less; there is no blind cruelty in hell, no gratuitous savagery. There is no desecration in hell. No trampled innocence. (*The Oath,* p. 253)

Our inability, even with the flawed imagery of hell, to establish rapport between *l'univers concentrationnaire* and our own, reminds us that what we see in the camps is not just the worst of our world intensified, but a new world, a world so base that not even our basest image—hell—is adequate to describe it. Wiesel:

> Turning point or watershed, [the Holocaust] produced a mutation on a cosmic scale, affecting all possible areas of human endeavor. After Auschwitz, the human condition is no longer the same. After Treblinka, nothing will ever be the same. The Event has altered man's perception and changed his relationship to God, to his fellow man and to himself. The unthinkable has become real. (*Days of Remembrance*, p. 16)

Even more sharply: the utter expendability of children. If one wants total reversal, here is the place to look. All cultures have instances of the base treatment of children, but they pale before the Nazi policy that Jewish children were to be exterminated. Even more: they were not simply victims like everybody else, but victims for whom special treatment was often reserved. It is impossible to understand; no categories will encompass it. Irving Greenberg describes an episode. Place: Auschwitz. Time: summer 1944. Situation: the gas chamber near the crematorium is out of order.

> The other gas chambers were full of the adults and therefore the children were not gassed, but just burned alive. There were several thousand of them. When one of the SS sort of had pity upon the children, he would take a child and beat the head against a stone before putting it on the pile of fire and wood, so that the child lost consciousness. However, the regular way they did it was by just throwing the children onto the pile. They would put a sheet of wood there, then sprinkle the whole thing with petrol, then wood again, and petrol and wood, and petrol —and then they placed the children there. Then the whole thing was lighted.[6]

Roy Eckardt comments on this unspeakable event: "There is in this world an evil that is more horrible than every other evil. This is the evil of children witnessing the murder of other children, while knowing that they also are to be murdered in the same way, being absolutely aware that they face the identical fate."[7]

No wonder Wiesel has commented that "[children] above all, were the principal victims of the annihilation. At Birkenau they were the first to disappear into the flames which black-

ened the skies. At Varsovie, at Biliastok and at Galicia, they
were the living targets for the German hunters."

When Wiesel thinks of children it is no longer of "inno-
cence, sunshine, happiness, play, laughter, teasing, dreaming,
simple chants. . . ." No. Now:

> Children for me evoke war, thunder and hate, shouts,
> screams, dogs howling, children in the street hunted, beaten,
> humiliated. I see them walking and running like the old men
> and women who surround them, as though to protest, as
> though to protect them without protecting them. There is no
> protection for Jewish children. . . . You watch them marching,
> marching, and you know they will never come back; and yet you
> go on seeing them, but they no longer see you. ("Then and
> Now," p. 271)

All mysteries lead up to this one:

> I write to understand as much as to be understood. Will I
> succeed one day? Wherever one starts from one reaches dark-
> ness. God? He remains the God of darkness. Man? Source of
> darkness. The killers' sneers, their victims' tears, the onlookers'
> indifference, their complicity and complacency, the divine role
> in all that: I do not understand. A million children massacred:
> I shall never understand. ("Why I Write," pp. 202–203)

In its treatment of children, the incommensurability between
l'univers concentrationnaire and ours is reached, and the breach
is total. The Event defies description: one cannot speak.

So much for the bind of the messenger.

More briefly, the bind of the listener.

The *inability* to hear is a byproduct of the incommensurability. One hears words but cannot take them in. Six million? A
number incapable of internalization. A special plan to exterminate the Jews? Unthinkable. Children tossed alive on bonfires?
Impossible to imagine. Not a part of our experience. *Not a part
of our experience.* . . . Here is a partial explanation; if there are
no analogies for the writer, there are even fewer for the listener. It is easier, Wiesel informs us, for those in Auschwitz to
imagine themselves free, than for others to imagine themselves in Auschwitz.

More serious than the inability to hear is the *unwillingness* to hear. It is not simply that we shy away from hearing ghastly things about others; indeed, we are sometimes a little too eager for just that—lusting for psychological voyeurism in observing another's pain. It is rather that we are afraid that what we hear about others will tell us something about ourselves that we do not want to hear. Who wants to hear about SS guards, when there is a not-quite-surfaced feeling that in similar circumstances we might have acted that way? The vehemence with which we deny the accusation may be a pointer to how close the thrust has come.

Indeed, we go out of our way to parry the thrust. Legitimate questions about the complicity of the spectators are turned into illegitimate indictments of the victims. The real question for us is surely: Why did the world stand by silently, giving no help to the Jews? Unwilling to face that question, the accused turns accuser: Why did Jews go submissively to their deaths? Why did they not rebel? And then, insidiously, seldom asked outright but often asked by indirection: And you, you who survived, at what price to your neighbor did you survive? From whose hands did you steal the bread that saved your life and cost the life of the other?

If there is a place for such questions, it is on the lips of survivors rather than bystanders—and survivors torture themselves with such interrogation. On the lips of bystanders, such questions are craven attempts to avoid the real question: Where were *you?*

Another reason for unwillingness to listen is trivialization: I have read a book about the Holocaust, I know about it, I saw the TV show, what else is new? Lawrence Langer sees this as a basic problem for writers:

> Perhaps never before in the history of literature have authors had to fight a reader reluctance based not on an inability to understand what they are about—this had been the initial fate of *Ulysses, The Sound and the Fury,* and *Waiting for Godot,* for example—but on the alleged assumption of the reader that he understood it only too well, that there is little need to burden the human imagination with further morbid explorations of a horrible reality which anyone with a long memory or a diligent curiosity is already acquainted with.[8]

Such persons will probably continue to evade the great reversal that took place in the kingdom of night. In our universe, the primal command was "Let there be light!"; in *l'univers concentrationnaire,* the primal command was, "Let there be night!" And there was night.

Fiat lux was replaced by *fiat nox.*

One must speak. One cannot speak. When one tries to speak one feels guilty of betrayal. Awesome dilemma for the user of words: words themselves betray.

The Event defies description: one cannot speak.

The Event suggests an alternative: one could choose silence

There is another alternative, a decision not to speak at all. The discussion has pushed us to the brink of one kind of silence, *a silence born of frustration* in the face of the incommensurability of the two worlds.

But there are other kinds of silence, and Wiesel explores several of them. There is, for example, *a silence born of respect,* a silence that honors the dead too much to profane their memory by using words already doomed to fail.

Wiesel imposed a ten-year vow of silence on himself after his release from Buchenwald "to be sure that what I would say would be true" ("Talking and Writing and Keeping Silent," p. 274). The decision itself indicates that he was already entertaining the possibility of speaking, but not too soon, not too glibly. There were reasons, he tells us, why the survivors did not initially speak, but exercised a silence born of respect. They were afraid that no one would believe them, and that as a result they would leave the dead doubly betrayed—first by the killers and then by those who made their deaths unbelievable ("it couldn't have happened") or even believable ("oh, now I understand"), both responses signalling that the hearer has heard nothing. Indeed, Wiesel writes, the survivors often did not speak for fear of committing sin by doing so. A silence born of respect was preferable to words that brought dishonor.

But there can also be *a silence of communicative power,* a silence that says something far more powerfully than words could ever do. Such silence might "tell" another generation things that could not be told in any other way.

> Twenty-five years after the event, I wonder whether we shouldn't have chosen silence then. For some reason, I believe that had all the survivors gathered in a secret conclave, somewhere in a forest, and decided together—I know it's a poetic image, unfeasible, but I feel this sense of loss of this opportunity—if we had then all of us decided never to say a word about it, I think we could have changed man by the very weight of our silence. ("Talking and Writing and Keeping Silent," p. 275)

The idea seems strange. Communicate by not communicating? No, Wiesel suggests, communicate by communicating in a different way. Let the silence bear the agony, transmit the agony, force others to confront the agony.

There are two forms this communicative silence could take, and Wiesel has explored them both. The first is subtle: a silence *within* speech. The second is not subtle at all: a silence that *negates* speech.

A musical analogy can help us understand the silence within speech. Composers employ sound to communicate with their listeners. But they also employ . . . silence. Without the "rest," the moment when there is no sound at all, the tools of melody, harmony and rhythm would be impoverished. Beethoven's second "Rasumovsky" quartet (Opus 59, No. 2) opens with two strong minor chords, followed by a full measure of silence. The silence seems unending. Finally there is a two measure theme, followed by another full measure of silence. The two measure theme is repeated, transposed, followed by another full measure of silence. Only after that does the principal theme return. Richard Wagner, commenting on this introduction, reflected that the silences are "as full of significance as sound." The silences are as important as the music itself. Better, *they are part of the music.* Remove them, and we do not hear what the composer wants us to "hear." The silence between the notes communicates to us.

So with Wiesel. It is the silence within his speech, the silence between the words, that communicates to us. What is not said is as important as what is said. Perhaps more so. He claims to have written only one book about the Holocaust, his autobiographical *Night,* and it is sparse, taut, and lean—communication by understatement rather than overstatement. What it does not say is fully as important as what it does. The five novels that follow are about post-Holocaust situations, and although the Holocaust pervades them all, its demonic power is likewise communicated by indirection. Wiesel has only to refer to what happened *there,* or speak of "the kingdom of night," for us to be immersed in a world of horror. He asks us to hear the sentences between the words he writes. In a short story, "The Graveyard Penitent," Rebbe Mendel is described as one who "would listen to the silence that followed words" (*A Jew Today,* p. 95), for it was then that true communication took place.

A reason to read Wiesel slowly: every word counts. So do the silences between the words.

In the "Dialogues" in *One Generation After* and *A Jew Today,* every unnecessary word has been excised. The reader has to intuit time, place, participants. There are only hints, allusions that grow in meaning with each rereading. Wiesel has called them "my most intimate form of writing." One of them (*A Jew Today,* pp. 149–152), which we gradually realize is an exchange between brother and sister, parted forever at the entrance of Birkenau, Elie and Tziporah, has a fearful beauty, a tenderness and poignancy that are almost unbearable, suffused with a love the brother and sister could later have shared. It is unutterably true even though it never happened—the supreme example of Wiesel's conviction that some events are true "although they never occurred" (*Legends,* p. viii). Ten times as many words would communicate one-tenth as much. It is the silence between the words that counts.

But even the silence within speech may fail. The distance between what the storyteller says through silence and what his listeners hear may be too great. There remains a yet more radical surgery, *a silence that negates speech.*

The proposal is no mere trial balloon, hoisted only for the purpose of being shot down. Wiesel takes it seriously enough to test it in book-length form. He has called *The Oath* his "most despairing book," written after he had written ten previous books that seemed to change nothing. So he asks himself: if testifying with words has been ineffectual, how about testifying with silence? *The Oath* examines such a possibility.

Its starting point is found in two earlier books. At the beginning of *The Gates of the Forest,* Wiesel inserted a Hasidic tale that has become justly famous as a key to understanding his own intent:

> When the great Rabbi Israel Baal Shem-Tov saw misfortune threatening the Jews it was his custom to go into a certain part of the forest to meditate. There he would light a fire, say a special prayer, and the miracle would be accomplished and the misfortune averted.
>
> Later, when his disciple, the celebrated Magid of Mezeritch, had occasion, for the same reason, to intercede with heaven, he would go to the same place in the forest and say, "Master of the Universe, listen! I do not know how to light the fire, but I am still able to say the prayer," and again the miracle would be accomplished.
>
> Still later, Rabbi Moshe-Leib of Sasov, in order to save his people once more, would go into the forest and say: "I do not know how to light the fire, I do not know the prayer, but I know the place and this must be sufficient." It was sufficient and the miracle was accomplished.
>
> Then it fell to Rabbi Israel of Rizhyn to overcome misfortune. Sitting in his armchair, his head in his hands, he spoke to God: "I am unable to light the fire and I do not know the prayer; I cannot even find the place in the forest. All I can do is to tell the story, and this must be sufficient."
>
> And it was sufficient. (*Gates,* pp. 6–9)

A beautiful story. Despite the apparent diminution from action to meditation to ritual to remembrance, "to tell the story" was sufficient. Wiesel did it superbly through book after book. It was sufficient.

Later on, in *Souls on Fire,* he retells the same story with the same ending, "It was sufficient," but adds, "It no longer is. The proof is that the threat has not been averted. Perhaps we are no longer able to tell the story" (*Souls,* p. 168).

Simply "telling the story" appears to have been ineffectual: "the threat has not been averted," the message has not been heard, communication has been inadequate. If "we are no longer able to tell the story," then the alternative must be explored: *not* to tell it. And that is the alternative *The Oath* explores.

There is going to be a pogrom in Kolvillàg. What else is new? There have been pogroms throughout Jewish history, and Jews have always chronicled them assiduously, hoping the chronicle would change history, induce repentance, and create a compassionate attitude toward Jews in the hearts of the instigators of pogroms. Moshe—a character we will meet many times—knows all the reasons for continuing to chronicle. "The enemy," he reminds the assembled Jews who are waiting for tragedy to strike, "can do with us as he pleases, but never will he silence us—that has been our motto. Words have been our weapon, our shield; the tale, our lifeboat" (*The Oath*, p. 238).

He makes the case with passion, a passion shared by his author-creator, who has exemplified it with every word he writes.

But then quite unexpectedly, Moshe shifts ground. Totally. "Now we shall adopt a new way," he continues angrily, "silence."

> "We are going to start on an unexplored path, one which does not lead to the outside, to expression. We shall innovate, do what our ancestors and forebears could not or dared not do. We are going to impose the ultimate challenge, *not by language but by the absence of language*, not by the word, but by the abdication of the word. . . . We shall testify no more." (*The Oath*, p. 239, italics added)

To Moshe, the logic is clear: "Here is the one solution we have not yet tried; that is its merit. It is the only one left that may work. I ask you to adopt it. No, I order you!" (pp. 239–240). It is a logic born of desperation, but a logic nevertheless: we have tried speaking and it has not worked; therefore let us try silence, perhaps it will work.

In desperate situations, a logic of desperation can be compelling. In this case it is. All the Jews in Kolvillàg bind themselves under the sign of the *Herem*, the dreadful agreement that anyone who breaks the oath shall be cursed. Moshe spares no pains: "May he who breaks this eternally sealed vow, he who defiles this oath be cursed!" (*The Oath,* p. 241). And the people are consenting.

The pogrom comes, and all the Jews are destroyed save Azriel, who escapes not only with his memories, but also with the chronicles of his father. He keeps both of them locked within his heart and memory for fifty years, faithful to the oath he had sworn. The burden is heavy; he seeks release from the oath at the hands of a *zaddik,* and is refused. He will die, it seems, with the secret of Kolvillàg unrevealed.

And then Azriel meets a young Jew, child of holocaust survivors. The young Jew cannot understand what happened to his parents, they cannot communicate with him, and his despair is so great that he is contemplating suicide. Azriel wonders: "Have I lived and survived only for this encounter and this challenge? Only to defeat death in this particular case? Could I have been spared in Kolvillàg so I could help a stranger?" (*The Oath,* p. 32).

How could he "defeat death in this particular case"? By breaking his oath, by telling the story. What would be the consequence? He muses to himself:

> I'll transmit my experience to him and he, in turn, will be compelled to do the same. He in turn will become a messenger. And once a messenger, he has no alternative. He must stay alive until he has transmitted his message. Azriel himself would not still be alive if his father the chronicler, his friends and his teacher Moshe the Madman had not made him the repository of their tragic and secret truths. By entrusting the Book to him, his father doomed him to survival. So this is the example to follow, Azriel pondered. I shall hold him responsible for Kolvillàg. (*The Oath,* p. 33)

He does so, giving the young man the liberating burden of responsibility for the story. "Now," Azriel tells him, "having received this story, you no longer have the right to die" (p. 282). And the young man accepts the burden. The book itself is his transmission of the message.

So an oath is broken, and for what purpose? To save a life, a single life. No oath is as important as a single life. No dedication to principle is higher than dedication to life itself. It is a heavy price: to save one life from death involves telling the story of many deaths. But whatever will save one life from death must be attempted, even if it means coming under the curse of the *Herem*.

After the book was published, Wiesel got an unsigned postcard. It said simply, *"The Oath* saved my life."

The oath of silence had to be broken because even a silence that communicates, by negating speech, is always in danger of becoming *a silence that betrays*. It can betray the dead by letting them be forgotten, but it can also—and this is the point of *The Oath*—betray the living. Azriel must break his oath of silence because failure to do so may lead to the death of his young companion. And no more offerings, anywhere, at any time, by anyone, should be made to death.

So perhaps Wiesel's "most despairing book," is not finally a despairing book, but, on however modest a scale, a hopeful book. If one life can be saved—the life of the youth to whom Azriel told the tale of Kolvillàg, or the life of the unsigned correspondent to whom Elie Wiesel told the tale of Kolvillàg—that both justifies and necessitates the telling of the tale.

The world knew what was happening in 1933–34–35–36—and remained silent. The world knew about the Warsaw ghetto uprising in 1943—and remained silent. The world knew about Auschwitz and Treblinka in 1943–44—and remained silent. Silence is no virtue; it is vice twice-compounded: indifference toward the victims, complicity with the executioners.

The Event precludes silence: one must become a messenger

The dilemma has been intensified: speech betrays so we must forswear speech, but silence also betrays so we must forsake silence. There is only one way to go: to break silence, to be a messenger.

We appear merely to have returned to our starting point, "The Event took place: one must speak." But we have become alerted to various betrayals and are forewarned to avoid them. And we can affirm silence *within* speech as part of the way to communicate.

One becomes a messenger, then, because one cannot *not* speak.

> When man, in his grief, falls silent, Goethe says, then God gives him the strength to sing of his sorrows. From that moment on, *he may no longer choose not to sing*, whether his song is heard or not. What matters is to struggle against silence with words, or through another form of silence. ("Why I Write," pp. 205–206, italics added)

At Treblinka, there is a memorial to the victims. It is many things: acres of stones, simulated railroad ties, charred bones on the site of a crematorium. In the midst of it all there are two words, carved in stone in six languages, the words *Never Again*. They answer the question, "Why must one become a messenger?"—so that *never again* can these things happen, so that *never again* can the world remain silent, so that *never again* will children be thrown alive on the flames, so that *never again* will a people be targeted for extermination simply because they are . . . a people.

To survive was one thing, but it alone was insufficient. It was necessary "not only to survive but to testify. The victims elect to become witnesses." (*Generation*, p. 38)

But what kind of witness, what kind of messenger? Elie Wiesel exemplifies at least four kinds of messengers:

1. He is *a messenger from the dead*. He speaks on their behalf, so they may be heard and so they will not be forgotten. Having returned from the kingdom of night, he must speak for those who did not: "Why do I write? To wrench those victims from oblivion. To help the dead vanquish death" ("Why I Write," p. 206). Often on their way to the gas chambers, victims would say to those still alive in the camps: remember everything, do not forget, tell the story, at any cost.

In a discussion of holocaust art, Wiesel writes:

> Let us tell tales so as to remember how vulnerable man is when faced with overwhelming evil. Let us tell tales so as not to allow the executioner to have the last word. The last word belongs to the victim. It is up to the witness to capture it, shape it, transmit it and still keep it as a secret, and then communicate

that secret to others. ("Art and Culture after the Holocaust,"
p. 403)

An uprising of the prisoners at Treblinka was undertaken
not only to destroy the camp, but also to make sure that at least
one person got away to tell the tale. Wiesel comments frequently about the number of chronicles left by those who died
in the Warsaw ghetto uprising. They, though doomed to die,
wanted the story to be told. Consequently, those who live must
continue to bring a message from the dead. The survivor may
not escape the curse—or mandate—scribbled on a latrine wall
in one of the camps: "May he be damned who, after regaining
freedom, remains silent."

It is not a vocation willingly assumed or joyfully maintained.
But it is inescapable, for the dead are inescapable. Where is
there a paragraph in modern literature to match the poignancy
of the following?

> I hear a voice within me telling me to stop mourning the
> past. I too want to sing of love and its magic. I too want to
> celebrate the sun, and the dawn that heralds the sun. I would
> like to shout, and shout loudly: "Listen, listen well! I too am
> capable of victory, do you hear? I too am open to laughter and
> joy! I want to stride, head high, my face unguarded, without
> having to point to the ashes over there on the horizon, without
> having to tamper with facts to hide their tragic ugliness. For a
> man born blind, God himself is blind, but look, I see, I am not
> blind." One feels like shouting this, but the shout changes to
> a murmur. One must make a choice; one must remain faithful.
> A big word, I know. Nevertheless, I use it, it suits me. Having
> written the things I have written, I feel I can afford no longer
> to play with words. If I say that the writer in me wants to remain
> loyal, it is because it is true. This sentiment moves all survivors;
> they owe nothing to anyone, but everything to the dead. ("Why
> I Write," p. 202)

"They owe nothing to anyone, but everything to the dead."

2. Not quite true of Wiesel. He feels an obligation to be a
messenger from the dead but also *a messenger for the living*. The
task of such a messenger is to warn of consequences and to
affirm possibilities.

He must warn of consequences. If the message "never again" is

from the dead, it is a message *for* the living, a warning expressed
in many ways: It could happen again. It must never happen
again. Watch for the tell-tale signs, signs that before were not
seen until too late. Next time there can be no excuse.

The warning is for all. When people can destroy Jews with
impunity, it is not long before they destroy other people as
well: "Whatever happens to the Jews happens to all mankind.
People thought they could kill Jews and remain alive, and they
were wrong. When they kill Jews, they kill themselves" (*Responses,* p. 13).

This is not just a figure of speech. Toward the end of the
pogrom in *The Oath,* the mob, having run out of Jews to kill,
sets fire to a building with Christians inside:

> Meanwhile, caught up in the frenzy, the killers were killing
> each other, senselessly, with swords, hatchets and clubs. Brothers and sisters striking one another, friends and accomplices
> strangling one another. (*The Oath,* p. 279)

The scene escalates in intensity. Soon the whole village is in
flames. "And suddenly," the narrator comments with frightening accuracy, "I understood with every fibre of my being why
I was shuddering at this vision of horror: I had just glimpsed
the future" (p. 281).

"Kolvillàg" is indeed, as its etymology indicates, "every
village." (An important rubric in reading Wiesel: analyze every
name.) The line from it extends to other villages and other
fires that were yet to come: Auschwitz, Treblinka, Coventry,
Dresden, Hiroshima, Nagasaki, Birmingham, Hanoi, Soweto.
Wiesel is fearful that accounts are not yet settled, and that if
the first Holocaust breeds a second one, it will take the form
of thermonuclear destruction, not just of Jews but of all the
human family. Before Auschwitz, no one could have predicted
the likelihood that crematoria flames would be a discriminate
destroyer of part of the human race. After Auschwitz, no one
can evade the likelihood that nuclear flames will be an indiscriminate destroyer of most of the human race. So:

> If the role of the writer may once have been to entertain, that
> of the witness is to disturb, alert, to waken, to warn against
> indifference to injustice—any injustice—and above all against
> complacency about any need and any people. If once upon a

time words may have been used by tellers of tales to please, they must be used today to displease, to unsettle. ("A Personal Response," p. 36)

A messenger to the living must warn of consequences. But such a one must also *affirm new possibilities.* The very decision to witness is an affirmation of new possibilities, an act of faith in people, faith that they might listen, faith that they can be touched, faith that words can still transform.

> I believe the purpose of literature is to correct injustice. People were killed . . . I try in my books to bring them back to life or at least to bring their death back to life. People suffered . . . I try to give meaning to their suffering. I write to surprise, not to inform. . . .
>
> My main obsession [is] how to transmit. If we cannot transmit, we are dead. The difference between death and life is that life transmits, death stops . . . What I try to say is this: Fate is cruel; what we can and must do is impose a human meaning on that fate. The moment I give my despair to someone that gift may become to him a reason for hope. (*Responses,* pp. 10, 13)

The mandate "to impose a human meaning on . . . fate" is stern but also liberating. It affirms that however much we have been crippled by the past we need not be immobilized by it. If out of one person's despair, hope can be born for another, then at least despair does not have the final word.

It is significant that the novel in which despair comes closest to having the final word, *The Oath,* is also the novel in which the affirmation of new possibilities is most clear. As Michael Berenbaum has pointed out, Wiesel's message in *The Oath* "involves a positive affirmation of life which moves beyond despair. Wiesel has moved from a protest against death to an outright appeal to life. . . . For the first time in any of Wiesel's novels, the major narrator clearly advocates life."[9]

When affirmation is possible in a world that seems to demand its denial, there is reason indeed to be a messenger.

Confirmation comes in a Hasidic tale about Rabbi Nahman that Wiesel frequently recounts. One version:

> Once upon a time there was a king who knew that the next harvest would be cursed. Whoever would eat from it would go mad. And so he ordered an enormous granary built and stored

there all that remained from the last crop. He entrusted the key to his friend and this is what he told him: "When my subjects and their king will have been struck with madness, you alone will have the right to enter the storehouse and eat uncontaminated food. Thus you will escape the malediction. But in exchange, your mission will be to cover the earth, going from country to country, from town to town, from one street to the other, from one man to the other, telling tales, ours—and you will shout, you will shout with all your might: Good people, do not forget! What is at stake is your life, your survival! So do not forget, do not forget! (*Souls*, p. 202)

The terms of the tale need revision for our time: rather than a granary where good food is plentiful, the kingdom of night was a place where not even bad food was plentiful. Through bitter induction into that kingdom, Wiesel was able to "escape the malediction," which for our generation can be defined as forgetfulness or indifference. Such a messenger has an obligation (which may also be a curse) laid upon him: to shout, "Do not forget! What is at stake is your life!"

3. In addition to being a messenger from the dead and a messenger for the living, Wiesel is also a *messenger to heaven*. Like most matters where heaven is concerned, this function of the messenger is harder to pin down. But for Wiesel to describe Leib the Lion at the end of *The Gates of the Forest* as a "messenger to heaven" (p. 223), is an astonishing advance beyond Eliezer, the "messenger from the dead" in *The Accident*.

Clearly to be a messenger to heaven means being charged with the exalted task of taking human messages into the divine presence and demanding a hearing. It can also mean the less agreeable task of contending with God, of holding God accountable for what has gone wrong in a world that is presumably under divine control.

But the task of messenger, in the divine context, can also mean carrying information in the reverse direction as well, as a messenger *of* God, or a messenger *from* God. Wiesel writes increasingly about such messengers, especially those found in the Hebrew Scriptures—Adam, Abraham and Isaac, Jacob, Jonah, Jeremiah, Job, Elisha, Saul. They all contend with God,

and by the seriousness with which they do so, become para-
digms for our own contention.[10]

Wiesel would not characterize himself as a "messenger of
God" but would insist that his commerce with God consists of
posing questions *to* God rather than purveying answers *from*
God. But even if we accept his disclaimer, it remains true that
such a one as he is a messenger to heaven, and a contentious
one at that, as we will later have occasion to document.[11]

4. The messenger has at least one more function. He must
also be *a messenger for the self,* his own self and other selves. He
must attain authenticity in his own inner being if he is to speak
authentically to others. If there is a danger of betraying the
dead, and the living, there is also a danger of betraying the
self. "In the beginning," as Wiesel frequently says, "I thought
I could change man. Today I know I cannot. If I still shout
today, if I still scream, it is to prevent man from ultimately
changing me."

Even with his sights thus scaled down, the messenger is able
to speak across barriers. His obligation to those who cannot
speak (the dead) is also an obligation to those who need to
hear (the living), and the messenger can thus fulfill an obligation to himself (a link between the dead and the living). Only
by being a vehicle of truth for others can he be true to himself.
Only by being true to himself can he be a vehicle of truth for
others. In a passage already cited, Wiesel says that the messenger is compelled to sing "whether his song is heard or not."
That is true enough, but if there is a choice it must always be
for songs that *can* be heard by others. It is a betrayal to do
otherwise. At an early age Wiesel learned an important lesson
from his grandfather: "Listen attentively, and above all, remember that true tales are meant to be transmitted—to keep
them to oneself is to betray them" (*Souls*, p. 7).

A messenger in isolation is no messenger. There must also
be someone to receive the message. A messenger can proclaim
from the housetops, but if no one is listening inside the
houses, the gesture is at best grandiloquent and at worst futile
—unless the messenger is addressing his message solely to
God . . . who may or may not be listening.

The Event suggests a certain kind of messenger: one can be a teller of tales

It is not enough to insist *that* the messenger must speak. It is also necessary to ask: *how* must the messenger speak? What will be his mode of communication?

Wiesel has made a clear decision to this matter: he has become a teller of tales. Perhaps, more accurately, the decision was made for him even before he was born. For Jews have always been tellers of tales. Their scriptures are not philosophical essays or logically constructed arguments in which premises are stated, implications explored, and conclusions reached. They are rather stories—told orally at first, gradually gathered together by this scribe and that, embellished here, revised there, retold a second time from a different point of view; stories of God, kings, rogues, women, and battles, in the form of epics, poems, songs, dynasties, real estate transactions, old men's memories, lovers' laments, and entreaties.

His Jewish heritage has bequeathed multiple benefits in Wiesel's case, for Hasidism, the particular strand of Judaism to which he belongs, abounds in storytellers. Hasidic literature is an intricate tangle of stories, tales, anecdotes, and legends, sometimes long and involved, frequently completed in a few pithy lines. Ask a Hasid a question and you get a story. Ask specifically for an answer to a question and you get another story . . . which turns out to be the answer . . . in the form of a question.

Irving Greenberg, in a provocative essay on Wiesel,[12] points out that *the prophet* used to be the one to confront Jews with the story of creation and redemption. The prophet spoke unequivocally: "Thus says the Lord . . ." But a time came when the story of God's redemptive action was shattered, or at least dramatically challenged, by the destruction of the temple. So the prophet was replaced by *the rabbi,* the one who searched, who questioned, who told the story "in a form believable after a catastrophe," in a world where the redemption the prophets believed in was no longer manifest.

But now there has been an even worse destruction, the Holocaust, which not only "dramatically challenges" the words of prophet and rabbi alike, but shatters them. The prophet cannot speak to the rabbinic world, nor can the rabbi speak to the Holocaust world. Another kind of teacher is needed. Greenberg feels that such a teacher has come "in even more secular guise—as *a teller of a tale.*" The story will continue to be told, but it will be told in a new form, and to Greenberg, Elie Wiesel is its prime examplar.

Although I later want to reclaim the mantle of prophet for Wiesel, I find Greenberg's analysis helpful because of his insistence that the Holocaust creates a totally new situation, not only for Jews but for all of us. Our old world has been shattered. So have our old ways of viewing it, let alone "explaining" it. And in that situation storytelling speaks as no other mode of communication can do.

To explore this claim, we must commit the ultimate sin against the storyteller and reflect systematically about what happens when stories are told:

1. The story teller creates *a bridge between two worlds.* His story brings us into contact with a world to which access is otherwise denied us. And this is no more than a recapitulation of his own experience, for just as we receive from another, so does he. His is not so much as act of creation, as an act of re-creation, of imaginative rearrangement. Wiesel got many stories from his grandfather, Dodye Feig, and through him from the entire Hasidic tradition. He is very honest about this dependency:

> You can invent a novel, but not a story. You think you invented it, but you didn't. . . . Whatever I have, I have received. Whatever I give belongs to who knows how many generations of Jewish scholars and dreamers and poets. I have received the words, and in combining them I am simply fulfilling the function of a messenger, which is to me as important as that of a storyteller. In fact, the story teller is important only as a messenger. (*Victory,* p. 24)

Storyteller and messenger are one, commissioned to open up to their listeners a message from another world than their own.

Must the story be "true" to communicate truth to us? Not an important question for the storyteller unless one insists on a positivistic notion of "truth," a framework alien to the storyteller. A rebbe once accused Wiesel of "writing lies" because he was creating fiction, i.e. writing about things that had not "really happened." Wiesel's response: "Things are not that simple, Rebbe. Some events do take place but are not true; others are—although they never occurred" (*Legends*, p. viii). It is the task of the storyteller to transmit events that never took place, but are true.

Is the Holocaust "true"? Wiesel confesses to wondering sometimes if it ever really happened. Does a Hasidic tale lose its "truth" if it appears in three different versions attributed to three different writers describing three different *zaddikim?* Perhaps it is all the more true for describing an aspect of the human situation that seems universally applicable. At all events, stories go far beyond what we limpingly call "mere factual truth." We hear that in Chelmno one man ordered another man to bury two Jews alive, and that after doing so both of them went home that night and listened to Mozart. We will never plumb the mystery of how one of them could give such an order and the other obey it. A story about the event will not dissolve the mystery or give us an answer, but it will juxtapose a world where such things happen with our own world.

2. But the story does not just juxtapose two worlds. It forces us to *confront the other world*. It suggests that the world in which we are comfortable, with which we are familiar, may not be the only world, may not even (terrifying thought) be the "real" world any longer. The story from elsewhere, precisely because it is a story and not an essay or a diagram, can be framed in the "logic" of another world, which is not our logic at all. It can have an inner consistency according to its own logic that seems alien and strange to us but then haunts us with a nagging fear: what if the logic that works there works here also? Words can do dangerous things to us. Wiesel recalls:

> It was the "Selishter Rebbe" who told me one day: "Be careful with words, they're dangerous. Be wary of them. They beget either demons or angels. It's up to you to give life to one or the other. Be careful, I tell you, nothing is as dangerous as giving free rein to words." (*Legends*, p. 31)

The logic of the Auschwitz world makes no sense in our world, but it makes perfect sense in the Auschwitz world. Try this: Jews are vermin, therefore Jews should be exterminated. Q.E.D. Or this: children are helpless, but children grow up and become strong, after which they are dangerous, therefore Jewish children should be exterminated before they are strong enough to be dangerous. Q.E.D. Absolutely.

Put together "Jews" and "children," arrive at "Jewish children," and the conclusion is that throwing them alive on bonfires is quite all right. It happened. You don't believe me? I was there. Let me tell you a story . . .

A story from the camps forces us to confront a world in which such logic is the order of the day. It is a report on what goes on in that other world of *l'univers concentrationnaire*. That world and our world do not "fit." The other is grotesque. Ours is reasonable. They have nothing in common.

3. But they do have something in common: the storyteller. The storyteller inhabits both worlds. He was in the other and now he is in ours.

This is disturbing. It means that we cannot dismiss his stories from one world as though they were unrelated to our world. What happens (unless we are immensely clever at safeguarding ourselves), is that the story not only confronts us; it also implicates us, involves us, *draws us into it*. Not very far. But far enough so that we can no longer live as though Auschwitz had never happened. Far enough so that we can imagine that had we been there we might have been among the SS guards, we might have unleashed the killer dogs, we might have bashed the babies' heads, we might have dropped the Zyklon B into the gas chamber . . .

The task of the storyteller is not to "entertain" us, but to engage us, to draw us in, so that the mad logic of the story from another world becomes a logic credible enough so that we can see that it could be the logic of our world.

We see ourselves in the stories of others. This is true even of the storyteller. When Wiesel recalls tales two centuries old, they become tales about himself. He offers this as a reason why he collected the Hasidic tales in *Souls on Fire:*

> In his role of storyteller, and that is the essential point—he has but one motivation: *to tell of himself while telling of others*. He wishes neither to teach nor to convince, but to close gaps and

create new bonds. Nor does he try to explain what was or even what is; he only tries to wrest from death certain prayers, certain faces, by appealing to the imagination and the nostalgia that makes man listen when his story is told. (*Souls,* p. 259, italics added)

What happens to the tellers of tales happens to the listeners as well:

True writers want to tell the story simply because they believe they can do something with it—their lives are not fruitless and are not spent in vain. True listeners want to listen to stories to enrich their own lives and to understand them. What is happening to me happens to you. *Both the listener and the reader are participants in the same story and both make it the story it is.* (*Conversation,* p. 86, italics added)

Some years ago I taught a class on Wiesel to undergraduates. When we finished *The Town Beyond the Wall,* with its powerful visions of madness, most of the students, products of "well-adjusted" upbringings, had difficulty relating even to the notion of madness. But one student, who had been up two nights in a row with a roommate on the verge of a breakdown, said of the conversations with the roommate, "She had told me everything I read in this book." The student could better cope with the roommate for having read *The Town Beyond the Wall;* the student could better understand *The Town Beyond the Wall* for having coped with the roommate. The storyteller brought her two worlds together.

Let the point be kept within the context of what Wiesel has repeatedly said elsewhere: one who was not *there* can ever understand it, and one who was there can never communicate it. But to whatever degree there is commerce between the two worlds, it is the storyteller who provides it.

4. After there has been such commerce, *we can never be the same again.* This is even more disturbing. One who has seen even the periphery of the kingdom of night will never again feel fully at ease in the center of the kingdom of light. Which means that how we think, feel, react, struggle, love, engage, will all be subject to new beginnings. Old categories will be inadequate, new categories frightening. "In the beginning there was the Holocaust," Wiesel once stated in a conversation

with other Jewish thinkers, "We must therefore start all over
again" ("Jewish Values in the Post-Holocaust Future," p. 285).
And starting all over again is the most disturbing thing possible. It means that we will spend more time asking questions
than offering answers. And it will be the contribution of stories
to intensify the questions rather than to offer answers. Repeatedly, Wiesel disavows answers; repeatedly he claims that it is
his vocation to raise questions, and then press them, not only
to human beings but to God as well . . . to God supremely,
since God has the most to answer for. Advice to the graduating
class at Manhattan College:

> Anyone who tells you he has the answers to the questions—
> with all apologies to your teachers, I do not believe them.
> There are no answers to true questions. There are only good
> questions, painful sometimes, exuberant at others. Whatever I
> have learned in my life is questions. And whatever I have tried
> to share with friends is questions. (*New York Times,* May 27,
> 1972)

This does not make human exchanges fruitless. It simply
means that to be fruitful they must be structured and resolved
in ways other than we had expected. Rabbi Nahman of Bratzlav: "Two men separated by space and time can nevertheless
take part in an exchange. One asks a question and the other,
elsewhere and later, asks another, unaware that his question
is an answer to the first" (*Souls,* p. 201).

Answers offered by some, may turn out to be new forms of
the question, and thus shed further light on the state of the
question. An example:

> The Messiah may come by accident, said a Hasidic Master,
> one hundred and fifty years ago. Today he would say: the end
> of the world may come by accident. How can it be saved? That's
> not for the novelist to say. There is a "Savior" for that particu-
> lar purpose. But the Savior, according to the tradition of my
> people, is not one person; he is in all of us. Which means: we
> can—we must—help him help us. Which means: we must ap-
> peal to our collective memory: only the tale of what was done
> to my people can save humankind from a similar fate. Which
> means: we must care—lest we fall victims to our own indiffer-
> ence.

Could this be the answer? No. But—it is the question. (Roth,
A Consuming Fire, p. 18)

5. All of which means that the story teller operates under
a moral constraint. He does not indulge in creation for the sake
of creating, or art for art's sake. He wants to open doors,
display new possibilities, press obligations, call for decisions.
Wiesel sees stories as agents of our humanization. He cites
with approval Rebbe Wolfe of Zhitomir, "the spoken word's
function is to humanize thought," (*Souls,* p. 87); and then later
offers a summary of his own: "The essence of a Hasidic legend? An attempt to humanize fate" (p. 257). Thought can be
impersonal; it must be humanized. Fate can be impersonal; it
must be humanized. Another way to state the imperative:

> To be a writer also means to correct injustices. The injustice
> in history is that some things are forgotten but others remain.
> People are dead but others survive who do not remember the
> dead. When entire communities are swallowed up and nothing
> remains, then it's an injustice. All this makes me into a writer
> but the word "writer" really does not apply. I see myself much
> more as a storyteller. (*Conversation,* p. 84)

To humanize thought and fate, to correct injustices. In neither case is the story an end in itself. It is an instrument
demanding response, which means responsibility to see that
injustices are corrected. Anything else is indulgence.

Wiesel tried to explain to the recalcitrant Rebbe who
thought he was writing lies that "some writings could sometimes, in moments of grace, attain the quality of deeds" (*Legends,* p. viii). He comments that the Rebbe didn't seem to
understand.

Poor Rebbe. He missed the whole point.

CHAPTER 2

Darkness That Eclipses Light
(a moral journey—1)

*The Holocaust is a sacred realm. One cannot enter
this realm without realizing that only those who were
there can know. But the outsider can come close to the
gates. One can never know and yet one must try.*
—Elie Wiesel, in *Counterpoint,* Fall 1980

There is a darkness that eclipses light. It is the darkness of
Auschwitz into which Elie Wiesel entered. The rest of us can
never enter that realm, can never know that darkness: "Only
those who were there can know." But those who were there
feel morally constrained to share what was there, so that we,
the outsiders, "can come close to the gates." We can never
know, and yet we must try.

Ten years after his liberation from Buchenwald—ten years
during which he lived out a vow of silence so that he would not
falsify—Elie Wiesel broke his silence with an account of the
kingdom of night. A Yiddish version, *And the World Has Remained Silent,* appeared in 1956, and a condensed version, *La
Nuit,* the version the world knows, was published in French in
1958, appearing in English in 1960 as *Night.* Once the authori-
al floodgates had been opened, five novels appeared in quick
succession: *Dawn* (1960), *The Accident* (1961), *The Town Beyond
the Wall* (1962), *The Gates of the Forest* (1964), *A Beggar in Jerusalem* (1968).[1] They conduct the reader on a moral journey of
awesome proportions.

The journey's starting point is *Night.* Every subsequent

50

book is commentary on that spare and unsparing text. Wiesel describes it as "a kind of testimony of one witness speaking of his own life, his own death," and then continues:

> All kinds of options were available: suicide, madness, killing, political action, hate, friendship. I note all of these options: faith, rejection of faith, blasphemy, atheism, denial, rejection of man, despair, and in each book I explore one aspect. In *Dawn* I explore the political action; in *The Accident,* suicide; in *The Town Beyond the Wall,* madness; in *The Gates of the Forest,* faith and friendship; in *A Beggar in Jerusalem,* history, the return. All the stories are one story except that I build them in concentric circles. The center is the same and is in *Night.* (*Conversation,* p. 86)

The reality of *Night* is the reality of the monstrous moral evil that was the Holocaust. Wiesel copes in each book with a possible answer to the question: *how do we respond to monstrous moral evil?* Most of the answers turn out to be destructive, as though monstrous moral evil retained final power over all attempts to challenge it, a darkness unremittingly eclipsing light.

Can light ever penetrate the darkness again? We are not entitled to anticipate an affirmative answer easily, as though we could eliminate the intervening steps on the journey, because they are so painful. Our guide did not have that privilege, and we must deny it to ourselves, walking one step at a time with him, remembering that we will always be "outsiders," and yet remembering also, with gratitude, that he will help us.

Victim

Of all of Wiesel's works, *Night* is the one that most cries out not to be touched, interpreted, synthesized. It must be encountered at first hand. The only justification for the following pages is to force that encounter.

How, then, do we respond to monstrous moral evil? Sometimes human beings are not even given the privilege of asking the question. The decision is already made for them by the practitioners of evil; they are designated in advance as *victims.*

It was a designation involuntarily assumed six million times during the reign of the kingdom of night by Jews in central Europe.

Many things happen to victims, so *Night* reports. At the heart of them all is shattering, a shattering of world, faith, self, and future.

The victim's world is shattered. The opening pages of *Night* breathe the serenity of a secure world. Sighet, nestled in the Carpathian mountains, is a town where Jews can live between memory and anticipation, drawing on the treasures of the past to create a hopeful future. Within Sighet there was a small boy who "believed profoundly," studying the Talmud by day and weeping over the destruction of the Temple by night. Praying was as natural as breathing to the small boy, who could await each Shabbat tremulous with anticipation that *this* might be the occasion of Messiah's coming. A secure world.

No, not a secure world. Instead, a world that was shattered, beginning with tiny actions at the edges that slowly accelerated, penetrating closer and closer to the vital center, until the entire world that was Sighet came crashing down. First it was the deportation of foreign Jews (Moché the Beadle, for one), followed by unbelievable stories of horrors being exacted against Jews outside the secure world; then, direct occupation by German soldiers, followed by the confiscation of the private property of Jews, the introduction of the yellow star, travel curfews, the creation of two ghettos, and finally, deportation.

The now-familiar scenario unfolded inexorably, but back then it was not familiar and therefore not seen as inexorable. Secure worlds do not shatter easily. Even as the screws of the Nazi machine were progressively tightened, Wiesel records three times with devastating honesty that it appeared that "life had returned to normal" (pp. 15, 16–17, 21).

It never did. It only got worse, even though right up to the time the cattlecars of deportees arrived at Auschwitz, the reluctance to believe the worst persisted. Only crazy people would believe the reports that were circulating, and only crazy people would circulate them. Moché, with tales of Jews digging mass graves, lining up in front of them and being efficiently machine-gunned into them? Moché must be mad.

Madame Schächter, screaming about fires and chimneys in the darkened cattlecar when everybody in the darkened cattlecar knew it contained nothing but frightened, thirst-crazed Jews? Madame Schächter must be mad. The real world was still Sighet, where God still dwelt and there were clean linens on Shabbat.

But the real world was no longer Sighet. The real world, which shattered the old world, was a railway station in upper Silesia, with a name no one in the cattlecars had even heard before. Auschwitz.

The last illusions disappeared when the cattlecar doors opened and the victims emerged on the platform at Birkenau —another unfamiliar name—the death camp of Auschwitz.

Close by were gigantic flames. The pious, deeply-believing boy reports: "They were burning something. A lorry drew up at the pit and delivered its load—little children. Babies! Yes, I saw it—saw it with my own eyes . . . those children in the flames" (p. 42).

What did that do to the piety and deep belief of the boy? In the most widely-quoted passage in holocaust literature, he tells us:

> Never shall I forget that night, the first night in camp, which has turned my life into one long night, seven times cursed and seven times sealed. Never shall I forget that smoke. Never shall I forget the little faces of the children, whose bodies I saw turned into wreathes of smoke beneath a silent blue sky.
>
> Never shall I forget those flames which consumed my faith forever.
>
> Never shall I forget that nocturnal silence which deprived me for all eternity, of the desire to live. Never shall I forget those moments which murdered my God and my soul and turned my dreams to dust. Never shall I forget these things, even if I am condemned to live as long as God Himself. Never. (p. 44)

Every word Wiesel has written since is commentary on that passage. Every bitterness and disappointment confirms it. Every sliver of light and hope is threatened by it. It is the end of a journey—not arrival at a promised land, but final expulsion from one. The exodus story in reverse.

* * *

The victim's faith is shattered. There is a shattering even more devastating than the shattering of one's world. It is the shattering of one's faith—in Wiesel's case the shattering of his faith in God.

He does not become an atheist or assert "the death of God" as many commentators assume. Years later, responding to Richard Rubenstein's assertion that Auschwitz has destroyed God and made denial of God morally mandatory, Wiesel said, "How strange that the philosophy denying God came not from the survivors. Those who came out with the so-called God is dead theology, not one of them had been in Auschwitz" ("Talking and Writing and Keeping Silent," p. 271). Even in the passage just cited, it is not God, but Wiesel's "faith" that is consumed by the flames. What has been "murdered" is "my God and my soul," the God conceived of by the pious Hasidic child of fourteen years. Indeed, the next sentence speaks of the anguish of being "condemned to live as long as God Himself." Do not assume, Wiesel reminds us in every book, that it is consolation to believe that God is still alive. Rather than solution, it simply states the problem. Ever since that first night, Wiesel has struggled with two irreconcilable realities— the reality of God and the reality of Auschwitz. Either seems able to cancel out the other, and yet neither will disappear. Either in isolation could be managed—Auschwitz and no God, or God and no Auschwitz. But Auschwitz *and* God, God *and* Auschwitz? That is the unbearable reality that haunts sleep and destroys wakefulness.

Auschwitz is not going to surrender its demonic power. Must God therefore be forced to surrender the divine power? Why should one say the *Kaddish,* the prayer for the dead, in a death camp? What is there to thank God for, in the land of burning children? (p. 43). He ceases to pray, and sympathizes with Job: "I did not deny God's existence, but I doubted His absolute justice" (p. 56).

The challenge comes to fever pitch at Rosh Hashanah, the Jewish new year. In a biting passage, the young boy records his reaction when ten thousand inmates repeat the ancient refrain, "Blessed be the Name of the Eternal."

Why, but why should I bless Him? In every fiber I rebelled. Because He had had thousands of children burned in His pits? Because He kept six crematories working night and day, on Sundays and feast days? Because in His great might He had created Auschwitz, Birkenau, Buna, and so many factories of death? How could I say to Him: "Blessed art Thou, Eternal, Master of the Universe, Who chose us from among the races to be tortured day and night, to see our fathers, our mothers, our brothers, end in the crematory? Praised be Thy Holy Name, Thou Who hast chosen us to be butchered on Thine altar?" (p. 78)

He even begins to feel strong in his quarrel with God: "I was the accuser, God the accused. . . . I had ceased to be anything but ashes, yet I felt myself to be stronger than the Almighty" (p. 79). On Yom Kippur, the day of atonement, he decides not to fast (grotesque world, in which starving men debate whether to eat or not), and his eating bread and swallowing soup when fasting is prescribed, is a bitter rebellion against God.

And likewise a bitter acknowledgement of God.

Devastating discovery: the comment of a faceless neighbor in the barracks, who had once believed in the promises of God: "I've got more faith in Hitler than in anyone else. He's the only one who's kept his promises, all his promises, to the Jewish people" (p. 92).

Almost at the end, during the long march through the snow, in the face of the betrayal of a father by a son, Wiesel writes, "And, in spite of myself, a prayer rose in my heart, to that God in whom I no longer believed" (p. 104).

Two incidents at Buna, a camp near Auschwitz, encapsulate the shattering of faith.

The first involves the hanging of a prisoner caught stealing during an alert. The others are ordered to stand at attention and witness the execution, after which they are marched past the dead face at close range before being dismissed for supper. A routine incident. Wiesel comments, "I remember that I found the soup excellent that evening" (p. 74).

The second hanging—one of the most devastating scenes in all holocaust literature—involves three inmates, one of them a child, who were suspected of blowing up the power station at Buna. As they approach the gallows, someone behind Wiesel asks, "Where is God? Where is He?" And then the chairs are toppled and the three victims are supported only by the ropes around their necks. Once again the prisoners are marched by the victims at close range so that all may see the dead faces and be deterred.

> The two adults were no longer alive. Their tongues hung swollen, blue-tinged. But the third rope was still moving; being so light, the child was still alive . . .
> For more than half an hour he stayed there, struggling between life and death, dying in slow agony under our eyes. And we had to look him full in the face. He was still alive when I passed in front of him. His tongue was still red, his eyes not yet glazed.
> Behind me, I heard the same man asking:
> "Where is God now?"
> And I heard a voice within me answer him:
> "Where is He? Here He is—He is hanging here on this gallows . . ."
> That night the soup tasted of corpses. (p. 76)

Commenting on this passage verges on blasphemy, and yet we must. Some Christians see God's "hanging here on this gallows" as a replication of Christ's hanging on the cross for the redemption of the world, God's presence in the midst of evil. But this is no replication of the crucifixion story. At best it is parody of that event, and its message is despair, not hope: God on the gallows, God subjected to human demonry, God at the mercy of evil, God embodying death and impotence rather than life and power, God whose "real presence" is such that soup is transubstantiated into corpses.

The victim's self is shattered. When a world is shattered and a faith is shattered, the self who lives in the world and shares the faith is likewise shattered.

The first night in camp has passed. It has been long enough to complete the shattering of the self. The evening and the morning are the first day. Only the first day.

> The night was gone. The morning star was shining in the sky. I too had become a completely different person. The student of the Talmud, the child that I was, had been consumed

in the flames. There remained only a shape that looked like me.
A dark flame had entered my soul and devoured it. (p. 47)

From now on there is no soul, no self. Only a number, tattooed on the left arm. A–7713.

The treatment of A–7713 involves dehumanization. Occasionally there is a kind word, and A–7713 tries to respond to it. But chiefly there are curses, intimidations, beatings, lines of numbers standing rigidly at attention . . . all night . . . in the snow . . . naked . . . Numbers are not supposed to have emotions, and although the number that is A–7713 tries to keep close to a father who has also become a number, and to protect a father progressively enfeebled, the father who is now a number becomes a liability and a burden to A–7713. It is the greatest triumph of the survival of the self that A–7713 retains a concern for the father, and has the self-incriminating honesty to say, when the father is bludgeoned before his eyes and later removed, that he feels a sense of freedom for the moment and of shame forever.

When the camp is evacuated in the face of the Russian offensive, A–7713 and all the other numbers can walk forty-two miles through the snow in a single night, not because they are selves any longer but because they have become machines, literally able to walk mechanically in their sleep. A–7713 and all the other numbers can walk over living bodies and corpses to find shelter in a shed, because in their eyes the living bodies and corpses are now only other numbers like themselves. The number who had once been a rabbi's son can abandon in the snow the number who had once been a rabbi, glad to be rid of the hindrance. In the ten-day trip in the snow in the cattle-cars, the number who had once been the son of Meir can kill the number who had once been Meir for the sake of a piece of bread, and in turn be killed before he can get the piece of bread to his lips, by other numbers who at one time had been fathers, sons, brothers, husbands, and whose lips had gently whispered the sacred words of the Torah.

To reduce persons to numbers is an efficient way to shatter a self.

The victim's future is shattered. The culmination comes at the

end of *Night.* But before we can look at endings, we must look
at beginnings.

Wiesel says that the beginnings of his novels are crucial: if
he gets the first sentence right he knows that the rest will
follow, and the reader will have an essential clue to the theme
of the book.

> They called him Moché the Beadle, as though he had never had
> a surname in his life. (*Night,* p. 12)
>
> Somewhere a child began to cry. (*Dawn,* p. ix)
>
> The accident occured on an evening in July, right in the heart
> of New York, as Kathleen and I were crossing the street to see
> the movie *The Brothers Karamazov.* (*The Accident,* p. 11)
>
> Outside, twilight swooped down on the city like a vandal's
> hand: suddenly, without warning. (*The Town Beyond the Wall,* p.
> 7)
>
> He had no name, so he gave him his own. (*The Gates of the Forest,*
> p. 13)
>
> The tale the beggar tells must be told from the beginning. (*A
> Beggar in Jerusalem,* p. 11)
>
> No, said the old man. I will not speak. (*The Oath,* p. 3)
>
> *Je n'ai jamais ri de ma vie* [I have never laughed in my whole life].
> (*The Testament,* as it begins in the French edition)

But if beginnings are crucial, endings are even more so.
Often, the meaning of the tale is not clear until the last pages,
the last sentences, even the last line. A stage direction on the
last page of *The Trial of God* reveals, with devastating impact,
the identity of Sam. Only with the last eight words of *The
Accident* is the full poignancy of Eliezer's plight brought home
to us. In the six books we are examining, the endings indicate
the measure of progress—or lack of it—that has taken place.

In *Night,* the culmination of the shattering of the victim's
world, belief, and self, is the shattering of the victim's future.
Six million futures were shattered beyond recovery. So were
the futures of those beyond the six million who survived. One
need not be killed to be a victim; one can be killed and still be
alive.

In Latin, *victima* is "an animal offered in sacrifice," which
Webster's *Dictionary* amplifies to read, "a person or animal

killed as a sacrifice to a god in a religious rite." That is an accurate definition of the victims of the Nazis, for in the most fundamental sense Nazism was a "religion," a collective obeisance before the god of race, blood, and soil, and deeds done in the name of that god were the exercise of a "religious rite," in which persons, reduced to the status of nonpersons, were offered up to appease the greed of the idol being worshipped.

To be fully victimized is not only to be dehumanized in the present by the removal of world, God, and self, but to be denied a future. That is true death, whether physical life is terminated or not.

At the end of *Night*, Buchenwald has been liberated, but in the wake of liberation A–7713 has contracted food poisoning and is in the hospital hovering between life and death. He finally summons enough energy to get out of bed and look in a mirror.

The book closes with the words:

> From the depths of the mirror, a corpse gazed back at me.
> The look in his eyes, as they stared into mine, has never left me. (p. 127)

A–7713 confronts himself. And death is all he finds. The future is destroyed as well.

Darkness has eclipsed light.

Executioner

Is there any place to go beyond the world of the victim? Is that the best that can be managed in the presence of monstrous evil?

There is another option. Rather than being victims, we might be executioners—better to kill and survive than be killed and succumb. The alternative is explored in *Dawn*, Wiesel's second book and first novel.

There is a similarity between the two alternatives. The victim has no choice: the role is imposed by another. The executioner, it might seem, does have a choice. True, the executioner is at least free enough to be held accountable. But the matter is more poignant. In addition to being dependent on each other—there can be no victim without an executioner, no executioner without a victim—the two share a further fate in common:

> What matters is the fact that each of them is playing a role which has been imposed on him. The two roles are the extremities of the estate of man. The tragic thing is the imposition.(*Dawn*, p. 86)

If the limits of human possibility are victim-executioner, then Wiesel tells us that a heavy hand is laid upon the destroyer as well as the one destroyed. We must later ask if there is a choice beyond the polarity; but within it, a tragic necessity is at work.

As the tragic necessity unfolds, Elisha (the name means "God will save") is a victim, a former inmate of Buchenwald, living in Paris after the war. He enrolls to study philosophy at the Sorbonne, "because I wanted to understand the meaning of the events of which I had been the victim" (p. 24). He plans to press his questions about God, suffering, rebellion, human nature, purification, bestiality.

So far the story parallels Wiesel's. But whereas Elie Wiesel did pursue philosophy, his fictional counterpart never gets the chance. For a "messenger" intervenes, one who in Hasidic tradition is a *Meshulah*, "the mysterious messenger of fate to whom nothing is impossible" (*Dawn*, p. 27). The messenger's name is Gad. The name is not a play on the word "God." Wiesel writes in French, and the words "Gad" and "Dieu" have no common linguistic ancestry. But Gad does possess a Biblical name, and both Gad and his scriptural counterpart are warriors. The earlier Gad is commissioned by Jacob to take military initiatives (Genesis 49:19); his tribe will have the east side of Jordan, an outpost subject to attack by pagan nations. When Moses gives his blessing to the tribes of Israel (Deuteronomy 33:20–21), he calls for the tribe of Gad to increase—the Gaddites are mighty warriors, and Gad himself is a brave leader.

The modern Gad lives up to his heritage. He has come to persuade Elisha to join the guerilla forces in Palestine, so that they can drive out the British and create a homeland for post-Holocaust Jews. Jews, he says, with fire in his eyes, will be victims no more. Rather than being fearful themselves, they will instill fear in others. If it is necessary to kill, they will kill. Since no one else has ever looked out for them, they will now look out for themselves. Elisha is enthralled:

> This was the first story I had ever heard in which the Jews were not the ones to be afraid. Until this moment I had believed that the mission of the Jews was to represent the trembling of history rather than the wind which made it tremble. (p. 29)

Elisha and Gad talk until dawn, a Parisian dawn, described as "a pale, prematurely weary light the color of stagnant water" (p. 31). Elisha accepts Gad's invitation, full of promise that there will be more vibrant dawns: "Here," Gad says, "the dawn is gray; in Palestine it is red like fire" (p. 31).

The student of philosophy becomes a terrorist. Instead of studying Plato and Spinoza, he studies the use of machine guns, hand grenades, and daggers; instead of learning aesthetics, he learns the fine arts of strangulation and prison escape. It is inhuman, Gad acknowledges, but no other choices are left; being more just than those who speak in the name of justice led to the abandonment of Jews in Hitler's camps.

> We can rely only on ourselves. If we must become more unjust and inhuman than those who have been unjust and inhuman to us, then we shall do so. We don't like to be bearers of death; heretofore we have chosen to be victims rather than executioners. The commandment *Thou shalt not kill* was given from the summit of one of the mountains here in Palestine, and we were the only ones to obey it. But that's all over; we must be like everybody else. Murder will not be our profession but our duty. In the days and weeks and months to come you will have only one purpose: to kill those who have made us killers. We shall kill in order that once more we may be men. . . ." (p. 41)

His training completed, Elisha takes part in a commando raid. A convoy is blown up and a whole truckload of British soldiers is machine-gunned to death; they run "like rabbits sotted with wine and sorrow" (pp. 42–43).

A blow for the cause of freedom. There is only one problem: "I imagined that I was in the dark gray uniform of an SS officer" (p. 42). Elisha is suddenly back in the Polish ghettos, where SS guards slaughtered the Jews, and where the Jews ran "like rabbits sotted with wine and sorrow" (p. 45). The script is the same: only the roles have been changed.

The British announce that they will hang David ben Mosche, caught during another guerilla raid. The guerillas retaliate by capturing a British officer, John Dawson, and announce that they will shoot him as a hostage if David ben Mosche is hanged. A perfect symmetry of reprisal. Neither side will back down; to do so, both affirm, might be interpreted as a sign of weakness. Both men will die.

Who is to murder John Dawson?

Elisha . . .

He is not thrilled by the assignment. Killing others in guerilla combat is one thing, killing a single defenseless human being in cold blood is another. The role of executioner is imposed on him, just as the role of victim is imposed on John Dawson.

An eighteen-year-old boy waiting for dawn, which will make him a killer, has various things with which to cope. He has to cope with *the intervening moments,* and he is helped in that by his friends, Ilana, Gad, Gideon, Joab. They rally around and share stories of how they were saved from death. Elisha too has been saved from death, but he realizes in retrospect that it is quite possible that he has "died and come back to earth, dead" (p. 71).

He has to cope with *the past.* The ghosts of his boyhood return and almost choke the atmosphere. Why have they come? As reminders that one never kills alone. When Elisha kills, he will make killers of them as well. Those who shaped and formed him will be re-shaped and re-formed by him. He feels judged by their presence; Jewish history has never glorified bloodshed and murder. His act will betray them, for there is no present without a past, and the past cannot be shed.

He has to cope with *John Dawson,* the man he is to kill. Considerably before the appointed hour of execution he goes down to the prison cell, "as if," he remarks with prescience, "I were going to my own execution" (p. 104). He realizes that it will be easier to kill John Dawson if he can hate him, if he can see John Dawson as a villain whose death will be a gift to humanity. They talk. And he finds to his dismay that he cannot hate John Dawson. In any other situation they would have

been friends. "There was harmony between us; my smile answered his; his pity was mine" (p. 111). (Wiesel comments
almost in passing that the inability to hate may have been the
presence of God in the prison cell.)

A tragedy: the lack of hatred makes it more difficult to kill.
A greater tragedy: in spite of the lack of hatred, to have to kill
anyway.

In spite of the lack of hatred, he has to kill anyway. Precisely
at 5 A.M. he pulls the trigger, while his name is still on the dying
man's lips. The episode is over. "That's it," Elisha says to
himself, preparing to go back upstairs. "It's done. I've killed"
(p. 126).

But he does not say, "I've killed John Dawson."

He says, "I've killed Elisha" (p. 126).

At the beginning of *Dawn* Elisha tells how a beggar once
taught him to distinguish night from day. "Always look at a
window. . . . If you see a face, any face, then you will be sure
that night has succeeded day. For, believe me, night has a
face" (p. xiii).

At the beginning of *Dawn* Elisha does look out a window.
And he sees a face, his own. So he knows two things: he knows
that it is still night, and he knows that the face of night is his
own face. And we know one thing: we know that Elisha is still
in the kingdom of night. The beginning of *Dawn* is the same
as the end of *Night*.

At the end of *Dawn*, Elisha goes to the window to see the
Palestinian dawn—a dawn that will not be like the gray dawn
back in Paris, like the color of stagnant water, but, as Gad had
promised, "red like fire." But the Palestinian dawn he sees has
"a grayish light the color of stagnant water" (p. 127).

It is still the tired dawn of Paris. Worse, it is not even dawn
at all. For as Elisha looks through the window, he reports,
"Fear caught my throat. The tattered fragment of darkness
had a face. Looking at it, I understood the reason for my fear.
The face was my own" (p. 127).[2]

The title *Dawn* is ironic. It is still night. The road to emancipation through becoming an executioner has been a cul-de-
sac, for murder is only another form of suicide. A corpse is

meeting the gaze of this beholder, too, and the beholder can see nothing else.

Darkness is still eclipsing night.

Flight

But do the roles of victim and executioner exhaust the alternatives? Could we decide (in the title of an essay by Albert Camus that strongly influenced Wiesel) to be "neither victims nor executioners"? Camus broke with his friends of the French resistance who decided after World War II that they could continue to justify collective violence for political ends. In "a world where murder is legitimate, and where human life is considered trifling," Camus responds that there are two questions we must face:

> Do you or do you not, directly or indirectly, want to be killed or assaulted? Do you or do you not, directly or indirectly, want to kill or assault?[3]

Those like himself who answer "no" to both questions must face some consequences. Pacifism, he feels, is unrealistic. But he insists: "People like myself want not a world in which murder no longer exists (we are not so crazy as that!) but rather one in which murder is not legitimate."[4]

Wiesel would agree. And having discovered that we must be "neither victims nor executioners," he searches for other options. They do not come easily, and most of them are unsatisfactory. But the search is a consuming passion.

The ghosts that haunted Elisha momentarily in *Dawn* obsess Eliezer unendingly in *The Accident;* how to deal with a destructive past, which is what the ghosts represent, forms the theme of the book. How could one deal with a destructive past? One might seek to run away from it, deny it, keep distanced from it. Common to all of these is the notion of *flight.* Conventional criticism describes *The Accident* as a testing of the option of suicide—the extreme instance of flight—but the book is also a series of variations on the overall theme.

This time the scene is New York City. The narrator is a newspaper correspondent at the United Nations. Crossing

Times Square to go to a movie, he is hit by a taxicab and almost killed. He is closely linked to the protagonists of the two previous books, sharing the history and deprivation of those who physically survived the death camps but remain psychically scarred. The wounds creating those scars are more clearly discerned by Eliezer than by either of his predecessors; areas of anxiety surface for him that were only latent in Elie and Elisha. Symptomatic is his sense of guilt that he survived while others did not, and his consequent sense of moral obligation to the dead, on whose unfinished lives he must impose a meaning. It is the sense of the impossible odds thus created, and the power of a destructive past to wipe out the possibility of a creative present, that is at the heart of his struggle.

Up to this point the story is autobiography as well as fiction, and the fact that the fictional counterpart is called Eliezer (Wiesel's own name), suggests the degree of identification he has with the creation of his pen. But further details in *The Accident*—that there was a girlfriend, and that "the accident" was not quite . . . an accident—are points at which autobiography has moved over into fiction.

Eliezer is taken to the hospital, and Dr. Russel, the surgeon, saves his life. After a few days, Kathleen, his girlfriend, begins to visit him, and most of the book is a series of flashbacks from the hospital bed—several extended ones with Kathleen, many brief ones with the dead but pervasively present grandmother, and one (which we will consider in a later chapter) with Sarah, who at the age of twelve was the sport of Nazi officers.

Eliezer's self-understanding poses the spectre of the past most graphically. He defines himself as "a messenger of the dead among the living" (p. 49), and is convinced that all he and those like him are capable of doing is to pour the filth of their own past on those around them. They are the living-dead. They may look like others, but they are not. Their lives are pretense: "Anyone who has seen what they have seen cannot be like the others, cannot laugh, love, pray, bargain, suffer, have fun, or forget" (p. 79). They have been "amputated," not of their limbs but of "their will and their taste for life" (p. 79).

At the beginning Wiesel draws on Kazantzakis' *Zorba the Greek* for an image:

> Man's heart is a ditch full of blood. The loved ones who have
> died throw themselves down on the bank of the ditch to drink
> the blood and so come to life again; the dearer they are to you,
> the more of your blood they drink.

And the problem is whether or not one can survive such an
assault. The incinerated forebears of Holocaust survivors had
no burial place; the living thus become "a grave for the unburied dead" (p. 53). They rob the living of what little was left
to them: "Our dead take with them to the hereafter not only
clothes and food, but also the futures of their descendents" (p.
113). After such pillage, nothing is left to the survivors. Others
may speak of love, or justice, or freedom, but "they don't know
that the planet is drained [by the dead] and that an enormous
train has carried everything off to heaven" (p. 114).

Fated with such a legacy, survivors feel that all they do is
contaminate others with their suffering. They provide a sour
taste and incur animosity. One night on shipboard, Eliezer,
after prodding from a stranger, pours out his story. The listener appears sympathetic, but at its conclusion he takes Eliezer's
measure and responds, "You must know this. . . . I think I'm
going to hate you" (p. 50).

Who would not flee a past that so shuts one off from other
human beings? Who would not flee even from oneself, as
Eliezer does when the nurse wants him to look in a mirror, and
he vehemently refuses? (pp. 59, 63).

Another image for the destructive and immobilizing past is
the image of Grandmother. Grandmother wears a black shawl.
She has no burial place; she too was wreathed in smoke ex-
haled from tall chimneys. She left her grandson on the station
platform when her train left and mounted the skies to heaven.
She is always present. Eliezer cannot be rid of her. She is there
when he makes love to Kathleen (p. 55), and when he does not
(pp. 34–36, 51). In his post-operational delirium he cannot
disentangle the two (pp. 39–40). When Gyula tries to destroy
Eliezer's past, it is Grandmother he is destroying for a second
time (p. 126). She is a constant rebuke. To affirm the living is
to deny her. She compounds guilt. She opens wounds that do
not heal.

Under whatever imagery, the past is a curse. How can one flee from its ongoing power to work evil?

There are many possibilities. Eliezer tries them all.

The simplest is to acknowledge that the destructive power of the past makes it impossible to share with those who were not there, and *exist alone,* cutting oneself off from others, acknowledging that real companionship is impossible. "A man who has suffered more than others, and differently, should live apart. Alone" (p. 112).

But one cannot really exist alone. The next best thing is to keep one's own world barred against invasion by others, and *live a life of pretense.* Eliezer's most frequent response to others is to employ deception as a means of survival. If the truth can only lacerate, perhaps falsehood can make relationship endurable. So Eliezer tells Dr. Russel what Dr. Russel wants to hear when the latter accuses him of having no desire to live. He tells Kathleen what Kathleen wants to hear, assuring her of a love he does not actually feel. When she urges Eliezer to forget the past and exorcize its demons with the help of their mutual love, he promises to do both things, all the while realizing that both are pretense: he cannot forget the past, and even her love will be impotent to exorcize its demons. Confirmation of the pretense: it is the day after making the false promises that "the accident" occurs.

Sometimes Eliezer tries *to thrust the past on someone else.* This also fails to work. The man on shipboard solicits this, and ends up hating. Kathleen solicits it; she wants to "know everything," to wallow in the misery of another, asking for more and more horror. Eliezer tries to comply: "I bared my soul. My most contemptible thoughts and desires, my most painful betrayals, my vaguest lies. I tore them from inside me and placed them in front of her, like an impure offering, so she could see them and smell their stench" (p. 54). It does not seal the relationship; without loving her, he "makes love" to her, trying to hurt her.

One can respond by *suicide:* admit total defeat, stop trying, succumb. The "accident" was really a conscious decision not to step out of the way of the taxi while there was still time. There is little to say about this option. Those who succeed are

not available for comment, and those who fail, like Eliezer, do
not often repeat the experiment.

The ways so far explored are negative. There are other ways
that appear to hold promise.

Dr. Russel's way, for instance. Dr. Russel counsels *struggle*.
Seize the initiative against whatever is threatening one. In
Eliezer's case it is the spectre of the past, in Dr. Russel's case
it is the spectre of death. The two spectres are finally one. Dr.
Russel confronts death every time he approaches the operat-
ing table. Sometimes he wins, a heady wine. But his is finally
a loser's game: "My victories can only be temporary. My defeats are final. Always" (p. 70). The option is reminiscent of
Albert Camus, so influential in Wiesel's life, and especially Dr.
Rieux in *The Plague*, who likewise fights against evil, even
though he too can ultimately know nothing but defeat. But for
Eliezer, the magnitude of ongoing defeat negates the possibility of tiny, temporary victories.

Kathleen has a second proposal more dignified than simply
soaking up Eliezer's filth like a vicarious sponge. She truly
believes that *love can conquer a loveless past,* and that two can
share burdens redemptively in ways that are impossible for
one alone. She refuses to believe that the dead, lacking love,
are more powerful than the living, possessing love. She proposes to take the place of Eliezer's fate. But the contest between Grandmother with the black shawl and Kathleen with
the good intention is not an even match. Grandmother wins
every time.

A final proposal is presented in the closing pages of the
book (pp. 115–127), by Gyula, a Hungarian portrait painter,
whose name means "redemption." He appears only in the
final episode, and dominates it totally. Gyula knows the burden of the past. He too had fought such demons. As a result,
he "had an obsession: to pit himself against fate, to force it to
give human meaning to its cruelty" (p. 119). He sets out to
share the obsession with Eliezer. His advice, nay, his command, is clear: *you must choose the present over the past, the living
over the dead, and do so by whatever means are necessary.*

Gyula comes to Eliezer's hospital room every afternoon,
having made a typically unilateral decision to paint the pa-
tient's portrait. When he finally shows it to Eliezer, a moment

of truth occurs, for Gyula has penetrated Eliezer's inmost being. There follows "a silent dialogue" between the two. The gist of it:

Gyula's mandate to Eliezer is unequivocal: "Maybe God is dead, but man is alive. The proof: he is capable of friendship. . . . You must forget [the dead]. You must chase them from your memory. With a whip, if necessary. . . . The dead have no place down here. They must leave us in peace. If they refuse, use a whip" (pp. 123–124).

Although Eliezer responds that he can't use a whip, Gyula is adamant: "Suffering is given to the living, not to the dead. . . . It is man's duty to make it cease, not to increase it. One hour of suffering less is already a victory over fate" (p. 124).

Eliezer acknowledges the importance of this insight. Gyula continues: "If your suffering splashes others, those around you, those for whom you represent a reason to live, then you must kill it, choke it. If the dead are its source, kill them again . . ." (p. 124).

Eliezer is not sure it can be done. And rather than pretending to do it, rather than lying, he would prefer lucidity.

Gyula is not for lucidity. "Lucidity is fate's victory, not man's. It is an act of freedom that carries within itself the negation of freedom" (p. 125). Lucidity stands for easy answers, finding ways to explain suffering, determining who God is, and other impossible things. Gyula prefers active questioning; indeed, it is the source of hope he offers: "Man must keep loving, searching, weighing, holding out his hand, offering himself, inventing himself" (p. 125). It means choosing the living over the dead. "Only the living can [suffer]. Kathleen is alive. I am alive. You must think of us. Not of them" (p. 125).

This is the choice Gyula forces on Eliezer: will he choose the living or the dead? Will he choose (and it is the same thing) day or night? Eliezer will be leaving the hospital tomorrow, on crutches. He is to lean (quite literally) on Kathleen. "She'll be happy if you lean on her. Receiving is a superior form of generosity. Make her happy. A little happiness justifies the effort of a whole life" (p. 126).

Is this the breakthrough we have been waiting for? We must move to the very end, for, as we have already seen, only at the very end of a Wiesel novel is the story complete.

At the end of *Night*, Elie Wiesel looks in a mirror and a corpse looks back at him.

At the end of *Dawn*, Elisha looks at a window and his own face stares back at him, which is the face of night, which is the face of death.

At the end of *The Accident*, Eliezer looks at a portrait of himself, and it too is the face of death, for in its eyes Gyula has captured the fact that "the accident had been an accident only in the most limited sense of the word" (p. 123). It is the face of death doubly, for in its eyes Eliezer also sees Grandmother, promising that next time she will take her grandson with her into the land of the dead.

When that twin revelation has registered on Eliezer's mind, Gyula lights the canvas with a match and it is consumed by the flames. It is Gyula's way of saying: destroy the past, flee from it, burn away your desire to die in front of a taxi or on a station platform with Grandmother, choose to live, choose the living over the dead, begin again.

It is the moment of greatest hope in all of Wiesel's writing thus far: a creative choice is offered that promises to overcome the destructive power of the past, in the name of friendship and love.

It is the moment of greatest despair in all of Wiesel's writing thus far. The book ends with words about Gyula's exit: "He had forgotten to take along the ashes" (p. 127). The experiment does not work. The past cannot be destroyed. The ashes remain. Grandmother's ashes are on the hospital floor just as they still float over all of Europe. Eliezer's face is still the face of death.

Wiesel has said that the entire book was written for the sake of that final line.

The title of *The Accident* in the original French is *Le Jour, Day*. Like the title *Dawn*, it, too, is ironic.[5] Day has not come. A false dawn and a false day are all that have intervened since the kingdom of night.

Darkness is still eclipsing light.

Spectator

Victim, executioner, flight—nothing works. Could one, therefore, simply disengage, refuse to get involved, remain on the sidelines? Could one become a spectator?

The option is explored in Wiesel's fourth book, *The Town Beyond the Wall.* The book as a whole is a turning point in his series of responses to monstrous moral evil, and it will engage us for the rest of this chapter and the first part of the next, for it confronts us with three further possibilities.

Michael, a post-Holocaust Jew like Elie, Elisha, and Eliezer, returns to the boyhood home, Szerencseváros (a name which means "the city of luck"), from which he had been deported by the Germans during World War II. Since Szerencseváros is now behind the Iron Curtain, the visit involves considerable risk. He is not sure what he is looking for, but he is convinced that whatever he needs to find can only be found in the town of his youth.

Once over the border and within the precincts of the town, Michael wanders about, gazing longingly at the old family home, visiting the shop his father had owned, and going to the site of the synagogue, which has been destroyed and replaced by a modern four-story building—symbol of the plight of Jews from Warsaw, Sighet, Szerencseváros.

Without warning a memory surfaces: on the day of the deportation he had seen a face in a window of the town square, watching the scene with utter indifference. The face of a spectator.

In a later conversation with Pedro he says, "Do you understand that I need to understand? To understand the others— the Other—those who watched us depart for the unknown; those who observed us, without emotion, while we became objects—living sticks of wood—and carefully numbered victims?" (*Town,* p. 159).

The reason for his return—a reason he had not previously been able to articulate—is now clear:

This, this was the thing I had wanted to understand ever since the war. Nothing else. How a human being can remain indifferent. The executioners I understood; also the victims, though with more difficulty. For the others, all the others, those who were neither for nor against, those who sprawled in passive patience, those who told themselves, "The storm will blow over and everything will be normal again," those who thought themselves above the battle, those who were permanently and merely spectators—all those were closed to me, incomprehensible. (p. 159)

The man in the window represents another way to deal with monstrous moral evil: "He was neither victim nor executioner; a spectator, that's what he was. He wanted to live in peace and quiet" (p. 161).

The spectator did not fill Michael with hatred. He felt only curiosity.

How can anyone remain a spectator indefinitely? How can anyone continue to embrace the woman he loves, to pray to God with fervor if not faith, to dream of a better tomorrow—after having seen *that?* . . . Between victims and executioners there is a mysterious bond; they belong to the same universe; one is the negation of the other. . . . The spectator is entirely beyond us. (p. 161)

Michael goes to the spectator's apartment explicitly to humiliate him. The spectator remains impassive, even as Michael splashes two glasses of wine in his face. He felt nothing then, he reports, he feels nothing now.

During an extended conversation, the ground shifts only when Michael, responding to a question, makes clear that he does not hate the spectator:

"No," I said. "I don't hate you." A pause; then: "I feel contempt for you. That's worse. The man who inspires hatred is still human; but not the man who inspires contempt. . . . Hatred implies humanity. . . . But contempt has only one implication: decadence." (p. 170)

Here, at last, is something the spectator cannot handle. Four times he insists that he will not accept such humiliation, and insists on being hated. Four times Michael refuses him the humanity such an emotion would confer.

But as Michael leaves, the spectator says, "I feel sure you'll hate me," and within minutes Michael is picked up by the police. Sitting in the front of the police car is the spectator,

sure that his act of betrayal will move Michael from contempt
to hatred. Michael refuses the offer.

The episode is disturbing. It reminds us of the strange bond
between victim and executioner ("one is the negation of the
other"), both of whom at least belong to the same universe—a
universe from which the spectator is excluded. It reminds us
further that none of the categories are mutually exclusive.
When the man in the window disavows the spectator role by
summoning the police, Michael must conclude, "He had
become human again. Deep down, I thought, man is not only
an executioner, not only a victim, not only a spectator: he is
all three at once" (p. 174). Michael, sitting in the police car as
victim, remains a spectator of the other's pain, thus acting as
his executioner.

It is lack of relationship, indifference, that characterizes the
spectator, and it is the most dehumanizing of all human acts,
for it destroys both the observer and the one observed. Martin
Buber, whose influence is apparent in *The Town Beyond the Wall*,
comments in *I and Thou:* "Whoever hates directly is closer to
a relation than those who are without love and hate."[6]

Spectators are without love and also without hate, and this
makes the spectator the most morally culpable of all, even
more than the executioner. For spectators, unwilling to do the
dirty work themselves, consent to letting others do the dirty
work on their behalf, encouraging them by silent complicity:
"Go ahead. We will watch. And while we will not participate,
neither will we condemn. You get our vote by default." So the
spectator is not really neutral. The spectator sides with the
executioner. Such a pose, masking silent support of evil, is
worthy only of contempt.

The indictment of a spectator in Szerencseváros is a mi-
crocosm of the indictment of a generation, and a God. Indifference, as far as Wiesel is concerned, is the greatest sin. The
title of his first book, *And the World Has Remained Silent*, encap-
sulates the concerns of every subsequent book. In later essays
he reminds us that it was the spectator attitude of the western
world that emboldened the Nazis to take the next step, and the
next . . . (see *Legends*, p. 226). He finds it "strange" (to use a
neutral word) that "the civilized world waited until it was too

late before expressing its moral indignation" (*Legends*, p. 204). Not only were principles betrayed, so were persons. One of his most poignant paragraphs:

> At the risk of offending, it must be emphasized that the victims suffered more, and more profoundly, from the indifference of the onlookers than from the brutality of the executioner. The cruelty of the enemy would have been incapable of breaking the prisoner; it was the silence of those he believed to be his friends —cruelty more cowardly, more subtle—which broke his heart. (*Legends*, p. 229)

Is God also a spectator? In the first quotation cited above, reference to "the other," the spectator, is followed by extending the description to include "the Other." God, too, is described as One who "watched us depart for the unknown," One "who observed us, without emotion, while we became objects—living sticks of wood—and carefully numbered victims" (p. 159). This is what Michael could not understand. Seen on the face of a human being, such indifference inspired only contempt. Seen on the face of God . . .

Could God, too, be worthy only of contempt?

Darkness is still eclipsing night.

Madness

No matter where he turns—whether his name is Elie, Elisha, Eliezer, or Michael—he finds nothing but darkness surrounding him. Why should he expect light to dawn? Why not surrender to the darkness? Why not sink into its arms? Why not acknowledge its sovereignty? Why not . . . go mad?

The epigraph of *The Town Beyond the Wall* signals the importance of this option. It is from Dostoievski's *The Possessed:* "I have a plan—to go mad." On a few occasions it is a potential agenda for Michael and on many occasions it is an actual agenda for others.

The sanest thing to say about madness is that it is complicated, and we must tentatively distinguish two interrelated kinds of madness that are operative in Wiesel's novels. One of these is what Abraham Heschel calls "moral madness," the madness of the Hebrew prophets, and what Wiesel calls "mystical madness." It characterizes those whom the world calls "mad," since they live by a different vision and challenge the existing order in the name of that vision. They are spokespersons for the divine and purveyors of a truth all persons need to hear. They offer a creative, indeed essential, contribution to human well-being, and we will explore their positive contribution in chapter 7.

But there is another kind of madness, sometimes called "clinical madness," which consists of being so out of touch with one's surroundings as to be unable to function within them, cut off from the ability to respond or communicate. When one's surroundings are threatening and destructive, it is a great temptation to deny the existence of what is threatening and destructive and substitute a secure and unthreatening world of one's own creation.

After his arrest, Michael is subjected to torture. The occupying powers have developed an exquisitely refined method for getting prisoners to talk; they simply stand them before a wall eight hours at a stretch until they break. During the first "prayer," as the sessions before the wall are ironically labeled, Michael recalls boyhood experiences in the town in which he is now imprisoned, a series of reminiscences that conjure up varieties of madness.

There is Martha. Ugly, obscene, insulting; the town drunk who flings her skirts up, and her curses out, to any who will come within seeing or hearing. Her life is submission to impulse, her organizing principle is chaos. She invites young Michael—eight, nine, ten years old—to make love with her. He runs home terrified. Actually, Martha doesn't need him. She sleeps with Satan, and the result of their union is the world itself, which therefore is not clean and pure, as its inhabitants think. "You stink of my blood, you're tangled in my guts," she tells all listeners (p. 10).

Madness. And yet, perhaps that *is* the world? The post-Holocaust world?

There is Moishe. We have met Moishe before and will meet him again. He is in most of Wiesel's novels. Moishe is a bridge between the two kinds of madness. He sees—perhaps even dwells—in a world inaccessible to those around him. Michael's father thinks the madness may be a protection for Moishe's friends rather than for Moishe, since seeing what he sees would be too dangerous for the others. Moishe asserts that "in this base world only madmen know" (p. 19). In Hitler's world, Moishe's credo goes, "These days honest men can do only one thing: go mad! Spit on logic, intelligence, sacrosanct reason! That's what you have to do, that's the way to stay human, to keep your wholeness!" (p. 20).

Michael comes to the disturbing conclusion that Moishe is not crazy. But if he is not, then the others are. And where does that leave Michael? With Moishe or the others?

There is old Varady. Old indeed. Over a hundred, and on record as having said—in the temple—that he would live forever. Varady preaches a human strength greater even than the strength of God. For such blasphemy Varady is ostracized, and accepts isolation as his lot. But whenever there is a death in the community, Varady's longevity becomes a disrespectful reminder of the mortality of others. He is disturbingly present in his very absence.

When the Germans come to deport the Jews, Varady kills himself.

Finally there is Kalman, who has three students, Hersh-Leib, Menashe, and Michael himself. If Varady wants to outwit death, Kalman and his protégés want to force the hand of destiny. Through prayers and asceticism they will hasten the time of Messiah's coming. He failed to come this week? Maybe by next week they will be strong enough. It is too great a strain. Hersh-Leib loses his mind first, then Menashe. Kalman must be mad as well, the townfolk say.

Michael alone is saved from madness . . . by the Germans, who thoughtfully occupy Szerencseváros in time to save him. (Of all the episodes in *The Town Beyond the Wall,* Wiesel says, this is the only one with an autobiographical base; he was the third student, the one the Germans "saved.")

They were all mad, Michael reflects later on to Pedro. Mad to think that people had any control over their fate, mad to imagine any possibility of redemption. There was no rational basis, in Hitler's world, for believing in God or humanity or any reconcilation between the two. So they defied the world, in their various ways, making an almost Promethean decision to assert themselves against all the outside forces—the world, death, God, evil.

And who is finally to say whether that is moral or clinical madness?

Out of the tutoring of his youth, Michael later faces the possibility of madness himself. He comes closest to it after the war in Paris, while waiting out the slow, agonizing death of Yankel. In the camps, Yankel had been a *pilpul,* a child whom fate had chosen as the darling of the Nazi guards, and who as a result had extraordinary power over the fate of fellow prisoners, a power he often exercised cruelly. He had been present at the death of Michael's father and had observed that Michael had been unable to cry. Yankel is Michael's alter-ego; Michael is afraid, as he tells Yankel, "of the bit of me that's part of you" (p. 58). As Yankel is dying, after being run over by a truck, Michael, outraged at the injustice in the world and looking for something to destroy, finds his hands around the boy's throat. He squeezes involuntarily, not so much to kill Yankel as "to strangle his own despair" (p. 96), which Yankel, vivid reminder of the past, represents to him. He is jolted out of his trance just in time by the entrance of a doctor.

Later, talking about the episode with Pedro, Michael twice acknowledges, "I was on the verge of madness" (pp. 99, 100). Trying to justify his own existence, he was creating a universe in which the one absolute value was the death of Yankel, which he saw as "the death agonies of a future that was, at bottom, mine too" (p. 99). Out of this, he says, "I wove a universe of hallucinations, I blended the past with the future. All the men on earth bore a single face: that of my dying friend. Their destinies were measured by his" (p. 99).

The temptation to enter this world is almost overpowering. Even as Michael recalls the episode, he feels its attraction once again. It would have provided entrance into a world without fear, release from misery. And it would have been so easy: "Just to say yes, to acquiesce with a nod, would have been enough; to roll on the floor, stick out my tongue, break into song, howl like a hurt dog: safety was there within reach, and detachment, deliverance" (p. 100).

Michael resists. He realizes that while it is true that "the choice of madness is an act of courage," it is also true that "it can't be done more than once. It's an end in itself. An act of the free will that destroys freedom" (p. 101). So he resists.

But such victories are never final. The temptation recurs, and must be resisted again. Michael and Pedro are walking along the waterfront in Algiers, where an old man drowned the night before. From the depth of his being Pedro shares an account of the rape—thirty-seven times—of the woman he loved, who died even before the multiple assault was over. Love and death, Pedro reflects grimly, can only be understood together. The story pushes Michael to the verge of madness. He wants to shake the universe, to dig up all the graves in Spain until her body is found, to create a world where one can make love . . . to a corpse. It is all he can do "to keep from dashing to join the waves and the man they had swallowed up the night before" (p. 127).

Later, in the prison cell, Michael is confined with two mad-men—the Silent One, living in a world so withdrawn that he is totally out of reach, and the Impatient One, living in a world where the only "truth" is a conviction that his cellmates are hiding a letter from him. Michael's almost uncontrollable impulse is to follow their example and enter a world not answerable to forces outside himself, a world in which all is permitted and all is possible.

> There A does not precede B, children are born dotards, fire produces cold, and snow becomes the source of desire. There, animals are gifted with human intelligence and demons display a sense of humor. There, all is impulse, passion, and chaos. There, the laws are abolished and those who promulgated them removed from office. The universe frees itself from the order in which it was imprisoned. Appearance snaps its ties with reality. A chair is no longer a chair, the king no longer king, the fool ceases to be a fool, or to cry. (p. 180)

Michael ponders: why not enter that world? Read the Impatient One the letter that doesn't exist. Construct a system all his own and nobody else's, where nobody can intrude and bother him.

He becomes furious as he remembers King Lear, who resists going mad, "who preferred suffering at the hands of men to flight into a trackless desert" (pp. 180–181). He could have protected himself from friends who betray as well as from cowardly enemies, "and yet [he] chose the least easy solution: he faced them directly" (p. 181). What folly, Michael feels, when there is such an easy way to avoid pain and injustice, by resigning from the struggle, by going mad.

But the old king refuses Michael's advice, and so does Michael.

Darkness is still eclipsing light.

But could such refusal, after gazing into the deep darkness, be the forerunner of light?

CHAPTER 3

Light that Penetrates Darkness
(a moral journey—2)

*"Look at the sky," Pedro said. "It's getting light. The
night's disappearing."*
—*The Town Beyond the Wall*, p. 123

*"The only valuable protest, or attitude, is one rooted
in the uncertain soil of humanity. Remaining human
—in spite of all temptations and humiliations—is the
only way to hold your own against the Other, whatever it may be."*
—Pedro to Michael, in *The Town Beyond the
Wall*, p. 183

In one of Albert Camus' short stories, the conclusion leaves
unresolved whether a word written in tiny letters on the center
of an artist's canvas should be read as *solitary* or *solidary*.[1] The
shape of one letter was the infinite distance between isolation
and community, between darkness and light. That is the distance traversed by Michael in the last half of *The Town Beyond
the Wall*.

Michael's confrontations with the spectator and the madman confirm what his precedessors had learned: darkness continues to eclipse light.

The villain who achieves ongoing victories for darkness is
the past. Each time, the past is a curse, containing a relentless
grip on the one who seeks to shake it, leaving the victim not
only powerless but alone. Solitude as well as impotence stands

80

at the end of each journey. Each predecessor sees only his own face, and in that face, death.

Could one, instead of fleeing from the past, turn about and confront it, seeking to wrestle it down to the beginnings of defeat, and thus initiate a journey away from darkness and toward light, from being solitary to being solidary? Could the villain itself lead the way toward liberation?

That, as we have seen, is the desperate gamble Michael undertakes: since his anguish began back in Szerencseváros, he will return to the scene of its inception and do battle with it there. If light is to penetrate darkness, it must be at the point where darkness first eclipsed light. It is indeed a desperate gamble, for up to now the embrace of the past has been lethal rather than life-giving.

He does not journey back to face the past and then discover that he is no longer solitary. Just the reverse: he discovers that he is no longer solitary, and can then journey back to face the past. It is the first journey by a Wiesel character that is not taken alone. The fact is celebrated by a stylistic shift; *The Town Beyond the Wall* is written in the third person.

There are a number of milestones on the journey.

Participant

The one attitude Michael and his predecessors could never summon toward another human being was trust. The possibility of trust had been effectively, and apparently permanently, destroyed by Hitler. Six million examples of broken trust sufficed to make the point: the British are not to be trusted, Kathleen is not to be trusted, the spectator is not to be trusted. Not-trusting was a way to survive, but at the cost of being cut off from the living, which meant being cut off from the possibility of loving. One dare not participate in the anguish—or the joy—of another.

Michael resists openness to others even before the Holocaust. As a boy he has ascetic tendencies, and sees his body not as a link to others but as something offensive. He will not hear his father:

"If the soul is the link between you and God, the body is the same between you and your fellows. Why destroy it? To kill the body, to remove a possibility of union between one human being and another, is as grave as destroying life. . . . Who does not live for man—for the man of today, for him who walks beside you and whom you can see, touch, love and hate—creates for himself a false image of God." (p. 48)

Michael and Milika

After the war, Michael is even less willing to risk relationship. In Paris, he has a chance encounter with Milika, a woman from Szerenscevános, who had given him his first kiss. They are both lonely and destitute. Something could come of the encounter. Something almost does. Indeed, Michael is surprised by the stirrings within him: "The emptiness within him became a fullness." He reflects: "I am, you are. That's enough. It means that man is not alone, that the scattered forces are somewhere reunited." He reflects further about "a liberating movement of the self which has suffered enough to be transformed into love" (p. 86).

These sound like the foreshadowings of a breakthrough. But Michael leaves Milika knowing that he will never see her again. Why not? Their puppy love had been experienced in Szerencseváros, and Szerencseváros is a city of the dead. "There is no loving in a graveyard" (p. 87). He will not risk exhuming a dead love from the graveyard.

Not even at the point of death. Ill with a terrible fever, he breathes her name. "It was as if Milika had sent her name as a messenger exhorting him to hold out, telling him, 'Don't go under! hang on; I'm here. I exist' " (p. 89). The landlady wants to summon the woman whose name has entered the sick room. And Michael "wanted to shout the name, to make it a prayer, an invitation." But, summoning all his strength, he does not do so: "with a savage effort of will he managed to keep his lips together" (p. 89).

End of the possibility of relationship between Michael and Milika.

Michael and Pedro

And so it might have been throughout a lifetime, had it not been for Pedro . . .

Michael first tries to rebuff Pedro. He is in Tangiers on a writing assignment, provided by a friend, Meir, who is a smuggler. Pedro is also a smuggler, working for Meir. Michael, urged by Meir to contact Pedro but reluctant to do so, postpones phoning until a few hours before his departure. Pedro rejects his regrets, sets a time and place for a meeting, and hangs up with the imperious command, "Be there."

The voice intrigues Michael. He decides "not to reject any encounter" (p. 110).

The meeting place is the "Black Cat." Pedro and his friends are telling stories. They do it whenever life gets too tough, in ways reminiscent of the night Elisha spent with Gad, Ileana, Joab, and Gideon telling stories before the shooting of John Dawson. Michael joins in, realizing that "sometimes it happens that we travel for a long time without knowing that we have made a long journey solely to pronounce a certain word, a certain phrase, in a certain place" (p. 118). This, he reflects, may be such an occasion. It is.

The stories completed, Pedro and Michael walk all night, sharing who they are in ways Michael has never done before. Something is happening, something new: "Michael thought of the road he had travelled. He had never suspected that at its end a friend would be waiting" (p. 122).

Before dawn, "Michael realized suddenly that he had reached a turning point: he was living through one of those moments when destiny sat up and took notice. He felt his heart leap. He was at a crossroads. Left or right? Whatever his choice, it would determine the future" (p. 122).

Pedro's offhand comment that "the night's disappearing" (p. 123) is fundamental in what it says on the deepest level about Michael's future—and the future of all who have walked Michael's path.

Michael, not yet ready to say everything to Pedro about the other night through which he has lived, can still say this about its impact:

"I want to blaspheme, and I can't quite manage it. I go up against Him. I shake my fist, I froth with rage, but it's still a way of telling Him that He's there, that He exists, that denial itself is an offering to His grandeur. The shout becomes a prayer in spite of me." (p. 123)

There have been earlier hints that rebellion can be an act of involuntary affirmation: Elie refusing to fast on Yom Kippur, Elisha unable to hate John Dawson. But up to now the consciousness of rebellion has far outweighed the consciousness of affirmation. Pedro wants to round it out—the conscious or unconscious acknowledgement of God must also be a conscious, not an unconscious, acknowledgement of humanity: "He who thinks about God, forgetting man, runs the risk of mistaking his goal: God may be your next-door neighbor" (p. 123). And Michael decides not to be guilty of "forgetting man." He cancels his departure plans and stays another week.

Out of this initial exchange grow seven nights of nocturnal wandering. At every point, human bonds are deepened. For the first time, Michael is drawn out of solitariness. "No," he reflects to himself, "you are not alone, but two, two, two." There is a presence even in silence, "when we are alone with someone who moves us, with someone who leans toward us" (p. 124). Never since the war had someone leaned toward Michael in such a way that he could reciprocate.

When Michael almost succumbs to madness after hearing Pedro's story of the rape of his lover, Pedro's words and presence save him:

"To say 'I suffer, therefore I am,' is to become the enemy of man. What you must say is 'I suffer, therefore you are.' Camus wrote somewhere that to protest against a universe of unhappiness you had to create happiness. That's an arrow pointing the way: it leads to another human being. And not via absurdity." (p. 127)[2]

Later on, when Michael has "to protest against a universe of unhappiness," it is Pedro's words that sustain him.

What is Pedro doing for Michael? Giving him back his past ("Michael realized that thanks to his friend he understood his own past better than before"), but more than that, instilling hope for the future, and nurturing him in the present—all by demonstrating that one and one are more than two, which, in the grace-filled mathematics of friendship, means that two are really one: "I won't forget last night," Pedro tells Michael just before they part. "From now on you can say, 'I am Pedro,' and I, 'I am Michael' " (p. 131).

The bridge from solitary to solidary has been constructed, and traffic is moving across it. No one walks alone.

It is Pedro who arranges Michael's return to Szerencseváros. It is Pedro who is waiting in the pullman car that escorts them to the border. And it is Pedro who is with him in the prison cell, even if—as the world measures distance—Pedro by that time is hundreds of miles away.

Michael/Pedro and Menachem

When the police, acting on a tip from the spectator, arrest Michael, he is tortured and then flung into a prison cell. The most important part of the action takes place there.

Two of his cellmates are completely out of touch with the world Michael still inhabits; they are trapped in self-constructed universes whose doors have no handles on the inside. But there is another prisoner, "a very handsome Jew, with the moving face of a Byzantine Christ" (p. 144), who sensitively recognizes Michael's relief that he held out under torture long enough for Pedro and the others to escape.

The Jew introduces himself: "Menachem. From Marmaroszighet" (p. 145). Before the introduction we knew nothing about him. Now we know a great deal; three words are sufficient. Menachem means "comforter." It can also mean "Messiah." And "Marmaroszighet" means Sighet in the province of Marmaros. Of Sighet we already know. Of comfort, nurtured in Sighet in the past, we also know. But of comfort, nurtured in Sighet in the present, we have not heard since the advent of the kingdom of night. Michael begins to draw strength from his past (the word "comforter," from *confortis*, means "with strength"); the introduction of a comforter *from Sighet* suggests that Wiesel is likewise beginning to draw on his own past. Menachem represents the explicit breath of a religious faith Wiesel had felt was gone forever.

But this is no easy resolution. Menachem's is a troubled faith; he voices the poignant question, "Why does God insist that we come to him by the hardest road?" (p. 146), and there are often tears in his eyes. Michael is at first scornful of Menachem's faith, particularly when Menachem affirms, with a certain serenity, that God is his caretaker and will restore his sanity. When The Impatient One tries to strangle Menachem, Michael intervenes in time to save his life. He cannot bear the look of gratitude and affection Menachem bestows on him, and cries for the first time in many years. This is gain, not loss, for tears represent a fissure through which light can penetrate the darkness of Michael's soul.

And then, abruptly, Menachem is transferred to another cell. As he is taken out, Michael sees only his back—replicating the scene on Sinai when Moses was granted only that much assurance of the divine presence.

Without Menachem, Michael almost succumbs to madness. He is jolted out of his increasingly private world only when The Impatient One tries to strangle The Silent One. Michael intervenes in time to save another life, although he continues impulsively to choke the assailant almost to the point of death.

Michael/Pedro and The Silent One

There follows a crucial "conversation" with Pedro:

> "You saved a human life, little brother. I'm proud of you."
>
> "I saved a body. A body with a sleeping mind and a dead soul. I'm not proud."
>
> "Save his soul. You can do it."
>
> "No, Pedro, I can't. I'm sinking fast too. A little while ago I almost killed a man. My own soul is blotting up madness and night. The whole universe has gone mad. Here and everywhere."
>
> Pedro smiled: he was remembering something.
>
> "You're smiling, Pedro, and I'm going mad. I have no strength left. I'm at the end of the line. I can't do any more. I'm alone. To stay sane I've got to have someone across from me. Otherwise my mind will rot, and smell of decay, and twist like the serpent that feels the earth and death."
>
> Pedro went on smiling: "That's exactly what I want you to

do: re-create the universe. Restore that boy's sanity. Cure him.
He'll save you." (p. 182)

Pedro's five-word injunction, "Cure him. He'll save you,"
sums up the wisdom he has bequeathed to Michael, both by
word and deed. We cannot exist alone. We must have an other
across from us. Only by reaching out to the other can we
ourselves be healed. The protest against solitude can only be
"rooted in the uncertain soul of humanity."

The conversation creates a new situation:

> Michael welcomed the dawn as a new man. His strength flowed
> back. He was suddenly responsible for a life that was an insepa-
> rable part of the life of mankind. He would fight. He would
> resume the creation of the world from the void. . . . (p. 183)

When the Impatient One is removed from the cell, Michael
is left alone with the Silent One. He moves to the corner where
Menachem had lived. Fortified by this symbolic recovery of his
heritage and by the conversation with Pedro, he embarks on
a task of mutual restoration, realizing that if relationship is not
established there will be two Silent Ones in the cell: "One of
us will win," he shouts in a moment of exasperation, "and if
it isn't me we're both lost!" (p. 185).

The journey ahead is the journey from solitary to solidary,
from spectator to participant, from one who stands aside to
one who stands beside. Michael embodies the words he keeps
saying to himself: "Jump onto the stage, mingle with the actors, and perform, you too. Don't stay at the window" (p. 188).
He knows who stayed at the window . . .

There is a phrase from a later novel, *A Beggar in Jerusalem*,
that helps us understand the shift in human values that is
occurring here. Writing about the gradual rallying of support
for Israel before the outbreak of the Six Day War, Wiesel
describes the shift as one from the role of "spectator" to that
of "witness," from passive indifference to active involvement
(*Beggar*, p. 139). There is no more crucial development of
moral sensitivity than this leap from *spectateur* to *témoin* (*Le
Mendiant de Jérusalem*, p. 105). Michael is now a witness to the
Silent One, sharing with him the supreme gift of which he has
been the recipient, and which he now has the privilege of
seeking to pass on.

The last eight pages of *The Town Beyond the Wall* are among
the most tightly packed pages Wiesel has written. They cannot
be summarized. They deserve careful study line by line, word
by word, to discover how Michael, to whom others had
reached out, himself reaches out to one apparently out of
reach, and painstakingly engages, tiny step by tiny step, in the
holy task of curing.

At the end of the earlier novels, each protagonist saw only
his own face, a face of death. It was still night.

At the end of *The Town Beyond the Wall*, Michael is looking,
not at his own face, but *into the face of another*. He has broken
out of isolation, into concern for, and relationship to, another
human being.

It is a quantum leap.

By taking up Pedro's challenge, "Cure him. He'll save you,"
Michael has put in motion forces that will bring about both of
the victories of which Pedro speaks. The cure of The Silent
One is already under way by the end of the book; recognition
of Michael's presence is being registered, as The Silent One
is gradually drawn out of a world in which he knew only of his
own existence. Doors from that world can only be opened
from the outside. And Michael is already being "saved" by the
other, for as Michael looks out he now finds . . . not himself,
but an other. By losing himself in another he finds himself. A
process is under way in which Pedro's gift to Michael is being
passed on to another, who will pass it on to still another.
Someday, Michael tells The Silent One,

> "You'll tell me your name and you'll ask me, 'Who are you?'
> and I'll answer 'I'm Pedro.' . . . Later, in another prison, some-
> one will ask your name and you'll say, 'I'm Michael.' And then
> you will know the taste of the most genuine of victories." (pp.
> 188–189)

Not very often have we seen the word "victories" in the
pages of Elie Wiesel. Its meaning is the greater for having been
withheld so long.

The name of The Silent One? We learn it in the last sentence of the prison scene, and it is a revelation deep enough
for tears: "The other bore the Biblical name of Eliezer, which

means *God has granted my prayer"* (p. 189). By introducing his own name, Wiesel indicates to the reader that he too has moved from solitary to solidary, and that in a world full of corpses, it is now more than corpses that he sees.

The earlier books ended with night still regnant; darkness had eclipsed light. The dawn and the day were both false. But in lines toward the end of this book we are told that "the night was receding, as on a mountain, before dawn" (p. 189).[3]

Infinitely hopeful words. For although night will never fully disappear, it is "receding," and dawn—a true dawn this time— is approaching. Yes, there will be a dawn. Even more, there will be a day.

Light has begun to penetrate darkness.

There is one more page, a legend we will explore in another place. It offers the most important ray of light. The book was written to give it flesh. In it, the dialogue within humanity turns out to be a dialogue between humanity and God as well. God, Pedro had previously intimated, might be found in the next-door neighbor; even, Michael can now affirm, in the cell-mate, for God is present at any point of meeting between two who reach out toward one another.

From solitude to a city

Michael's journey is the only one thus far with a creative resolution. New life, he discovers, can come through participation in the plight and possibilities of another human life.

The theme is enriched—and severely tested—in *The Gates of the Forest,* which draws us beyond a world of one-to-one relations (all that was possible to Michael in the prison cell) into a world of communal interaction. The book consists of four self-contained episodes that build on each other to a climax. The first and last concentrate on inner transformations, while the second and third are action-filled narratives, full of drama and surprise.

In the Garden of Eden, one of Adam's important tasks was naming the animals, and names have been important in the Jewish tradition ever since. To know the name of God is crucial to the mission of Moses (Exodus 3:13–15); a change in name can mean a change in destiny (Abram to Abraham, Jacob to

Israel); a name can symbolize a message—Hosea names his children Jezreel ("God sows"), Lo-ruhamah ("not pitied"), Lo-ammi ("not my people").

Wiesel carries on this tradition. The names of his major characters all contain the Hebrew name of God (El): ones we have met (El-iezer, El-isha, Micha-el), and ones we are still to meet (Gavri-el, Katri-el, Azri-el, Palti-el). Other characters' names have biblical counterparts: Moshe (Moses), David, David ben Moshe, Gad, Gideon. The names of central non-Jewish characters often have a biblical ring as well: Pedro (Peter), Petruskanu (Peter), Maria (Mary). Even a lowly insurance representative in *The Accident* is named Mark.

Consequently, if there is lack of clarity about names in a Wiesel novel, that is a sure pointer to lack of clarity about destiny, and one could hardly communicate such lack of clarity more clearly that Wiesel does in the opening sentence of *The Gates of the Forest:* "He had no name, so he gave him his own" (p. 13). How do all those personal pronouns untangle?

Not very easily. But we gradually piece together that a Jewish boy is hiding in the forest from Germans who have rounded up his family and all the other Jews in the village. His name is Gregor. But that is not really his name. His real name is Gavriel ("man of God"), but he has discarded his Jewish identity and taken the non-Jewish name of Gregor—his bid for survival in a world where it has been decreed that Jews shall not survive.

A stranger, also Jewish, finds him. The stranger does not have a name. He lost it somewhere. Who is he? Clearly a messenger, possibly Elijah, perhaps an angel. Whoever he is, he needs a name, so Gregor gives him his old one.

Gavriel, as we now know him, tells Gregor that in the world above the forest, the floating clouds are all that remain of the Jews who were rounded up and sent to the crematoria. While they talk of these and many other things—laughter, friendship, responsibility, the Messiah—a cordon of soldiers is tightening its noose around the forest. The hideout will soon be discovered. But Gavriel has a plan. As the soldiers approach, he steps out and gives himself up. The soldiers are satisfied. They had been looking for one Jew. Mission accomplished. Gregor has a reprieve. And a responsibility. He can no longer hide in the solitude of the forest.

He makes his way to a nearby village where the old family servant, Maria, hides him. She makes him assume the role of a deaf mute and passes him off as the son of her departed sister Ileana, whose reputation was such that almost every male in the village could have been named defendant in a paternity suit over Gregor.

Gregor soon comes to know more about the village than anyone else; people will talk frankly with someone who can neither hear what they say nor repeat it to others. Most of them confess to illicit affairs with Ileana. Even the priest changes places with Gregor in the confessional booth. However, "the priest had committed no carnal sins. He was against sin, but not against crime" (p. 91). He confesses to having betrayed a Jew seeking refuge because the Jew would not accept Christ as a condition of survival. And now the priest is afraid . . . not of a man but of God.

The episode in the village is Wiesel's first significant treatment of Christianity. There is anger, ambivalence, gratitude. *Anger:* what the priest does to one Jew is no more than what most Christians are doing to most Jews. When the priest professes not to have known whom he was sending to certain death, Gregor wants to respond (but holds his tongue, remembering that he is a deaf mute), "You don't know who it was that you chased away; well, I'll tell you. It was I, it was Gavriel. I curse you, and may my curse precede and follow you all the way to the grave" (p. 93). *Ambivalence:* when Maria murmurs "Sweet Jesus . . ." in prayer, Gregor reminds her that Jesus too was changed into a cloud, like all the other Jews. "He let himself be killed one day and since then there's been no end to the killing" (p. 66). *Gratitude:* it is Maria, a Christian, who protects Gregor, and it is Petruskanu, a non-Jew, who later saves his life.

The issue is dramatically joined—literally. At the end of each school year the children give a play. In the spirit of the times the play this year is about Judas Iscariot, paradigm of Jewish baseness. Gregor is tapped for the villain's role, despite Maria's misgivings. It is felt that a mute Judas will be particularly appropriate.

The account of what follows is one of the most powerful and painful scenes Wiesel has constructed. A new version of the passion story unfolds on stage, in which Jesus' disciples decide to avenge their master's death by punishing Judas, the quintessential Christ-killer. The confrontation is severe, and paradigmatic. All the epithets piled onto Jews ever since are piled onto Judas: "You betrayed the Son of God! You killed the Savior!" The actors begin to beat Judas, pouring out all the anti-Semitism that two thousand years of Christian history have provided them.

So appealing is the theme that the members of the audience get into the act, first by shouting encouragement to the actors, and then by going onstage themselves, where, "delirious with an ancient hate, suddenly reawakened" (p. 110), they rain blow after blow on Gregor. They enjoy a double pleasure: not only can they batter Judas, they can also batter the son of a woman many of them had loved and all have reason to hate.

By this time Gregor's face is streaming with blood. In an unspoken understanding with the mayor, Petruskanu, who takes no part in the mob scene, Gregor suddenly shouts at the top of his voice: "Men and women of this village, listen to me!" The men and women of the village freeze in terror.

That the deaf mute can speak is the first surprise. The immediate reaction of the villagers is to call it a miracle, fawn over "our dear Gregor," "our beloved Gregor," and ask forgiveness. It is Judas they were after. Gregor is a saint, Judas the villain.

Gregor turns the tables on them. He is not a saint, Judas is. They want forgiveness? Judas is the only one who can forgive. "He is the victim; not Jesus: he is the crucified; not the Christ" (p. 116). Caught up in the trauma of the event, the villagers agree that they have been guilty of injustice toward Judas. Even the priest finally joins the litany.

This bizarre twist in the story drives home that the "injustice toward Judas" is being replicated six million times, a further replication of two thousand years of victimizing members of the race of Judas (and Jesus), fastening on them the epithet used in countless passion plays, "Christ-killer, Christ-killer, Christ-killer!"

A fitting conclusion. The tables have been turned. But Gre-

gor surprises the crowd a second time. Not only is he not
Judas, "I'm not Ileana's son" (p. 117). Consternation among
the villagers. And Gregor, fully in control now, weighs two
possibilities: he can curse or he can forgive. The temptation
to vengeance is strong: tell to all the secrets each confided to
him alone—of one that he was lusting after his wife's sister, of
another that he was the informer who betrayed his best friend
to the police, of a third . . .

But, again catching the eye of Petruskanu, Gregor decides
not to betray their confessions. Instead he makes another
confession of his own: "My name is not Gregor. I am a Jew and
my name is a Jewish name, Gavriel" (p. 118).

The spell is broken. The villagers have but a single thought:
"We are the victims of a Jew who holds us in his hands" (p.
118), a Jew who knows enough secrets to destroy us all. There
is only one thing to do: brand him a liar and traitor, and treat
him as liars and traitors deserve to be treated. The men in the
audience press forward, knives in their hands, egged on by the
women: "Go on! Give it to him! Make him dumb again! Cut
out his tongue!" (p. 119).

Gregor believes he is going to die, and although he does not
know it, he would not have died alone: "At the same moment,
in the crimson fields of Galicia, smartly turned-out officers
were shouting the order: 'Fire! Fire!' A hundred Jews, ten
thousand Jews were tumbling into the ditches" (p. 119).

Petruskanu finally intervenes, rushes Gregor off stage and
into his carriage, whips the horses, and helps Gregor establish
contact with a band of partisans in the forest.

At first we want to discredit the scene. It is too unbelievable.
People don't act on such multiple levels of savagery. But Wiesel, by the faintest allusions here and there, links it so inexorably with other instances of Jewish persecution that at the end
we also want to discredit the scene. It is too believable.

The episode with the partisans is straightforward and devastating. Gregor is now with other Jews, who have a sufficient
cache of arms to defend themselves, but who are out of touch
with what is really happening. Gregor shares what he learned
from Gavriel: Jews are not going to "work camps," Jews are
going to crematoria.

The head of the partisans is Leib the Lion, an old boyhood

friend of Gregor's; at age ten the two of them had successfully
defended themselves against taunts of "Christ-killer." Leib's
response to Gregor's news is clear: if Gavriel is still a prisoner,
he must be freed, not only for his own sake but so he can tell
other Jews what he has seen at first hand.

A plan is worked out: Gregor and Clara, Leib's lover, will
go to the town, ingratiate themselves with a prison guard and
get information about the whereabouts of Gavriel so that an
escape can be planned.

But the plan misfires. Leib himself is captured, tortured,
and sent off on a transport to a death camp.

The denouement is devastating; the partisans have lost
their leader, Clara has lost her lover, and Gregor has not only
lost a friend but feels guilty of betrayal. The partisans share
the latter judgment and put him through a fearful grilling from
which he is finally extricated only by the intervention of Clara.

The dilemma in which Gregor is caught—guilt that he is
alive when others are dead—is the experience of most "survivors," exemplified by Eliezer in *The Accident* and elaborated in
many of Wiesel's essays. Not only does it heighten the complicity of the spectator, it also heightens the importance of
being a participant. The stakes are high and cruel: "He who
is not among the victims is with the executioners. This was the
meaning of the holocaust" (p. 168). Gregor will continue to
feel, in the future, "To live is the betray the dead" (p. 174).
A frightful dilemma: to be surrounded by death and to feel
responsible for death, to believe that the very drawing of a
breath denies that possibility to another. And at precisely this
juncture occurs one of those critical exchanges that shifts the
balance of the universe.

Yehuda, twenty years old, is on sentry duty. He feels that his
death is imminent—feels it in his bones, his dreams, his intui-
tions. So, in the face of death, what does he talk about to
Gregor? Love. People are being murdered in the valley below
. . . and he speaks of love. He observes that Gregor already
loves Clara, a reality Gregor has been trying to hide even from
himself. And Yehuda, twenty years old with the wisdom of
twenty centuries at his command, urges Gregor to affirm that
love. "Above all in time of war, when men are filled with death.

This is the time to love. This is the time to choose. An act of love may tip the balance" (p. 178).

Not only tip the balance; create a new universe:

> "You say, 'I'm alone.' Someone answers, 'I'm alone too.' There's a shift in the scale of power. A bridge is thrown between the two abysses." (p. 178)

This is more than Gregor can cope with. Love? Now? So soon after Leib's death? By what right could he . . . ?

Yehuda persists: "You mustn't be ashamed of your love; you should be proud of it. In an inhuman world like this one love is the great reward and the greatest of victories" (p. 180).

And there is something more, about drawing good even out of the midst of suffering:

> "It's inhuman to wall yourself up in pain and memories as if in a prison. Suffering must open us to others. It must not cause us to reject them. . . . God chooses to suffer in order to better understand man and be better understood by him. But you, you insist on suffering alone. Such suffering shrinks you, diminishes you. Friend, that is almost cruel." (p. 180)

The message Gyula could not get through to Eliezer in *The Accident* is a message Yehuda gets through to Gregor. "You're right," Gregor answers. "I do love Clara."

Yehuda is right about another thing, too. His death *is* imminent, and death and love do go together. A few nights later he is stabbed in the village, the partisans return and shoot the one who stabbed him, and Gregor tells Clara that he loves her.

Fourth episode: the Williamsburg section of Brooklyn. It is the shortest and the most important. Separated from one another after the war, and meeting by chance in Paris, Clara and Gregor are married soon after. It is a disaster.

Clara is living in a fantasy world where Leib is still her lover. She loves Gregor only by pretending he is Leib. Gregor had realized it might be this way. He had exhorted her before the marriage:

> "Often I feel pain just as you do. But I work to tame and disarm my suffering, whereas you give in to yours and often summon it. Both attitudes are human, but one is a link with strength and life, the other [to] resignation, to death." (p. 211)

More specifically: "Let's leave the graveyard, Clara. Let's try to walk together. I know how to sing, and listen, and wait. I offer you my song and silence and my hand" (p. 211).

A tremendous advance. We recall Michael, who was also in Paris after the war, who also had a chance reunion with a woman he had known before, who also came from "the graveyard." Michael closed the door on Milika in advance. Gregor not only keeps the door open but implores Clara to walk through it with him. He stakes his future on a belief that when two walk through the door together marvelous things can happen:

> "There is more of eternity in the instant which unites two people than in the memory of God, more peace in a gaze into a beloved's heart than in the kingdom of heaven." (p. 212)

Not everyone, however, will take the risk. Mendel, a friend of Gregor's, loses a son. He does not want to share his loss. Gregor tries to make friends with him: "No one can fight the night by himself and conquer it, Mendel. Victory would be meaningless even if he won. For two persons together victory is possible" (p. 193). Such victory has happened before: between Pedro and Michael, between Michael and the Silent One. But not between Gregor and Mendel, for Mendel will not open himself. He wills defeat instead: "I have no wish to conquer the night" (p. 193).

Nor does Clara. Gregor tries, desperately, to draw her out of her immersion in the past. The situation in *The Accident* is reversed: Gregor is like Kathleen, convinced that love can conquer the dead past; Clara is like Eliezer, trapped in the past and unwilling to come to terms with the present.

Gregor finally gives up. The only solution is to leave Clara. He decides to do so.

But along with the deterioration of his relationship with Clara, something else is happening to Gregor. He is beginning to rediscover his Hasidic roots. He goes to the synagogue to argue with the rebbe, and is caught up in the celebration of those who rejoice when there is no reason to rejoice. The rebbe insists that there are reasons to rejoice even when there is no reason to rejoice:

"There is joy as well as fury in the *hasid's* dancing. It's his way of proclaiming, 'You don't want me to dance; too bad, I'll dance anyhow. You've taken away every reason for singing, but I shall sing. . . . You didn't expect my joy, but here it is; yes, my joy will rise up; it will submerge you.' " (p. 196)

Gregor and the rebbe have a number of conversations. Gregor wants the rebbe to scream out against God. No, Gregor really wants the rebbe to teach him to cry . . .

On another occasion the rebbe speaks of suffering, but then moves on to get them all to sing, a bawdy Army song, as it turns out. But the words don't matter, for through the act of song, pure joy invades the hearts of the singers. Gregor is almost over the threshhold, ready to affirm that joy "is man's ally and not his mirage" (p. 201), when Gavriel enters.

Gavriel? Gregor can't be sure, and Gavriel (if it is he) remains as enigmatic as he was back in the forest. There is a long exchange, and as a result of telling Gavriel (if it is he) about Clara, Gregor realizes that he cannot, after all, leave her. He cannot return to the solitude that the forest represented. To choose solitude is to act against humanity. He is committed to another.

Gavriel has reminded him of his past. Gavriel *is* his past, the past that was there even before the forest. He must reclaim it now, and live with the power it represents.

He asks Gavriel to give him back his name.

Whatever lack of clarity Gregor had had about his destiny is resolved by that action.

It is morning now, and Gavriel (if it was he) has gone. A young boy tells Gregor they need a tenth man to say morning prayers, particularly the Kaddish, the prayer for the dead. Will he join them? They can provide the phylacteries, and he can even keep them afterwards.

"What's your name?" asked the boy.
"Gregor." He blushed and corrected himself: "Gavriel. Gavriel's my name. Gregor isn't a Jewish name, you know that." (p. 222)

He affirms to himself that after the prayers he will go back to Clara. And back there he will say such things as these:

"Let's resume the struggle. . . . It's better to sleep on the

trodden ground, if the ground is real, than to chase mirages.
. . . Know then that all of us have our ghosts. . . . They'll
continue to haunt us, but we must fight them. . . . The struggle
to survive will begin here, in this room, where we are sitting."
(pp. 222–223)

He goes in to recite the Kaddish.

At the end of *The Town Beyond the Wall* Michael is gazing into
the face of another and the beginnings of redemption are
present. A concluding legend even hints that God is present
in the midst of any such exchange.

That hint is made explicit at the end of *The Gates of the Forest*.
When Gregor joins the others in the Kaddish, he is no longer
looking simply at another human being, but, in the posture of
prayer, looking into the hidden face of God, reciting a prayer
which Wiesel describes as "the solemn affirmation, filled with
grandeur and serenity, by which man returns God his crown
and his scepter" (p. 223).

Those unfamiliar with the text of the Kaddish need to bear
that description in mind, for though it is indeed "the prayer
for the dead," its text deals not with dead human beings but
with the living being of God:

Be His Great Name praised forever and for all eternity.
. . .
The Name of the Holy One, praised be He, be blessed, praised,
honored, magnified, exalted, glorified, extolled and lauded.
. . .
May abundant peace from Heaven . . . be for us and for all
Israel. . . .
May there be revealed the greatness and holiness of His Great
Name in the world. . . .

Within the prayer are many specific petitions—for health,
comfort, forgiveness, raising the dead, rebuilding the temple.
But the accent is always on the greatness of God, and Gregor's
recital of the Kaddish is no perfunctory exercise of conventional piety: "He recited it slowly, concentrating on every sentence, every word, every syllable of praise" (p. 223).

In that context, Gregor prays especially for the soul of his
comrade Leib, asking God to do what he, Gregor, has been
unable to do for Clara, namely so order it that Leib "cease to

cause suffering to those who once loved him and still love him" (p. 223). Which is also a prayer for Clara, to whom he will now return to carry on the struggle—fortified by the rebbe, the newly-discovered community, Gavriel (if it was he), and the heritage of prayer and commitment to which he has found a means of return.

Here is a rounding out of the moral journey—not only an affirmation of humanity, won back by Michael at so great a cost; not only an affirmation of God, won back by Gregor at so great a cost; but an affirmation of humanity and God together, won back by Elie Wiesel at so great a cost. It has been a long journey, described by Irving Halperin as moving "from Buchenwald to the synagogue, from the image of a corpse-like face in a mirror to the grandiloquent and serene words of the Kaddish."[4]

Light continues to penetrate darkness.

From a city to The City

Wiesel had intended *The Gates of the Forest* to conclude a series of novels dealing with the Holocaust and its aftermath, and embarked almost immediately on a different project, a large and ambitious novel about the plight of Jews in Russia, sparked by a visit there in 1965 and reported in *The Jews of Silence* (1966).

But an unexpected event intruded, and the large and ambitious novel was put aside (it was finally published in 1980 as *The Testament*), and replaced by another one. The unexpected event was the Six Day War of 1967, and the novel—actually more than a novel—was *A Beggar in Jerusalem,* written at white heat during the latter part of 1967 and early 1968. Although not part of the sequence Wiesel originally projected, it provides an even more fitting culmination than *The Gates of the Forest.*

We have seen that the cumulative journey of the first five books was from solitude to solidarity, from looking into the visible face of death to looking into the invisible face of God, and (in the last book) from being alone in a forest to being surrounded by others in a city—Brooklyn, yet.

What better symbol of the necessity of shared humanity

than a city? But . . . what better city to exemplify both the
possibilities and the perils of a shared humanity than the city
of peace, Jeru-shalom, a city that has so often been a place of
both human warfare and divine benediction?

So the ugly reality of the Six Day War elicited a book from
Wiesel in which the journey begun in Auschwitz finally culminated in Jerusalem. Which means, as Wiesel might suggest,
that it probably began there also.

Had Wiesel created the design, it would have seemed con-
trived. Imposed on him, it seems inevitable.

On any estimate, *A Beggar in Jerusalem* is Wiesel's most difficult book. At first reading it seems a *pastiche,* almost a grab bag
of ideas, stories, aphorisms, tales ancient and modern, curious
conversations, vivid war scenes, all strewn across a landscape
of 255 pages during most of which the reader is never absolutely sure who is speaking or what is going on.

The narrator is David, who may really be Katriel. Katriel is
killed in the war. Or maybe David was. Malka is married to one
of them. Or both. The time frame is the present, the distant
past, and everything in between, simultaneously. Also the future. The action takes place in Jerusalem, Auschwitz, Sighet,
an insane asylum, mass graves in Poland, Washington, Rome
—all at the same time. Mosche the madman is back, supremely
at ease (as might be imagined) in such a setting, with a whole
host of friends similarly afflicted.

Wiesel himself has described the book as "neither novel nor
anti-novel, neither fiction nor autobiography, neither poem
nor prose. It is all this together." He set out, he tells us, to
write a tale that would be "all-encompassing, on all levels." He
succeeded.

Yes, he succeeded. For as one reflects on the subject matter,
it becomes clear that this is the only authentic way Wiesel
could write about Jerusalem. For the Jew, Jerusalem encom-
passes all time, invades all space, is one place and everywhere,
is temporal and eternal. Such statements are descriptions, not
contradictions. To be fighting for Jerusalem now is to be
standing alongside warriors from the time of King David; to
light the candles for Shabbat anywhere in the world is to be
lighting them also in Jerusalem; to describe a six day war

means to describe six thousand years of history; to locate the final resting place of six million Jews from all over Europe requires only a tiny patch of land in the Old City in front of the Wall.

No "straightforward" novel could convey such things. Only by plunging the reader into the breakdown of all conventional schemes of time and space can Wiesel communicate the "logic" of Jerusalem. It takes a "beggar," a madman, to do it.

Precisely because it is such a novel, or more than a novel, we are absolved of the necessity of summarizing the plot—which, needless to say, would resist summarizing. Instead we shall explore how earlier themes are brought to greater fruition. We shall refer to a parable, a relationship, a vision, and a mystery.

A parable. Katriel's parable (pp. 148–150) is initially an occasion for David's anger, but gradually becomes an instrument of self-understanding:

A man leaves home seeking adventure and a magic city. He spends the night in a forest, and points his shoes in the direction he should follow upon waking. During the night a prankster turns the shoes around so that next day the promised city seems amazingly familiar. The traveler discovers that he can anticipate the streets, the location of the buildings, the gardens. He is surprised that the fabulous city is so ordinary—exactly like his own. He makes his way unerringly to a house just like the one he used to live in, even to the broken lock on the front door. A woman who looks like his wife serves him a meal with children who bear an uncanny resemblance to his own. The smallest climbs up in his lap and pleads, "You'll stay with us, won't you? You won't leave us, will you?" And the stranger ends up promising them everything.

The story gnaws at David. It seems familiar and yet he cannot place it. He starts to needle Katriel for telling it, and becomes angry and uneasy before the exchange is over. Why does it disturb him? Where has he heard it before?

He remembers a beggar once telling him to remember that *"the day someone tells you your life,* you will not have much longer to live" (p. 159, italics added). And that triggers a realization that the traveler in the story might have been himself. The "real" David (who, like all other protagonists, is a holocaust survivor) might actually have remained "in the kingdom of night, a prisoner of the dead" (p. 159), and the life he is now living might be just as full of pretense as that of the traveler.

> "The living person I was, the one I thought myself to be, had been living a lie; I was nothing more than an echo of voices long since extinguished. . . . I thought I was living my own life, I was only inventing it." (pp. 159–160)

Another beggar—or was it the same one?—had told David on another occasion that "the day your life will be told to you . . ." (p. 224), and the same reference is picked up about thirty pages later: "When your tale will be told to you . . ." (p. 253). On the latter occasion (which is the occasion of his wedding to Malka), David responds to those ominous ellipses with their implication that he has not much longer to live:

> "When your tale will be told you . . ." Yes, the prediction is proven correct. This war too will have left its mark on the lives of more than one person. Someone died inside of me, I still don't know who. But I do know this: Whether Katriel is alive or not is not important. I shall unlearn being jealous of his past, of his innocence. What is important is to continue. It will take time and patience. . . . (p. 254)

David comes to an important insight through this progression. Yes, the parable upsets him because it *is* his own story and it is a disturbing story. But to recognize one's own story is a step toward self-understanding. Like Katriel's traveler, he is permanently exiled, a stranger in the world around him, appearing to be someone other than he truly is. And now that "his life has been told to him," which the beggar said was a foreshadowing of death, he is able to acknowledge that "someone died inside of me." He doesn't know who died, but the fact that he is going to "unlearn" his jealousy of Katriel's past (a matter we shall presently explore) suggests that the death has been liberating, and that a new creature is being born who will be able to live an authentic life rather than having to invent a false one.

A relationship. The beginning of an escape from the clutches

of the past receives further resolution in the complex relationship between David and Katriel.

We have already established that David is the narrator, the
"beggar" who has gone to Jerusalem at the time of the Six Day
War, to help others and solicit help for himself. We have noted
that Katriel (whose name means "crown of God") is essential
to any understanding of David. Whoever else he is in addition
to being the son of a rabbi in Safed, the husband of Malka, and
a friend of David, Katriel is clearly David's alter-ego, the one
apart from whom David cannot be understood. Sometimes,
indeed, we wonder if there is any Katriel apart from David, or
David apart from Katriel, and even David the narrator is not
always sure—unless, of course, Katriel is the narrator. Katriel
is the side of David, or any human being, that is firmly rooted
in the past. When he has to confront the modern world, in this
case by being called up for military duty, he abhors what he
finds, and the fact that he kills another human being in combat
almost unhinges him. He has suffered (he and Malka have lost
a child), he has been angry with God (complaints that will
concern us in another place), and he has killed. Perhaps it is
the sum of all those things that ordains that he too is killed,
or at least declared "missing in action"; one never knows for
sure about Katriel.

David has to wrestle with this side of his being. Like all of
Wiesel's "survivors," he must struggle with the reality that to
be alive when other Jews have died puts an intolerable burden
on the survivor. How can one be happy, without seeming to
forget and thereby dishonoring those who can never again be
happy?

In David's case the problem is intensified; he falls in love
with Malka, Katriel's widow. Here is where the heavy hand of
the past is cruel, just as it was for Gregor when he fell in love
with Clara. For if one pays appropriate homage to the dead,
that seems to affirm that love among the living is selfish. A
familiar bind: it destroyed Eliezer in *The Accident* and fore-
closed the possibility of Michael's relating to Milika in *The
Town Beyond the Wall*. (It is worth noting that Milika and Malka
have the same name—"queen"—but that they are queens with
very different destinies.) And even David, as he professes his

love for Malka, is at that very moment reminded of Ileana, a woman of the resistance who gave her life to save his.

But a new future beckons: "The war is over," Katriel reflects to himself, "and I am alive, ready for peace and love. Every limb of my numbed body is ready to make peace and to love gently" (p. 174). David and Malka affirm that a relationship between them is possible. We are even present (prospectively, at least) at their wedding. To be able to marry, or even contemplate marriage when they are tied to the devastation of the past, and to determine to forge a new future together, is a tremendous step for David and Malka. And it is Wiesel's way of affirming symbolically that it is possible to escape from the clutches of the past.

A vision. With an acknowledgement that we can escape the clutches of the past, we are on the verge of the biggest breakthrough thus far in Wiesel's writing. It is this: *the past, which has been the enemy, can now be invoked as an ally.* One can not only "escape its clutches," one can enlist its support. The theme emerges in the account of the capture of the Old City and the recovery of access to the Wall, Judaism's most sacred spot. A straightforward description of military action escalates into a vision, based on an experience Wiesel himself had, described in a preface to the French edition of *A Beggar in Jerusalem* that is not included in the English translation. In it, Wiesel comments that the relationship between the Holocaust and the liberation of the Old City gives the latter event a moral and even a mystical dimension. He understood this when he visited the Old City and saw thousands of men and women marching past the wall. He suddenly saw them in a new light: mixed in with the living were the dead, coming from the four corners of the exile, freed from all the cemeteries and all the destructive memories. Some of them were out of his youth, others out of his imagination. Madmen, beggars, teachers, students, cantors, children, drunkards, tellers of tales—he even saw the characters from his books, who had followed him there to put in an appearance and to testify like him, and through him. Then they left, and he had to summon them back and put them within the pages of a new book, which he called *A Beggar in Jerusalem* (see *Le Mendiant de Jérusalem,* p. 11).

As David, part of the army still fighting to regain the Old City, approaches the wall, he too sees "all those who had stood here before me, bent with humility or touched with ecstasy. . . . Kings and prophets, warriors and priests, poets and philosophers, rich and poor" (p. 239). Meanwhile, the soldiers are singing, everyone is dancing, a few are weeping. The crowd gets larger. People are streaming in from everywhere, wearing every kind of dress, speaking every kind of language, scholars, rebels, rabbis . . . and a little girl, thirsty in the midst of deportation, given no name here, but possessing a name we already know: Tziporah.

Aware that he is in a kind of trance, David "by inviting hallucination and then rejecting it," plunges once more into the reverie. He sees before the Wall all the dead, from all the dead towns of Europe, all who had no place beneath the soil because of chimneys that offered them no cemetery save the sky.

"Do you know why Jerusalem was saved?" a questioner asks in the vision, and there is an answer from within the vision: "Because this time the towns and villages, large and small alike, by the hundreds and thousands, rose up in its defense" (p. 244). Those towns and villages had been emptied of Jews, and the Jews had become a pillar of protective fire around Jerusalem, whether the towns and villages were Warsaw or Bratzlav . . . or Sighet.

The preacher, who is standing by David during the vision and is part of it, continues, "Israel defeated its enemies—do you know why? Israel won because its army, its people, could deploy six million more names in battle" (p. 244).

In Europe, during six years preceding war, and during six years of war, no one came to the defense of the Jews; in Israel, during a six day war, six million Jews came to the defense of Jerusalem. This is the first time the dead have been a *living* presence. This is the first time the past has been invoked as an ally. This is the first time that ghosts from the past have been other than a source of terror; recall only the ghosts that condemned Elisha in *Dawn*, that drank the blood of Eliezer in *The Accident*, that immobilized Clara in *The Gates of the Forest.* This is the first time that out of irredeemable evil, good has come. It does not make the evil good, but it does say that there is no

evil that cannot be used, somehow, for ends other than the
perpetuation of evil, for ends—yes—designed for good.

One time, visiting a kibbutz in the far north of Israel, within
artillery range of guns on the other side of the border, I recounted this episode to a Jewish woman who at that time had
read only *Night* and did not know that there were words of
hope in the writings of Elie Wiesel. As I described the vision
in which the dead became allies of the living, I could see tears
form in her eyes. And where before, as she later acknowledged, there had been room only for tears of sorrow, now
there was also room for tears of joy.

A mystery. The ending of *A Beggar in Jerusalem* is not as clearcut as the endings of Wiesel's earlier novels—which should
not surprise us, since the novel as a whole is not as clearcut
either. Nevertheless, the last eight and a half pages form a
reflective epilogue that is a fitting summary of where the entire
journey has led us.

The other endings brought us to the place where the
protagonist was looking into the eyes of another—and an Other—and *A Beggar in Jerusalem* confirms that reality, with the
added dimensions that in this case, for the first time, he is
looking into the eyes of a woman, and that in this case, also for
the first time, he specifically asks for reciprocity. He needs to
have her look at him as well, if he is "to find himself, to define
himself" (p. 251).

There are other notes that have not previously been sounded. The dead need no longer be a curse. They can even be a
source of liberation and empowerment. David will put a note
in the Wall in the Old City:

> Addressed to the dead, it will ask them to take pity on a world
> which has betrayed and rejected them. Being powerful and
> vindictive, they can do whatever they please. Punish. Or even
> forgive. (p. 252)

Or even forgive. The dead have done a lot of punishing up to
this moment. We have not before this moment heard of the
possibility of forgiveness on the part of the dead. Or of the
living.

A further note of hope emanates from Jerusalem, the city

of peace. David tells us that "a page has been turned. The beasts in the heart of man have stopped howling, they have stopped bleeding. The curse has been revoked in this place, and its reign terminated" (p. 252). Signs of such hope? "The orphans are learning to smile again, the victors to weep" (p. 253). We had always thought it could only be the other way around: orphans are supposed to weep, victors to smile. A page has been turned indeed.

No, the future is not yet fully clear. But what is fully clear is that there *is* a future, and a future worth having—a future concerning which it is enough to know that "what is important is to continue" (p. 254). If an agenda of continuance sounds too simple, we need only remember that the fifteen-year-old boy at the end of *Night* had no desire to follow it, nor did Elisha in *Dawn* or Eliezer in *The Accident*. Gregor, in *The Gates of the Forest,* did, but not Clara, not Mendel. For David, however, the word "victory," so sparingly employed up to this point, can again be invoked, although he is at immediate pains to remind us that its coinage is always in danger of being debased:

> Victory does not prevent suffering from having existed, nor death from having taken its toll. How can one work for the living without by that very act betraying those who are absent? The question remains open and no new fact can change it. (p. 254)

But a "new fact"—or rather, an old fact rediscovered—makes it possible to live with the question, to keep it "open" without being destroyed by it. It is not so much a fact as a mystery:

> Of course, the mystery of good is no less disturbing than the mystery of evil. But one does not cancel out the other. Man alone is capable of uniting them by remembering. (p. 254)

This may be the most important statement Wiesel has yet made, the wisdom he has distilled out of a long and painful journey. The mystery of evil has been explored in pitiless detail through six books. It has seemed all-encompassing. But now we are told that it is not. There is a residue. The mystery of good does not cancel out the mystery of evil—a self-evident truth if there ever was one. But the reverse is also true—and it is far from self-evident: *the mystery of evil does not cancel out the mystery of good.*

How is such an affirmation possible? How can the two mysteries be "united"? Wiesel has already told us. There is a capacity in human beings that makes it possible, a capacity that up to this point has been only a source of terror: the act of remembering. Memory, we noted at the beginning of our study, is both a graveyard and a kingdom. It has been a graveyard; now it can begin to be a kingdom, opening up a future "whose newness," David confides to us, "still makes me dizzy" (p. 255). A blessed state. Better than the equilibrium of despair.

Light continues to penetrate darkness.

CHAPTER 4

From Auschwitz to Mount Moriah—And Return
(a historical journey)

My goal is always the same: to invoke the past as a shield for the future; *to show the invisible world of yesterday and through it, perhaps on it, erect a moral world where just men are not victims and children never starve and never run in fear.*
—"A Personal Response," p. 36, emphasis added

After Auschwitz everything brings us back to Auschwitz. When I speak of Abraham, Isaac and Jacob . . . it is the better to understand them in the light of Auschwitz.
—"Why I Write," p. 205.

We know [Job's story] for having lived it. . . . Whenever we attempt to tell our own story, we transmit his.
—*Messengers of God,* pp. 211–212.

One of Elie Wiesel's tales is entitled "Testament of a Jew in Saragossa" (*Legends,* pp. 93–102). The narrator, a Jew visiting the Spanish city of Saragossa, is given the services of a young Spanish guide, who proudly shows him the cathedral and the city. Upon learning that the visitor is a Jew, able to read many languages, the Spaniard invites him to his home, complete with crucifix and portrait of the Virgin, and asks he can translate a yellowed parchment handed down in his family from father to son for many generations. It is in Hebrew.

As the narrator reads the text he is overcome with emotion. It dates from the time of the forced conversion of Jews in Spain. The author was a Marrano, a Jew who had publicly converted, but had actually kept alive the faith and practices of his ancestors:

> I, Moses, son of Abraham, forced to break all ties with my people and my faith, leave these lines to the children of my children and to theirs, in order that on the day when Israel will be able to walk again, its head high under the sun, without fear and without remorse, they will know where their roots lie. Written at Saragossa, this ninth day of the month of *Av*, in the year of punishment and exile. (*Legends*, p. 97)

The young Catholic learns from hearing the text that he is a Jew. "It had taken four centuries for the message of Moses, son of Abraham, to reach its destination" (p. 98).

The young Catholic is not enchanted by the discovery. Indeed, he is indignant. But he still wants to learn more than is contained in the statement of his ancestor, Moses, son of Abraham. The narrator describes the Spanish Inquisition. More still, the Spaniard demands. So the narrator tells the ancient story of persecution, resistance, renaissance, to the young man for whom the previously unknown history is now suddenly and catastrophically his own.

They part. But the story does not end there. A year later the narrator, visiting Jerusalem, is accosted by a stranger who addresses him in halting Hebrew. The narrator does not recognize the stranger until the latter mutters the word "Saragossa." It is the Spaniard.

Once again he takes the narrator to his dwelling, this time unadorned by crucifix or Virgin. The young man brings in a framed fragment of yellowed parchment. This time he reads the Hebrew text himself. They talk. When it is time for the narrator to leave, the young man, after letting the suspense build up, finally reveals who he is: "My name," he says, "is Moshe ben Abraham, Moses, son of Abraham" (p. 102).

The story, and the dynamics working within it, are central

for Wiesel. Sometimes we arrive at a certain place at a certain time to fulfill a certain mission of which we were previously unaware, a mission of *Tikkun*, restoration. The narrator is the vehicle through whom a Jew, dead four centuries, brings restoration and new life to another Jew living in the twentieth century. We who live in the present can discover who we truly are only by exploring the past; the past, seemingly over and done with, may receive its meaning and fulfillment only when something new happens in the present.

And the storyteller is a link between the two.

Necessity: the journey to the past, where the present is recovered, not evaded

The moral journey on which we have been accompanying Wiesel soon becomes a historical journey. In his tales about contemporary post-Holocaust Jews, we begin to be aware of references to the past—Hasidic stories, tales from the Midrash, episodes and characters from the Hebrew scriptures. The process reaches a culmination in *A Beggar in Jerusalem,* where events from the past are hard to disentangle from events in the present. We are irritated by our inability to separate them until we realize that they cannot be separated . . . because they are inseparable. We cannot deal with the present without also dealing with the past.

Concern for the past is not evasion of the present; it is how we understand the present and use it creatively. The past provides "a shield for the future," without which we are vulnerable to the destructiveness of the present.

Wiesel's recognition of the need for interaction between present and past is characteristically Hasidic. The Baal Shem Tov, founder of Hasidism, not only stressed Jewish solidarity but also taught that the companionship embraces past as well as present. Ancestors stand behind contemporaries; they meet each other.

> Whatever they did, they did for us. Whatever we do, we do for them. Long ago, in Egypt, every one of us strove for the preservation of the holy tongue, the names of our ancestors and their

descendents, and the memory of the Covenant. Every one of us
sat at the Prophets' feet to receive their teachings. Every one
of us marched through the desert, to Sinai and from Sinai.
Every one of us watched the splendor and desolation of Jerusalem. We all followed Reb Yohanan Ben-Zakkai into exile; we all
shared his anguish and pride. And that is why we must stay
together. (*Masters*, pp. 7–8)

From his earliest days in Sighet, Wiesel internalized this reality:

On the morning of Shavuoth there I was with Moses receiving
the Law. On the even of Tishah b'Av, seated on the floor, my
head covered with ashes, I wept, together with Rabbi Yohanan
Ben-Zakkai, over the destruction of the city that had been
thought indestructible. During the week of Hanukkah, I rushed
to the aid of the Maccabees; and on Purim, I laughed, how I
laughed, with Mordecai, celebrating his victory over Haman.
And week after week, as we blessed the wine during Shabbat
meals, I accompanied the Jews out of Egypt—yes, I was forever
leaving Egypt, freeing myself from bondage. To be a Jew meant
creating links, a network of continuity. (*A Jew Today*, p. 6)

The process goes both ways. Not only does the past help us
understand the present, the present helps us understand the
past. Reflecting on Cain and Abel, Abraham and Isaac, Wiesel
writes:

In Jewish history, all events are linked. Only today, after the
whirlwind of fire and blood that was the Holocaust, do we grasp
the full range of implications of the murder of one man by his
brother, the deeper meanings of a father's questions and dis-
concerting silences. Only as we tell them now, in the light of
certain experiences of life and death, do we understand them.
(*Messengers*, pp. xiii–xiv)

If the story starts with Auschwitz, scene of a contemporary
Holocaust, it will not be understood until it has led back to
Mount Moriah, scene of an ancient potential Holocaust. And
if the story leads to Mount Moriah, it will not end there but will
lead us back to the contemporary world in which Auschwitz
occurred, the same world seen differently.

To emphasize this historical journey, Wiesel extends the

scope of his writing to include tales from his upbringing, his Hasidic heritage, the Midrash, and the Hebrew scriptures.[1]

Reverence: the journey to Sighet,
where lost reality is more haunting than a severed dream

The immediate past, in Elie Wiesel's case, is irredeemable. It is the world of Auschwitz, a world of nihilistic proportions, capable only of destroying the ability to believe, even the will to live.

But behind the memories of an eternity in Auschwitz are the memories of a boyhood in Sighet, a little town "somewhere in the Carpathian mountains of Transylvania," that had earlier provided a fulcrum of meaning. Sighet is now a lost reality, shattered by Auschwitz, but a reality Wiesel constantly seeks to piece back together and reclaim. Sighet may well loom larger in Wiesel's future writing; it haunts him, not so much as a dream from which he was irretrievably awakened, but more as a reality from which he was irretrievably snatched— elusive because never fully recoverable, always to be sought.

Wiesel writes with a photograph of his boyhood home on the desk before him. The reality emanating from that haunting photograph through his pen and onto his pages, will never receive adequate replication. He has set himself an unattainable goal, which therefore becomes an unending project. The rest of us are beneficiaries of his creative anguish.

Auschwitz . . . Sighet. Irreconcilable realities. Incapable of existing in the same world. At first the destructive flames of hatred and dispassion in Auschwitz extinguished the creative flames of love and ardor in Sighet. But they could not fully do so. For although the flames of Sighet are searing, seeking to revive a people destroyed by the other flames, they also contain foretastes of healing, as Wiesel recreates that world of his childhood for us—glancing references here, allusions there, stories *of* Sighet on one page, stories *from* Sighet on another, this character reanimated, that character redrawn. The rest of us are beneficiaries of his anguished creativity.

We will not understand the rest of his journey if we do not linger in the place to which he is always returning; a place where it sometimes seems that "the whole universe is but an extension of that little town" (*Legends*, p. 26).

One can never "systematize" Sighet, but one can record impressions. Above all, Shabbat:

> I shall never forget Shabbat in my town. When I shall have forgotten everything else, my memory will still retain the atmosphere of holiday, of serenity pervading even the poorest houses; the white tablecloth, the candles, the meticulously combed little girls, the men on their way to synagogue. When my town shall fade into the abyss of time, I will continue to remember the light and the warmth it radiated on Shabbat. (*A Jew Today*, p. 8; see also *Generation*, pp. 13–15)

That light and warmth, he remembers, changed things:

> The jealousies and grudges, the petty rancors between neighbors could wait. As could debts and worries, the dangers. Everything could wait. As it enveloped the universe, the Shabbat conferred on it a dimension of peace, an aura of love. (*A Jew Today*, p. 8)

His grandfather, Dodye Feig, the most important influence on his life:

> Whenever I felt sad or guilty or misunderstood, I would seek refuge with him. I would go and knock at his door or simply imagine him standing before me: "Are you unhappy, little one? Do you have complaints against life? But then, what are you waiting for to change it? Come, I shall help you. Have I ever told you the marvelous story of . . ." Yes or no, it made no difference; the small schoolboy forgot his sorrow. . . .
>
> The stories that I most like to tell are the ones I heard from my grandfather. I owe him my love of tradition, my passion for the Jewish people and its unfortunate children. (*A Jew Today*, pp. 67, 69)

Sometimes the memories are clear:

> That town. I see it still. I see it everywhere. I see it with such clarity that I often mock and admonish myself: continue and you'll go mad; the town no longer exists, it never did. But I can't help it. (*Generation*, pp. 12–13)

When memories grow dim, it is the writer's task to recreate them:

> The act of writing is for me often nothing more than the secret
> or conscious desire to carve words on a tombstone: to the
> memory of a town forever vanished, to the memory of a child-
> hood in exile, to the memory of all those I loved and who,
> before I could tell them I loved them, went away. (*Legends,* p.
> 26)

Yes, the words are carved. Elisha, in *Dawn,* speaks of a time
when "I was twelve years old, my parents were still alive, and
God still dwelt in our town" (*Dawn,* p. x).

Why is it so yearned for? Because it represents a world now
gone, but a world infinitely to be desired, a world against
which one must measure all worlds that have succeeded it:

> At that time, in that universe, everything seemed simple.
> . . . In my small town somewhere in the Carpathian Mountains,
> I knew where I was, I knew why I existed. I existed to glorify
> God and to sanctify his Word. I existed to link my destiny to
> that of my people, and the destiny of my people to that of
> humanity. I existed to do good and to combat evil, to accom-
> plish the will of heaven: in short, to fit each of my acts, each of
> my dreams, each of my prayers into God's design. ("Recalling
> Swallowed-up Worlds," p. 609)

All shattered. But the fragments must be lovingly gathered
up and shared. And so Sighet, and the small boy who lived
there one time, many lifetimes ago, remain constant reference
points. Even in prayer:

> I ask you, God of Abraham, Isaac and Jacob, to enable me to
> pronounce these words without betraying the child that trans-
> mitted them to me: God of Abraham, Isaac and Jacob, enable
> me to forgive You and enable the child I once was to forgive
> me too.
>   I no longer ask You for the life of that child, nor even for
> his faith. I only beg you to listen to him and act in such a way
> that You and I can listen to him together. (*Generation,* pp. 189–
> 190)

Wiesel goes back to Sighet, twenty years later, to see if he
can recapture the lost reality, having earlier imagined such a
return in one of his novels. Can the real Sighet be recovered?
It cannot. The fictional journey, which describes the beginnings of redemption, outstrips the actual journey, which

brings no redemption, but only the recognition that "one cannot dig up a grave with impunity" (*Legends,* p. 146). The real
Sighet is no longer "somewhere in the Carpathian Mountains."

> Sighet, the real Sighet, was elsewhere, somewhere in Upper
> Silesia, near a peculiar little railroad station called Birkenau,
> near a great fire lighting up the sky; the real Sighet formed part
> of an immense city of ashes. (*Legends,* p. 150)

He had been wrong to return, Wiesel concludes, and cuts his
visit short. "For it had never existed—the town that had once
been mine" (p. 164).

Five years later there is another return. It is no more fulfill-
ing. There is a visit to the family home. The old furniture is
still there, the same chairs and beds. The same, yet not the
same at all.

> I look at the wall and find the nail I drove into it in 1936—yes,
> I remember it clearly—in order to hang the portrait of the
> Wizsnitzer Rebbe, who had just died. I see the nail and I look
> for the portrait; it has been replaced by a cross. (*A Jew Today,*
> p. 60)

The same, yet not the same at all.

Today Sighet represents "a world that no longer exists,"
and it represents a world being sought. In 1981 Wiesel writes,
"I am seeking my childhood. I will always be seeking it. I need
it. It is necessary to me as a point of reference, as a refuge"
("Recalling Swallowed-up Worlds," p. 609).

There is pathos here. Let us pause before it . . .

But there is also a dynamic. The search for the unattainable
continues. And if Elie Wiesel cannot go *to* Sighet, he will go
through it, every day, to what lies beyond it—the Hasidic world
he first encountered there, the world of stories old Dodye Feig
shared with a young grandson sitting enthralled on his knee,
the world where celebration is not a hollow word, the world
where stories draw generations together across the bands of
time, across the bonds of death.

> My father, an enlightened spirit, believed in man.
> My grandfather, a fervent Hasid, believed in God.
> The one taught me to speak, the other to sing.

Both loved stories.
And when I tell mine, I hear their voices.
Whispering from beyond the silenced storm, they are what
  links the survivor to their memory.
                                    (dedication of *Souls on Fire*, p. 1)

Celebration: the journey into Hasidism,
where dancing counts for more than prayers

When Wiesel chose to gather some of the riches he had
rediscovered in Hasidism, he called his collection *Célébration
hassidique*. In the wake of all the chimneys and the burnings,
"celebration" is the last word we would have expected him to
use. And yet, such is the power of the tale, that celebrations
from the past can trigger celebrations in the present. Any
ambivalence in the word (for "celebrations" can occur against
sombre backdrops), is well transmitted in the English title,
Souls on Fire. In the wake of all the chimneys and the burnings,
"fire" is the last image we would have expected Wiesel to use
as a equivalent of "celebration"; "souls on fire" would seem
capable only of invoking images of human life being extinguished forever.

But Hasidism looks at our expectations, scoffs at them, and
tosses them aside. We missed the point: the image of "souls
on fire" is positive—souls ablaze with the glory of God, souls
fired up to a spiritual intensity beyond the reach of others,
souls in the warmth of whose presence we too are called to
celebrate.

Too quick a transition? Perhaps. The title may still have
ironic overtones. Celebration can be defiance as well as exu-
berance, even wrested out of something close to despair, and
Wiesel captures *that* side of Hasidism in the full title of his
second Hasidic book, *Four Hasidic Masters and Their Struggle
Against Melancholy*. Sometimes, as Wiesel discovered in Russia,
Jews must be commanded to engage in celebration. But to
claim celebration as one pole of existence is to claim at least
a modest victory, and Hasidism enables Wiesel to do so. Let
all the titles stand.

What is Hasidism? Definition is betrayal. Hasidism is a protest against formalization, abstraction, a scholastic set of mind that asks for . . . definitions. It began as a movement within middle European Jewry in the eighteenth century, when Judaism was getting abstract, scholastic, definitional. It does not deal with world views as much as with worldly creatures. It disavows philosophy in the name of fervor. Instead of systems, it transmits stories.

Wiesel is a quintessential Hasid. He tells Hasidic tales and puts his own stamp upon them; he tells his own tales, and they are stamped with a Hasidic imprint. It is the tale, not abstraction, that communicates. To hear ancient tales is to hear what Hasidism is. After recounting a long one, Wiesel comments:

> This tale is characteristic because it contains most of the basic elements of Hasidism. The fervent waiting, the longing for redemption; the erratic wanderings over untraveled roads; the link between man and his Creator, between the individual act and its repercussions in the celestial spheres; the importance of ordinary words; the accent on fervor and on friendship too; the concept of miracles performed by man and for man. It is also characteristic because it may well . . . not be true. (*Souls,* p. 5)

A few short tales and anecdotes from *Souls on Fire* will communicate better than many long paragraphs and analyses:

> [Of the Maggid of Mezeritsch, the mysterious Leib, son of Sarah, said,] "I came to the Maggid not to listen to discourses, nor to learn from his wisdom; I came to watch him tie his shoelaces." (p. 61)

> In an inn somewhere, a wealthy guest mistakes [Rebbe Zusia] for a beggar and treats him accordingly. Later he learns his identity and comes to cry his remorse: "Forgive me, Rebbe, you must—for I didn't know."
>
> "Why do you ask Zusia to forgive you?" Rebbe Zusia said, shaking his head and smiling. "You haven't done anything bad to him; it is not Zusia you insulted but a poor beggar, so go and ask the beggars, everywhere, to forgive you." (p. 126)

> [Nahman of Bratzlav] ridiculed a famous Tzaddik who for nine years had prayed with fervor thinking that his Hasidim were listening in the anteroom; he thought he could hear their whispers. At the end of nine years he opened the door. A cat was scratching the floor. (p. 194)

[The "grandfather of Schpole"] was the first Rebbe to turn
dance into a ritual. Watching him sway and turn, the son of the
great Maggid of Mezeritch exclaimed, "Your dancing counts
for more than my prayers." (p. 46)

A favorite:

Before Rebbe Zusia died, he said: "When I shall face the celestial tribunal, I shall not be asked why I was not Abraham, Jacob
or Moses. I shall be asked why I was not Zusia." (p. 120)[2]

But Wiesel does more than tell stories. Sometimes he reflects on them, drawing what he has learned into a synthesis.
One such moment:

God is not indifferent and man is not His enemy—this was the substance of the Hasidic message. It was a message against despair,
against resignation; it sensitized the individual Jew to his own
problems and made him aware of his ability to solve them. It
taught him that hope must be derived from his own history, and
joy from within his own condition. (*Masters,* p. 15, italics added)

Célébration hassidique . . .

The celebration is a celebration of humanity, and only because of that a celebration of God.

It is in man that God must be loved, because the love of God
goes through the love of man . . . The name of man's secret is
God, and the name of God's secret is none other than the one
invented by man: love. Who loves, loves God. (*Souls,* p. 31)

There is no elitism, no cult of the favored few, no class on
whom the rest must depend for salvation:

Every woodcutter may be a prophet in disguise, every shoemak-
er a Just Man, every unknown the Baal Shem. . . . A shepherd
plays a tune—the Baal Shem relates him to King David. A
stranger in rags provokes laughter—the Master refers to him as
Abraham. (*Souls,* p. 33)

Out of many characteristics of Hasidism, let us isolate one—
humor—to illustrate the rest. Humor is a way of introducing
unexpected logic into a situation, thus making the situation
transformable. It introduces a sense of proportion; those who
can laugh at themselves are not likely to take themselves too
seriously, a cleansing discovery. It serves as a source of

strength: those who can laugh at their enemies are not so likely
to be cowed by them. It enlivens reports about the founder of
Hasidism, the Baal Shem Tov:

> Some [historians] go so far as to deny his very existence. They
> would like us to believe that he was—quite simply—invented by
> his disciples, whose own existence they fortunately do not
> doubt. Others, to restore the balance, claim that . . . there were
> actually two Baal Shem Tovs and that the Hasidic movement
> was founded . . . by the other. (*Souls*, pp. 9–10)

Humor is one of the secrets of Jewish survival:

> [The wife of Rebbe Barukh of Medzebozh] complained:
> "The children have nothing to eat; go get them some bread."
> Hershele went to the marketplace with a whip in his hand,
> shouting: "Who wants to go to Zhitomir for half the price?" So
> some people, to save half the fare, flocked to him instead of
> taking the coach. He made them pay, and then said: "Follow
> me." He led them out of town, and farther. Midway, the "pass-
> engers" asked him: "Hershele, where are the horses?"
>   "Who spoke of horses?" he said. "I spoke of half fare
> . . ." (*Masters*, p. 55)

It is a frequent vehicle for communicating truths about
human nature . . .

> [The Baal Shem Tov] warned them to be suspicious of anyone
> claiming to have all the answers: "You want to know if a particu-
> lar Rebbe is genuine? Go ask his advice. Ask him if he knows
> a way to chase impure thoughts from your mind; if he says yes,
> you'll know he is a fake." (*Souls*, pp. 25–26)

. . and the interrelation between the human and divine:

> [Levi-Yitzhak of Berditchev] offered God a bargain: "We shall
> give You our sins and, in return, You will grant us Your pardon.
> By the way, You come out ahead. Without our sins, what would
> You do with Your pardon?" (*Souls*, p. 108)

What has the journey into Hasidism done for Wiesel?

First, it has helped him reestablish his identity, after that
identity was stripped from him by the fires of Birkenau, and
has repositioned him in the tradition of his father and grandfather. He started telling Hasidic tales not only to rehabilitate
the *zaddikim*, but to rehabilitate himself. Referring to himself

in the third person, Wiesel writes at the end of his first book on Hasidism: "In his role of storyteller, and that is the essential point—he has but one motivation: *to tell of himself while telling of others*" (*Souls*, p. 259, italics added). The impulse remains. Near the end of his second book on Hasidism, it reappears: "A Hasidic story is about Hasidim more than about their Masters; it is about those who retell it as much as about those who experienced it" (*Masters*, p. 121).

Second, Hasidism has helped Wiesel recover a perspective on the world that empowers celebration, community, humor, an ongoing struggle with God, and a recognition that events are never closed to the emergence of new possibilities. Nothing in the post-Auschwitz world suggests that such things are still possible. Everything in the Hasidic world insists that such things are still mandatory. To be able to laugh and sing and dance—when there is every reason not to do so—is a gift from Hasidism. Not to cry and mourn and withdraw—when there is every reason to do so—is a gift from Hasidism. Only a Hasid could see the future as utterly bleak, all the evidence negative, and yet begin his next paragraph with the words "And yet . . ."

Third, Hasidism has provided Wiesel with his vehicle of communication—the tale. Not only is Hasidism a repository of endless tales he has rediscovered and retold, it is also the inspiration for new tales of his own creation. As he acknowledges, when reflecting on the great Hasidic masters, "Consciously or not, I have incorporated a song, an echo, a word of theirs in my own legends and fables" (*Masters*, p. 123). Sometimes, as in the opening of *The Gates of the Forest*, an ancient tale, Hasidic in origin, is woven into the texture of the tale of modern Jews. Sometimes the Hasidic ethos casts its spell more indirectly on the modern tale, in ways that have the quality of healing. We discover, for example, that the turning point in the moral journey recounted in the two previous chapters owes its power to the dynamic of Hasidism:

[In *The Town Beyond the Wall*] I imagined a man who one day finds himself sharing a cell with a madman. After a while, he feels his reason failing; he knows that he is going to lose it completely. Exposed to madness, he will ultimately become its

victim. And so, in order not to go mad, he sets out to cure his
mad cell-mate. Were the hero of my tale but aware, would he
have understood that he was only following in the steps of the
Hasidic Masters whom . . . I have tried to evoke? (*Masters,* pp.
123–124)

Reflection: the journey into Midrash, where every thought is worthy of embellishment

The journey into the past does not end with the recovery
of Hasidism. For just as Wiesel's life is embedded in something wider and deeper than contemporary experience, so the
Hasidic tradition is embedded in something wider and deeper
—the whole Jewish story, spread over the centuries. The next
step is a journey into Midrash.

Midrash means "investigation," and midrashic texts are
investigations of the ancient biblical texts. The principle of
midrashic writing is to explore every possible nuance of a text,
seeking deeper and more elusive meanings than are immediately apparent. Every detail is significant, both what is said and
what is not said.

There is ample biographical material about one character,
and a paucity of information about another? A midrash will
explore the reasons for such discrepancy. There is a break in
the continuity of the narrative? A midrash will propose the
missing links. The same verb is repeated in the same narrative
to describe the same action by the same people, but once in
the plural and once in the singular? Ah, there must be deep
reasons for this; a midrash will supply them.

Within texts of divine origin, nothing is irrelevant. Because
the counsels of God are unfathomable, there will never be an
end to insights derivable from them. A text elliptical to one
generation will possess devastating clarity to another. The
midrashic task will never be completed, for the Hebrew Scriptures contain, germinally at least, all that can ever be thought.
And every thought is worthy of embellishment.

So midrashic materials are made to order for Wiesel. Byron
Sherwin, interpreting Wiesel, indicates why this is so: "Midrash provides a link between a biblical text and a contempo-

rary situation. It binds the experiences of the patriarchs and the prophets to our experiences, to our lives, to our times. Midrash provides a means by which our story may become incorporated into the continuing story of Jewish experience."[3]

Two things happen in Wiesel's journey into midrash. One is that he makes extensive use of midrashic materials in all of his biblical writings, as we shall presently see. And he has written the text of a cantata, *Ani Maamin,* out of a well-known midrashic tale, describing how in times of crisis, Abraham, Isaac, and Jacob are dispatched from heaven to roam the earth, report to the divine throne what is happening, and make recommendations for divine action.

And what Wiesel does with that ancient tale illustrates the second result of his encounter with midrash. For he does not simply retell an ancient midrash, he creates a new one. He moves the pilgrimage of the patriarchs to the time of the Holocaust, and he omits the speculations of the traditional midrash—that the covenant has been broken or that the devastation anticipates Messiah's coming—offering a new resolution of the tale that relates God to the ongoing suffering of the Jewish people in a new way.[4]

Wiesel's own midrashic contributions are not limited to his dealings with earlier texts. His entire literary output is *a new midrash,* a new "investigation." Often he is responding to texts of the past—most notably in his retelling of Hasidic and biblical stories. But always he is responding to the text that is the history of a people, all of whose experiences—joys and sorrows, weeping and laughter, "hope turned to dust and dust turned to hope"—cry out for "investigation." Other Jewish thinkers do this philosophically, or theologically, or historically. Wiesel does it through tales. And tales are the distinctive form of midrash.

Contemporaneity: the journey into Scripture, where stories of the past describe the present

Since midrashic materials have their base in the Hebrew scriptures, they point us inescapably to the biblical texts, and Wiesel's attention more and more comes to focus directly on them. Three books thus far retell the biblical stories: *Messengers of God* (1976), *Images from the Bible* (1980, a commentary on biblical scenes painted by Shalom of Safed), and *Five Biblical Portraits* (1981). There will be more.

In the first of these, Wiesel does for biblical characters what he had already begun to do for Hasidic characters—retelling their stories so that they become contemporary. The chapter on Job is called "Job: Our Contemporary," but the title applies to every biblical character from the beginning:

> Embodying man's eternal quest for meaning, justice and truth, Adam remains the contemporary—and the companion—of all men, of all generations. Every one of us yearns to recapture some lost paradise, every one of us bears the mark of some violated, stolen innocence. All our passions and sorrows, all our failings, Adam already knew. (*Messengers*, p. 7)

To read about Adam is to read about ourselves. At only one point is he truly different from us: he did not have to deal with an Oedipus complex . . . (p. 7).

Cain and Abel? Our story as well. "Their behavior is familiar to us: every one of their impulses prefigures our conduct in stress situations. Ultimately we are confronted by them, or rather by their image, the image of a man with two faces we cannot contemplate without fear" (p. 39). Their story is a tragedy; in it we see the lineaments of our own tragedy. We know the tragedy of Cain, the first murderer, but there is tragedy for Abel as well, not simply the tragedy of being killed, but the tragedy of being chosen by God. There is a poignancy for those who stand in the succession of Abel's spiritual heirs:

> Cain should have understood his brother's tragedy: to be chosen by God is no less painful and restrictive than to incur His wrath. Man punishes those who love him, God chastises those He loves. In either case, the punishment is unjust: to live with God carries no less anguish than to live without Him or against Him. (*Messengers*, p. 57)

"The agony of the believer" in the present generation is as deep as that of the children of the second generation.[5]

One of the most gripping and terrifying of the biblical stories is the *akedah*, the story of God's demand that Abraham sacrifice his son by fire. That ancient story became both gripping and terrifying to Wiesel on his first night in Birkenau. Standing in the glare of the fires of the crematoria, Wiesel and his father were met by fellow Jews. Speaking in the third person, Wiesel recollects:

> Suddenly people began coming to him and those who were with him and began telling him and his father, "You know these flames? These are human beings. Do you know that people are being destroyed here? Do you know that the *akedah* is once more at the heart of Judaism? Abraham and Isaac both go to the altar, and both will be consumed." ("Freedom of Conscience—A Jewish Commentary," p. 71)

There is no better way to see the contemporaneity of the biblical stories than to follow Wiesel through his own analysis of the *akedah,* the story of Abraham's near-sacrifice of Isaac. For as he says, "If Isaac's averted sacrifice had involved only Abraham and his son, their ordeal would have been limited to their own suffering. But it involves us" (*Messengers,* p. xiii). Indeed, it involves us so much that sometimes the two tales can scarcely be disentangled. The tale of Abraham and his son Isaac walking toward a holocaust, and the tale of Shlomo Wiesel and his son Elie walking toward a holocaust, are the same tale. Save for the outcome.

> Somewhere a father and his son are heading toward an altar in flames; somewhere a dreamy boy knows that his father will die under the veiled gaze of God. Somewhere a teller of tales remembers, and overcome by an ancient and nameless sadness, he feels like weeping. He has seen Abraham and he has seen Isaac walk toward death; the angel, busy singing the Almighty's praises, did not come to wrest them from the hushed black night. (*Messengers,* p. xiii)

To Wiesel, the *akedah* is "a survivor's story." The very choice of words links past and present. All significant Jewish themes find embodiment in it, including "the need to obey God's will and the need to rebel against it" (p. 69). All Jews are bound to it: "every one of us, at one time or another, is called to play a part in it" (p. 70).

We know the story: God decides to test Abraham, who is to make an offering, a holocaust, of his first-born son, Isaac. Dutiful to God's will, Abraham journeys with Isaac to Mount

Moriah, binds the victim and prepares to use the knife, preparatory to lighting the flames. An angel stays the executioner's hand, barely in time. A ram, conveniently caught in a tangled thicket, is substituted.

As a child, Wiesel had great difficulty with this tale. Who does not? Who needs gods who would order murder? Who needs fathers who would acquiesce in such a demand? Who needs sons who limply accept such a destiny?

Not only is the story a problem, so is its subsequent use in Jewish tradition. Why is Abraham, a would-be slaughterer, affirmed in Jewish prayers as the symbol of love and grace? Why is Isaac called *Yitzhak*, "he who will laugh"? Such a one with such a fate can laugh?

Wiesel traces midrashic materials that explore God's reasons for testing Abraham. Important consideration: God tests only the strong. Subsequent reflection: Abraham was tested both for his own good and to serve as an example to later Jews. Final appraisal: "Of course, this does not satisfy everyone: the idea that suffering is good for Jews is one that owes its popularity to our enemies" (p. 79).

Still, at the end of the ordeal there has been no murder. Abraham has passed the test and Isaac is still alive. But as Wiesel points out perceptively, "the tale ends with a strange sentence which opens rather than heals the wounds" (p. 83). On the journey to Moriah, Abraham and Isaac had traveled together. They did everything together, even to the gathering of wood for the holocaust. But on the return journey, the verb is in the singular: "He [not they] returned to his servants, waiting at a distance at the foot of the mountain." What pathos, in the space of a single verb form. Isaac was alive, but Isaac was no longer journeying with his father. It is not hard to fathom the reason . . .

A Jew can identify with Isaac. But who can identify with Abraham? Wiesel, with the help of the midrash, makes a case for Abraham. Not only did God test Abraham; Abraham, in turn, tested God. It was as though he had said, "I defy You, Lord. I shall submit to Your will, but let us see whether You shall go up to the end, whether You shall remain passive and remain silent when the life of my son—who is also Your son— is at stake!" (p. 91).

It appears to be a draw, this battle between God and Abraham. But when it comes to the showdown, God backs off. Abraham wins. Which is why, Wiesels suggests, the biblical text reports that it is an angel who tells Abraham to stay the execution. Why not God? He is too embarrassed.

The midrash tells us that Abraham is not content with one victory. His momentum aroused, he pushes his advantage. It is not enough to get word from an angel. The command to stay the execution must come directly from the one who ordered the execution. Abraham prepares to pick up the knife once more. Hastily, God concedes a second time, and the command now comes not from an intermediary, but from the mouth of God.

Abraham presses his advantage once more. God must promise to forgive the children of Israel when they break the law in the future. God's promise must be more powerful than God's commandment. Or else . . . And the hand is raised once again. God acquiesces a third time.

So Abraham *can* be understood as the symbol of love and grace; he is charitable toward God, if not noticibly so toward Isaac. Abraham calls God's bluff and threatens to expose God for some mixed-up priorities about the relationship of demand and promise. Such an Abraham can indeed be a model for Jews who feel called to question, challenge, shout defiance. And God—as Wiesel also establishes at the end of *Ani Maamin*—"loves to to be defeated by His children" (p. 93).

It is not, of course, quite that neat. It never is. If "God loves to be defeated by his children," Satan never does. So Satan, in another midrash, tells Sarah the whole story, and Sarah, unable to handle the thought that Abraham was willing to kill their first-born son, falls dead. Comments Wiesel: "In the end someone else pays the price—and that someone is almost always innocent" (p. 94).

A cruel twist. Abraham, despite a heavenly victory, is twice defeated on earth: he returns alone, and he returns to an empty home. Abraham is a loser as well as God—another consistently Jewish story.

> All the pogroms, the crusades, the persecutions, the slaughters,
> the catastrophes, the massacres by sword and the liquidations

by fire—each time it was Abraham leading his son to the altar,
to the holocaust all over again. (*Messengers*, p. 95)

Countless Abrahams have witnessed their children's deaths;
countless Isaacs have lived the *akedah* in their flesh, and died.
But the biblical story has a resolution usually denied those who
subsequently reenact it: Isaac survives.

What is one to do with such an unexpected ending? In two
packed pages Wiesel shows how the ending speaks with new
power to succeeding generations.

A sampling.

Isaac "had to make something of his memories, his experience, in order to force us to hope" (p. 96). He does not "break
with society" or "rebel against life." Instead, he becomes a
model for survivors of later holocausts: "He married, had
children, refusing to let fate turn him into a bitter man. He felt
neither hatred nor anger toward his contemporaries who did
not share his experience" (p. 96).

Isaac becomes "the defender of his people . . . entitled to
say anything he likes to God, ask anything of him" (p. 97).
Why?

> Because he suffered? No. Suffering, in Jewish tradition, confers
> no privileges. It all depends on what one makes of that suffer-
> ing. Isaac knew how to transform it into prayer and love rather
> than into rancor and malediction. (*Messengers*, p. 97)

A recipe for any future worth savoring.

But we are not even yet done with the story. There is still
the matter of the name *Yitzhak*, "a name which evokes and
signifies laughter" (p. 97). For what reason could a survivor of
the Holocaust and the experience of laughter possibly be
joined? There is a beautiful reason:

> As the first survivor, he had to teach us, the future survivors of
> Jewish history, that it is possible to suffer and despair an entire
> lifetime and still not give up the art of laughter. (*Messengers*, p.
> 97)

In spite of everything that happened to him—the trauma, the
violation, the disillusionment—Isaac "remained capable of
laughter."

*   *   *

I was in the audience when Wiesel gave the lecture that became the substance of this material in *Messengers of God.* Our gradually dawning recognition, as the lecture unfolded—that the story of a father and a son going toward a holocaust was both a biblical and a contemporary story, and that the participant in the contemporary story was the teller of the tale— spoke to us with transfixing power.

The lecture concluded with words omitted from the printed version, words that held us in their grasp, as the messenger, with every reason to despair, to succumb to tears, showed how the power of the ancient story was working even today: "Thus we have learned that each of us is both Abraham and Isaac. To be a Jew is to see what they have seen, remember what they have said, and lived, and endured, and indicated, and do what they have done, and go on doing it, or at least telling about it to some friends, sometimes, and to tell it all the time, not with tears, not with tears. But with laughter."

For Elie Wiesel, the journey that began at Auschwitz led to Mount Moriah. But it could do so only because another journey that began at Mount Moriah led to Auschwitz. And every point in between . . . and beyond.

Challenge: journeys into the present, where any human need is paramount

The journey to the past does not end there. It leads back to the present, empowering those on the journey to refashion the present in ways not possible before. The agenda is clear: responding to human need wherever it confronts us. Cambodia, Russia, Israel, Washington, wherever . . .

Cambodia. In February 1980, Wiesel (in company with Bayard Rustin, Marc Tannenbaum, Liv Ullmann, members of the French parliament and others) went to the Thai border of Cambodia, seeking to deliver twenty truckloads of food and medical supplies to starving Cambodians. Denied access, they spoke by loudspeaker across the border. Reflecting on his own confinement and starvation, Wiesel remarked, "One thing that is worse for the victim than hunger, fear, torture, even humiliation, is the feeling of abandonment, the feeling that nobody cares, the feeling that you don't count."

Why was he on an Asian border? "I came here," he said over the loudspeaker, "because nobody came when I was there."

The occasion was the thirty-sixth anniversary of the death of Elie Wiesel's father. He found enough Jews in the group to form a *minyan*. They recited the Kaddish, the prayer for the dead, in memory of his father. And not only his father.

> Suddenly I noticed a young French doctor who was repeating the same prayer, in tears. "Who is your Kaddish for?" I asked him.
>
> "For them," he answered, and he pointed toward the border, the other side of the border. (*San Francisco Examiner and Chronicle,* April 27, 1980, p. 2; also *New York Times,* February 7, 1980, p. A3)

A past to be recovered, a present to be redeemed.

Russia.[6] Wiesel's first trip to Russia, during the High Holy Days and Sukkot in 1965, has left an indelible impression on his life and writing. He had not believed all the stories of persecution and revived anti-Semitism and went to find out. He discovered fear, and tremendous courage. He witnessed despair, and celebration. Normative experience: thousands of Jews, dancing in the streets of Moscow on the eve of Simchat Torah, rejoicing when there was no reason to rejoice, rejoicing because there was no reason to rejoice, an act of defiance that was an exercise in definition: "They danced until midnight without rest, to let the city know that they are Jews" (*Silence,* p. 84; see pp. 58–84). Wiesel later called it a second visit to Jerusalem (see *A Jew Today,* pp. 24–25).

The Russians, he discovered, committed a tactical blunder in trying to destroy the Jewish consciousness of Russian Jews. "We are Jews for spite," one student told Wiesel, who adds, "For want of better teachers, it is the anti-Semites who are making them Jews" (p. 82).

The title of the book about the visit, *The Jews of Silence,* was misunderstood, despite a statement at the very end, "What torments me most is not the Jews of silence I met in Russia, but the silence of the Jews I live among today" (p. 127). Many people thought Wiesel was charging Russian Jews with lack of courage. Writing later "To a Young Jew in Soviet Russia," he explains:

> I implied that the real "Jews of Silence" were those who, smug and unconcerned, on the other side of the borders did nothing to come to your rescue. The title referred to us, established and complacent Jews, who did not respond to your appeals. (*A Jew Today*, p. 115)

Wiesel has not been "smug and unconcerned." He has sounded the trumpet of alarm on behalf of Jews in Russia, not only in essays and plays, but in his most ambitious piece of writing, *The Testament*, the novel he was working on when the Six Day War interrupted him back in 1967.

The Testament represents a new direction in Wiesel's writing. It is painted with a wide brush on a vast canvas. The Holocaust is there—it will always be there in Wiesel's writings—but so are many other things. The action covers half a century of European history. The protagonist, Paltiel Kossover (Paltiel means "God is my refuge"), is a Russian Jew. He endures a pogrom in his youth, migrates to Germany after embracing communism, works for the party in France after Hitler comes to power, fights in the Spanish Civil War, is with the Russian troops in World War II, and establishes himself in post-war Russian literary society as a poet. Ah! for once a Jewish success story? No. For the party line changes and Paltiel is a victim of an anti-Semitic Stalinist purge. The book is his "testament" before the court that eventually executes him on orders from above.

It is the story of hundreds of Russian Jewish artists after World War II. But it is more than the story of a ruthless state destroying a sensitive person; it is also the story of a sensitive person struggling with the conflicting claims of his Jewish faith and his embrace of communism. Fairly early in his communist career Paltiel sheds his phylacteries. But he never disposes of them, and they reappear when his son is born, just before the fateful knock on the door in the dead of night. As he testifies before the court, Paltiel comes to an ironic realization: "I lived a Communist and I die a Jew" (*Testament*, p. 21). An outer story of activity, fighting, hating, and loving, the book is also an inner story of mounting tensions, ideological and theological conflicts, hopes, and disappointments. In Paltiel's "testament," we are told, "every word contains a hidden meaning" (p. 29). It is also true of the book as a whole. Christian readers have to cope with the observation that for a Jew to live in a Christian world is to know the meaning of fear; all readers have to confront what it means to visit Majdanek; everyone has to struggle with the image of God as a "grave-digger," not one who kills, but one who rounds up and disposes of corpses. Is a more hopeful image of God possible after World War II? The burden is on those who say so.

The Testament is thus a story of actions full of devastating consequences. But it is something more. The important thing for Wiesel is that the story be told, for when it is told, its power is sufficient to produce change. Tyrants must therefore suppress the story. The Stalinist court thought it had done so *in re* Paltiel Kossover: the purgers would be purged, Paltiel's testimony never read, his story never told.

But it is. And this became an occasion for laughter. The book begins with lack of laughter: "I have never laughed in my life," old Zupanev tells us (p. 28). And throughout the book he never laughs, until the very last page. It is laughter signaling a cunning victory, laughter revealing something more powerful than the NKVD and the Politburo, more powerful even than Stalin. And that something is the insignificant court stenographer, who, by his very insignificance, survives the purging of the purgers and tells the story nobody was supposed to hear.

During the liquidation they forget about Zupanev. And so he, the invisible one, makes the story visible, passing on the "testament" to Paltiel Kossover's son. It is Zupanev's only victory. An occasion for laughter.

The irony is compounded. Grisha Kossover, son of Paltiel, has bitten off his tongue rather than speak of his father to one whom he fears is an informer. But because he receives the story Zupanev alone could communicate, Grisha, the mute, will share the story with others. The one who cannot be seen, sees. The one who cannot talk, tells.

It is Wiesel's way of reminding us of the power of the tale.

No story is ever lost. It will reappear, it will be told, in some fashion or other. There is always an invisible Viktor Zupanev, or a mute Grisha Kossover, or an articulate Elie Wiesel.

An occasion for laughter.

Israel. "Israel . . . a distant dream filling the veins of reality with sacred blood" (*Silence*, p. 98).

So Wiesel describes Israel's place in the hearts and minds of Russian Jews. Alongside the "distant dream" there is, of course, the immediate reality of a nation-state among other nation-states, involved in day-to-day decisions about power politics . . . and survival. There is no spot in the contemporary world where dream and reality are more intertwined. Or more essential to one another.

The creation of the state of Israel, heralded in *Dawn*, took form when Jews stopped counting on others and decided to take destiny into their own hands. The preservation of the state of Israel, celebrated in *A Beggar in Jerusalem*, was reaffirmed when Jews—six million and more—rallied to ensure that dream and reality would not be severed. The ongoing significance of the state of Israel, dramatized in *The Testament*, is renewed every time a plane touches down at Lod airport in Tel Aviv, with Jewish refugees arriving to begin life anew.

Wiesel describes three visits to the heart of Israel, which is Jerusalem. We have read about the visits earlier, although we were not sure the first two visits were to Jerusalem. The first visit was in 1944 in a place called Birkenau. Jews from every land were pouring in there, the ingathering of exiles was taking place. Perhaps redemption was at hand, as the earthly and heavenly Jerusalem opened its doors . . .

The second visit was in 1965 in Moscow, as Jews danced defiantly on the eve of Simchat Torah. A land and a city were reclaimed that night as an invisible Jacob's ladder carried everything but the bodies of the dancers up to heaven. Jerusalem.

The third visit was in 1967 when the Old City was reclaimed at the end of the Six Day War, the occasion of the vision when Jews from the four corners of the exile streamed into the city: "Jerusalem was bringing us closer to all the provisional Jerusalems-in-exile that the enemy had covered with ashes" (*A Jew Today*, p. 26; see Chapter 3 above).

The state of Israel came into being while Elie Wiesel was a stateless person living in Paris.

Miraculous? A thousand times yes, he thought. But a teacher disabused him: "Call it miraculous, that I refuse. We have paid too dearly for it. To be a miracle, it would have had to happen a little sooner" (*Generation*, pp. 127–128).

Israel a compensation for the Holocaust? A thousand times no. Such an equation is too easy, too scandalous. It suggests that because Auschwitz led to such an outcome, Auschwitz was "justified," an appropriate bit of moral leverage on the conscience of the world. Nothing is an "answer" to Auschwitz, which negates all answers. But many good things did emerge out of the Jews' concern for a homeland in the postwar years. They did not seek vengeance against their executioners, for one thing, but turned their attention in new and positive directions. About which people, after which wars, can it likewise be said that "they did not seek vengeance against their executioners"? (see *Generation*, pp. 126–130). So although Israel does not help Wiesel understand Auschwitz, there *is* a miracle (*pace* the teacher in Paris) in the fact that the creation of Israel enabled Jews "to transform the hate imposed upon it into a craving for solidarity with the world."

> Israel . . . represents a victory over absurdity and inhumanity. And if I claim it for myself, it is because I belong to a generation which has known so few. (*Generation*, p. 131)

This does not exempt Israel from the problems that beset other states, save that in Israel's case sheer survival is a daily problem; one successful military foray by a bordering power could destroy the reality and perhaps even the dream. War is not an appealing option to Israelis, and Wiesel invokes a long history of Jewish aborrence of war as a sign other nations could rely upon. The maxim, "Better to prevent war than to win it," was true even in Joshua's time (*A Jew Today*, p. 172). And war is never to be glorified: "War? Yes, if there is no alternative, but praise of war? Never" (p. 177).

An episode during the Six Day War epitomizes the attitude Wiesel believes is endemic to Israelis:

The battle for the Old City is still being waged when an Arab appears, asking to speak to an Israeli officer. His wife is about to give birth; he needs a doctor. The officer is struck by the incongruity. At a moment when his own men are wounded and still need help, he should spare a doctor to help give birth to a child who might grow up and stab his own son? But he makes a decision, and a Jewish doctor from the medical corps is dispatched to assist the woman in labor. Comments Wiesel:

> Why would you expect this officer, returned to civilian life, to discover in himself, now, an inclination toward hostility, an instinct for torture? (*Generation,* p. 149)

That was yesterday. What about today?

In the midst of increasingly exacerbated tensions, Wiesel writes "To A Young Palestinian Arab" (*A Jew Today,* pp. 101–106), exemplifying a concern stated earlier: "I hope with all my heart that one day, Jew and Arab, reconciled for the sake of their children, will live in peace, without the aspirations of the one limiting the other's" (*Generation,* p. 153).

It is an effort at conciliation, "hoping only to ascertain whether bonds might still be formed that would transcend mistrust, in spite of the blood that has been shed" (*A Jew Today,* p. 101).

He does not offer political solutions and proposes instead that Jews and Arabs "look at our relations from an exclusively human point of view" (p. 103). He offers a confession and an acknowledgement: "I am irritated by your threats but overwhelmed by your suffering; I am more sensitive to that than you imagine. The people of my generation cannot be otherwise" (p. 103). In the midst of unremitting devotion to the cause of Jewish survival, Wiesels still turns his eyes toward the Arabs. He can understand the anger of his correspondent. But both Jews and Arabs are suffering, and suffering should unite people instead of dividing them. Perhaps they have different understandings of suffering.

Wiesel believes that Jewish suffering has been used creatively since the Holocaust, not to spit on the killers or despise the spectators, but "to opt *for* man" rather than against. Wiesel finds the lack of vengeance on the part of the survivors almost without historical precedent. With rare exceptions, vengeance was not exacted. The suffering of Jews was not used against others.

To Palestinian Arabs Wiesel says, "I do feel responsible for what happened to you, but not for what you chose to do as a result of what happened to you. I feel responsible for your sorrow, but not for the way you use it" (p. 106). He feels that Arab suffering has been used to terrorize, to murder, "from Munich to Maalot . . .", and even though such acts may be the work of extremists, they win approval from their compatriots.

The issue, finally, is how suffering is to be used. If it cannot be obliterated, it can at least be humanized. He pleads for initiatives to turn suffering "into dialogue rather than sword," a decision that depends on both Jews and Arabs, and on nobody else. "And then perhaps, out of our reconciliation, a great hope will be born" (p. 106).

There is a corresponding letter "To a Brother in Israel" (*A Jew Today*, pp. 107–113). Originally a talk given in Jerusalem ("I never criticize Israel outside Israel," is one of Wiesel's principles), it asks what comments diaspora Jews (those who live outside of Israel) can address to Israelis, while acknowledging that Israelis feel that other Jews are not fully faithful to the vision Israel represents, since they do not live there.

The overall comment seems unfair, Wiesel concedes, but, in the nature of the case, unavoidable: "I expect more from Israel than from any other nation" (p. 111). He goes on:

> Not only do I wish to love Israel, I want to admire it, hold it up as an example, find there what cannot be found elsewhere: a certain sense of justice, a certain sense of dignity. I want to find there a society ruled by a vision of probity, justice and compassion. (p. 111)

Diaspora Jews want Israel to be everything they are not. They want Israel to be what the rest of the world is not, "a haven where the cycle of cynicism and nihilism will be broken" (p. 112).

"From Israel," Wiesel concedes, "we expect no more, no less than the impossible" (p. 112). Israelis should disagree less noisily, should welcome immigrants more openly, "adopt a more Jewish attitude toward Palestinian Arabs and, particularly, toward Israeli Arabs," and overall "be less intransigent, more receptive" (p. 111).

Unfair. And yet Israeli and diaspora Jews might develop a working agreement, since they are responsible for one another:

> If the principal task of the Diaspora is to protect Israel, yours should be to become a new source of life to the Diaspora. . . . Without the Diaspora, Israel would have no one to question and no one to be questioned by. Without Israel, the Diaspora would know nothing of victory but the anguish that precedes it. (p. 113)[8]

Washington. The assumption that more can be expected from Israel than from any other nation, is an assumption Wiesel makes about every member of the human family as well. People are called by him to become more than there is any reasonable expectation they will become. Concern for Jewish destiny leads to concern for human destiny.[7] This universal outreach is symbolized by Elie Wiesel's chairmanship of the United States Holocaust Memorial Council, charged with proposing a suitable memorial in Washington to holocaust victims. A memorial to the six million, of course, but, as Wiesel has said, "through them and beyond them but not without them," a memorial to *all* who were victims of the Nazi savagery. The memorial is not only to be a reminder of the past, but a warning for the future, a means of creating an "early warning system" to detect any actions anywhere that could lead to genocide against any people.

"Another holocaust" could take many forms; one in particular increasingly occupies Wiesel's attention. He is rightly disturbed by the way the word "holocaust" is cheapened by overuse. Such concern does not diminish the tragedy that befalls others; it only pleads that the word be reserved for the burning *(kaustikos)* of all *(holos)* the Jews.

There is one exception, however. One can imagine a second holocaust that would be worse than the first, and it is the single instance in which the same word can appropriately be used. This would be a nuclear holocaust, the only event that would literally fulfill the definition: the total consumption by burning of all that is.

Those like Wiesel, who went through the first Holocaust, and have taken a vow that "never again" shall it be repeated, are increasingly committed to averting a nuclear holocaust, which is the threatening counterpart in our time to what happened in their time. As Wiesel put it, in one of his most "public" appearances, the Day of Remembrance ceremony in the rotunda of the U.S. Capitol on April 24, 1979:

> Let us remember for their sakes, and ours: memory may perhaps be our only answer, our only hope to save the world from the ultimate punishment, a nuclear holocaust.

When the narrator in *The Oath* saw destruction of the Jews in Kollvillàg turn into the destruction of others as well, he trembled, for he realized that he saw the future: what human beings first do to Jews they later to do others. The observation, written in 1972, is even more relevant a decade later. The journey from Auschwitz back to Mount Moriah has not only led us back to the present, but has turned our faces toward a future terrifying beyond description.

Unless . . .

CHAPTER 5

The Silence of God, and
the Necessity of Contention
(a theological journey)

*Why does God insist that we come to him by the
hardest road?*
—Menachem, the believing Jew from Sighet
(*The Town Beyond the Wall,* p. 146)

*You don't understand [those in the camps] when you
say that it is more difficult to live today in a world
without God. NO! If you want difficulties, choose to
live* with *God. . . . The real tragedy, the real drama,
is the drama of the believer.*
—Wiesel, the believing Jew from Sighet and
Auschwitz ("Talking and Writing and
Keeping Silent," p. 274)

On speaking of God while speaking of humanity

Elie Wiesel does not think of himself as a theologian, nor
is he attracted by the discipline of theology.

I don't like the word "theologian." I find it disturbing. What
is a theologian, really? Someone who knows things about God.
But who knows what God is? Kafka once said, "Man cannot
speak *of* God. If at all, he can speak *to* God." So I'm still trying
to speak *to* Him. How can we speak *of* Him? (*Victory,* p. 13)

139

God cannot be expressed, Martin Buber once said, God can only be addressed.

Wiesel not only stands in the heritage of Martin Buber and Franz Kafka, but exemplifies an important part of the heritage of the Hebrew Scriptures: what we know of God receives expression through what we know of God's children. Consider the talmudic account of the giving of the Ten Commandments. All Israel stands at the foot of Mount Sinai; there is thunder, lighting, every accoutrement of divine manifestation.

> Then, abruptly, there was silence. And in this silence a Voice was heard. God spoke. What did He speak of? His secret work, His eternally imperceptible intentions? No, he spoke of man's relationship to man, of one individual's duties toward others. At this unique moment God wished to deal with human relations rather than theology. (*Messengers,* p. 195)

Two conclusions: (1) God is more concerned with how we treat human beings than with what we think about God, and (2) how we treat human beings will *indicate* what we think about God. For Wiesel, the second is considerably more important than the first.

> For the Jew, Judaism is the only possible way to humanism. It stresses human relations even more than God-man relations. There is no word, for example, in Hebrew, the sacred tongue, for the atheist. . . . The closest term would be *kofer be'ikor,* "someone who denies the essential" or God. But if we check the Talmudic sources we see that whenever the term appears it deals with relations between man and man or man and woman, not with God. *Whoever betrays humanity, whoever torments one's fellow man, denies the existence of God.* ("A Personal Response," p. 37, italics added)

In a lecture at Stanford University in 1974, Wiesel elaborated this point:

> There is no Jewish theology for a very simple reason: God wants man to be concerned with human things, not with godly things.
>
> I remember when I was a child and I prepared myself for the section in the reading of the Torah which deals with the Ten Commandments. And I remember I asked my teacher, "Why did God speak of such mundane things?" After all, for the first

time, for the very first and last time, God was going to manifest Himself and speak to His people. I had hoped that God would speak about the mystery of the beginning, or would reveal the secrets of how His work is being done, or at least He would give us a course in theology, which, after all is His field. Instead, what He did was come out with such simple everyday matters: you shall not steal, you shall not lie, you shall not violate Shabbat. For this we need the voice of God?

And the answer is Yes. Jewish theology is human relations. I believe it is God's way of saying, "I can take care of My own ideas, images, theories—you take care of My creation." (Slightly abridged from a taped transcript)

This explains some apparent contraditions in statements Wiesel makes about his writing. Challenged by a questioner for not having talked about God during a panel discussion, Wiesel responded, "As for God, I did speak about Him. I do little else in my books. It's my problem, and His, too" ("Jewish Values in the Post-Holocaust Future," p. 298).

And yet he will also say, "I really never speak about God. I have enough trouble speaking of myself—I cannot speak about God" (*Victory*, p. 18).

In conversation, Wiesel explains, "I cannot speak of God without speaking of man, or of man without speaking of God. God has always been my central problem in everything I have written." "In [*The Town Beyond the Wall*]," he explained on another occasion, "I tried to deal with man's relation to God, because God is always there. When man talks to man, somehow, God is there" (*Responses*, p. 151).

So there is no real contradiction. Wiesel seldom writes "about God." But he always writes about men and women who believe in God, or deny God, or quarrel with God. Surely there is no other way to write "about God." Whatever we learn about engagement with God will come out of what we learn about engagement between human beings.

The agony of the believer

For Wiesel, it is God's existence rather than God's nonexistence that is the problem. The dilemma is created by belief, not

disbelief. His agony over the question of God is the agony of
the believer.

Contrary to much popular interpretation, Wiesel's indictment of God does not constitute a denial of God. The fact that
it is not a denial only adds to its poignancy. If only one *could*
deny and have it over and done with—God disposed of,
pushed off the scene, no longer around to haunt and terrorize
—at least the ground rules would be clear: expect nothing,
trust no one, do not hope. A dreary prospect but a manageable
one.

But God is not so kind to Elie Wiesel as to be deniable, and
unless God is powerful and malevolent (a possibility and a
nightmare), God appears weak and victimized by a world that
has slipped out of divine control. If the latter, God can be
pitied. But if God is really in control, what has happened in
God's universe is monstrous. Either way, God must be called
to account: where was God when children were being thrown
on bonfires, when killer dogs were unleashed against naked
women as SS guards leered and laughed?

It would be hard to live in the world without God, Wiesel
concedes, but it is even harder to live in the world *with* God.
And it is the latter difficulty with which he has to deal. The
tension is never overcome. It exists in the very first book,
Night, and persists through the very latest book—whatever its
title. The questions come from within belief. "The agony of
the believer equals the bewilderment of the non-believer"
(*Generation,* p. 166).

"The Jew," Wiesel insists, "in my view, may rise against
God provided he remains within God. One can be a very good
Jew, observe all the *mitzvot,* study Talmud—and yet be against
God . . . as if to say: You, God, do not want me to be Jewish?
Well, Jewish we shall be nevertheless, despite Your will"
("Jewish Values in the Post-Holocaust Future," p. 299). To
stay within the community even provides certain privileges:
"From inside his community [the Jew] may say anything. Let
him step outside it, and he will be denied this right. The revolt
of the believer is not that of the renegade; the two do not speak
in the name of the same anguish" (*Souls,* p. 111). Menachem,
the believing Jew in the prison cell with Michael—the same
Menachem who asks that most poignant of all questions, "Why

does God insist that we come to him by the hardest road?"—recognizes that he may be insane, and responds, "And yet, Michael, my friend, I prefer to be insane with God or in Him—than without God, or far from him." When Michael calls this blasphemy, Menachem responds, "There, too, I prefer to blaspheme in God than far from him" (*Town*, p. 176). The agony of the believer is never overcome.

A complication: the consolations may make things worse:

> The Midrash tells us that when Pharaoh ordered that Jewish children be walled in alive in the pyramids, the Angel Michael siezed one of them and held it up to the heavenly court. When God saw the frightened child, he was moved to such compassion that he decided then and there to bring the exile to an end.
>
> I loved to read this Midrashic tale. I was as proud of the angel because he cared as of God because He acted. I now reread the tale and desperately try to understand. One Jewish child succeeded in moving God, but one million Jewish children did not. I try to understand—and I cannot. (*A Jew Today*, p. 179)

The agony of the believer is compounded: not only do we fail to understand why one child moves God and a million do not, but if we could understand, it would be worse. Wiesel describes a conversation with one of the judges in the Eichmann trial. Asked if he understood the Holocaust better, now that a verdict against Eichmann had been rendered, the judge replied, "Understand the Holocaust? I hope I never understand it. To understand would be worse than not to understand." By which he meant that if one could understand a universe in which the Holocaust made sense, or develop a concept of God in relation to whom the Holocaust could be "justified," that would be a universe in which the judge would not care to live, that would be a God in whom he would not want to believe.

"Perhaps some day someone will explain how, on the level of man, Auschwitz was possible; but on the level of God, it will forever remain the most disturbing of mysteries" (*Legends*, p. 20).

The questions mount. Questions about human nature, questions about the divine nature. Questions without answers. Fortunately.

Jews, Wiesel insists, are those who continue to ask questions. What kind of questions? An infinite variety of questions, but surely such questions as these:

> Why and how survive in a universe which negates you? Or: How can you reconcile yourself with history and the graves it digs and transcends? Or: How should you answer the Jewish child who insists: I don't want to suffer, I no longer want to suffer without knowing why. Worse: How does one answer that child's father who says: I don't want, I no longer want, my son to suffer pain and punishment without knowing that his torment has meaning and will have an end? And then, the big question, the most serious of all: How does one answer the person who demands an interpretation of God's silence at the very moment when man—any man, Jew or non-Jew—has greater need than ever of His word, let alone His mercy? (*Generation*, p. 166)

The latter question is indeed "the big question, the most serious of all," and it poses most squarely the agony of the believer. It is not even that God exists that is the problem. It is that God exists . . . and remains silent. When people cried out, why did God not answer? When there were prayers from earth, why was there silence from heaven? God's silence defines the agony of the believer.

The silence of God

It is the agony of the believer to have to cope with silence. Not the silence of emptiness, not the silence of a void, not the silence of human perplexity. The silence of God, which is also the absence of God.

The scene: a ghetto that has stopped living. The protagonist: a beadle who has lost his mind:

> It was the beadle's custom to rush to the synagogue each morning, to ascend the bimah and shout first with pride, and then with anger: "I have come to inform you, Master of the Universe, that we are here."
>
> Then came the first massacre, followed by many others. The beadle somehow always emerged unscathed. As soon as he could, he would run to the synagogue, and pounding his fist on

the lectern, he would shout at the top of his voice, "You see, Lord, we are still here."

After the last massacre, he found himself all alone in the deserted synagogue. The last living Jew, he climbed the bimah one last time, stared at the Ark and whispered with infinite gentleness: "You see? I am still here."

He stopped briefly before continuing in his sad, almost toneless voice: "But You, where are You?" (*Generation*, p. 68)

Infinite pathos. God *is . . .* That used to be the summation of ontological wisdom. But, in relation to the children of the world, the summation of ontological wisdom has become deficiency. God is . . . silent. God is . . . absent. "You, where are You?"

Perhaps God cannot provide an answer. But we must pursue the question. Wiesel pursues it in a poem set to music by Darius Milhaud, *Ani Maamin: A Song Lost and Found Again.* "Ani maamin beviat ha-Mashiah" was one of Maimonides' thirteen Articles of Faith. It became the text of a Hasidic chant, sung by Wiesel in his childhood: "I believe," it affirms, "in the coming of the Messiah, and though he tarry yet will I wait for him." "As a child," Wiesel writes, "I believed fervently. I still believe, but now chiefly in the hope that faith will restore the old fervor" (*Legends*, p. 89). That is one reason he wrote the poem. The song was "lost" in the camps; could it be "found" again?

For me it was an appeal to faith, to hope; an affirmation that even though the Messiah was late in coming—I believed that he would come . . . one day. Then I heard it sung inside the kingdom of madness by the Jews who knew they were on the threshold of death. How could they believe in the Messiah over there? How could they go on waiting for him? They should have known better. . . When you think of the Holocaust, you are inevitably confronted by the questions: Where was God? What did he know? What did he do? These questions are at the core of this poem—or tale, for it is also a tale, naturally. (Dust jacket of *Ani Maamin*)

The cantata retells the old story of Abraham, Isaac, and Jacob wandering the earth, only this time they are doing it during the Holocaust. They return to the heavenly precincts to plead the cause of Jews in their time of greatest persecution.

Each recounts a crucial event from his own past—Abraham, the first to affirm God as the redeemer of humanity; Isaac, the one who faced his own sacrifice uncomplainingly; Jacob, the one who dreamed of a ladder to earth from heaven. All insist that God has abandoned the future promised to them and their children, a future that has turned to ashes. Jacob asks:

> You promised me to watch over Israel—
> Where are You? What of your promise?
> You promised me blessings for Israel—
> Is this your blessing?
>
> [p. 23]

The patriarchs weep. The angels weep. But God does not weep. God remains silent.

Again they implore him:

> Faithful God, behold the torment
> That bears your seal,
> As does the faith
> Of your victims.
>
> [p. 27]

The slaughter continues, even as they speak. And with each Jewish death, another fragment of the Temple goes up in flames. Hope is being murdered as never before. But from the celestial tribunal, only silence . . .

The pleaders intensify their urgency. Abraham did not know that the road from Ur to Canaan would end in Treblinka. Isaac did not know that the vision from Mount Moriah would include Majdanek. Jacob on his way to Bethel did not know

> That every road
> At dusk
> Would lead to Auschwitz.
>
> [p. 33]

Each gives an example of the destruction the Holocaust has brought: a bunker in Warsaw where a Jewish hand had to silence forever the cry of a Jewish child, a death march in a forest where a father cannot console a son, a despairing suicide in a concentration camp. The Chorus supports the patriarchs and cries out to heaven: "Your children implore you: Hear and answer!" (p. 47). But heaven remains silent.

Finally the silence of heaven is broken, not by God, but by an angel come to plead God's cause: who are you to question the divine power or plan? God has his reasons. You are not to challenge but accept. There will be salvation in the end.

Abraham interrupts with the crucial question:

> You showed me messianic times—
> But what kind of messiah
> Is a messiah
> Who demands
> Six million dead
> Before he reveals himself?
>
> [pp. 69, 71]

The angel can only respond:

> God consoles.
> That is enough.
>
> [p. 71]

At that, the pleading turns to anger. It is *not* enough! It can never be enough. Abraham, Isaac, and Jacob respond that they and their people will never be consoled. It is impossible to be "consoled" for Belsen, or "rewarded" for Birkenau, or "forgetful" of Majdanek.

They decide to leave heaven. All they can do is return to earth and tell their people not to hope: "For now it is clear: God knows—and remains silent. God knows—so it must be his will" (p. 75). The executioners win, for God is silent. The patriarchs step back to leave, and God is still silent . . .

Which would, of course, be a dramatic place to conclude. Who could blame Wiesel for concluding there? A plea has been made to God, and the plea has been met by God's silence.

The poem does not conclude there, but we will defer consideration of its conclusion until later. For the moment, let it stand as an underlining of the agony of the believer.

But how much of this sort of treatment can the believer take, and still remain a believer? Only so much. A time comes when patience is torn away, and what is underneath is not more patience but deep anger. Things are intolerable. A quarrel ensues. God is accountable. Silence is not a satisfactory rendering of accountability. God must be put on trial.

The necessity of contention: putting God on trial

To quarrel with God is to pay God the supreme compliment: it is to take God seriously. It is to say that God matters enough to be worth some anger.

To be indifferent to God is to pay God the supreme insult. It is to say that nothing of consequence is at stake.

We may not be aware, at the beginning of a quarrel with God, that we are paying God the supreme compliment, but, along with Michael in *The Town Beyond the Wall*, we are likely to find out. Spiritually crippled by his time in the camps, Michael says to Pedro, in words with which we are already familiar, but can never hear too often:

> I want to blaspheme, and I can't quite manage it. I go up against [God], I shake my fist, I froth with rage, but it's still a way of telling Him that He's there, that He exists, that He's never the same twice, that denial itself is an offering to His grandeur. The shout becomes a prayer in spite of me. (*Town*, p. 123)

There are a number of concerns that justify "the shout [that] becomes a prayer." When there is manifest evil in the world, the shout is morally necessary. One of Wiesel's teachers engraved on the heart of his pupil the realization that "only the Jew knows that he may oppose God as long as he does so in defense of His creation" (*A Jew Today*, p. 6).

Yet more. "Jewish tradition allows man to say anything to God, provided it be on behalf of man. Man's inner liberation is God's justification" (*Souls*, p. 111).

In defense of creation, on behalf of humanity—even for the sake of God may human contention against God be justified. Wiesel tells a tale: a group of Jewish exiles were left in the desert without food and drink.

> One evening they collapsed with fatigue. They were four to fall asleep; they were three to rise. The father dug a grave for his wife, and the children recited the Kaddish. And they took up their walk again.
>
> The next day they were three to lie down; only two woke up. The father dug a grave for his older son and recited the Kaddish. And with his remaining son he continued the march.
>
> Then one night the two stretched out. But at dawn only the

father opened his eyes. He dug a grave in the sand and this is how he addressed God: "Master of the Universe, I know what You want—I understand what You are doing. You want despair to overwhelm me. You want me to cease believing in You, to cease praying to You, to cease invoking Your name to glorify and sanctify it. Well, I tell you: No, no—a thousand times no! You shall not succeed! In spite of me and in spite of You, I shall shout the Kaddish, which is a song of faith, for You and against You. This song You shall not still, God of Israel." (*A Jew Today*, 135–136)

It has a long Jewish history, this quarrel with God—Abraham intercedes against God for Sodom, Moses intercedes against God for those who built the golden calf, Job calls God to account for personal indignities, Jeremiah lives his life as a perpetual quarrel with God. The quarrel bursts the bonds of genteel discourse when outrages against God's children go unchecked.

The bonds can be burst when private sorrow is engulfing. Katriel and Malka lose a son. They cannot understand. Malka sobs, but Katriel keeps sorrow and outrage locked inside him, until he loses control:

We love you, God, we fear You, we crown You, we cling to You in spite of You, yet forgive me if I tell You my innermost thoughts, forgive me for telling You that You are cheating! You give us reason, but You are its limit and its mirror. You command us to be free, but on condition that we make You a gift of that freedom. You order us to love, but You give that love the taste of ashes. You bless us, and You take back Your blessing. Why are You doing all this, to prove what? What truth do You wish to teach us about whom? (*Beggar*, p. 120)

The bonds can be burst when public disaster is imminent. A *tzaddik*, on the eve of the Six Day War, reminds God that he has never before questioned God's love or mercy, he has "let pass under silence the death of one million children," he has strangled his outcry and anger over the Holocaust, he has sought "to transform into song the dagger You have so often plunged into my submissive heart." No more.

"I cannot go on. If this time again You desert Your people, if this time again You permit the slaughterer to murder Your children and besmirch their allegiance to the covenant, if this time You let Your promise become mockery, then know, O Master of all that breathes, know that You no longer deserve Your people's love and their passion to sanctify You, to justify You toward and against all, toward and against Yourself; if this time again the survivors are massacred and their deaths held up to ridicule . . . before dying I shall shout as no victim has ever shouted, and know that each of my tears and each of my shouts will tarnish your glory, each of my gestures will negate You and will negate me as You have negated me. . . ." (*Beggar*, pp. 140–141)

Wiesel has encapsulated the necessity of contention in *The Trial of God*, a play in which the whole history of moral outrage is embodied in one man, Berish the inkeeper. It is the evening of the festival of Purim in the town of Shamgorod in 1649, where not long before, during preparations for the wedding of Berish's daughter Hanna, a pogrom erupted. All the Jews were killed save Berish and Hanna, who were not so fortunate. Berish was forced to watch the rape of his daughter, who was driven mad by the succession of violators. Berish is now consumed by anger, not only against Christians who destroy Jews, but against the God who permits such destruction.

Purim is a feast of masks, improvisations, and imbibing, celebrating one of the few occasions in Jewish history when the oppressors were outmaneuvered and the Jews were saved. A wandering band of minstrels comes to the inn to entertain local Jews in the spirit of the holiday. Embarrassed to discover that only two Jews remain alive and that festivity is hardly the order of the day, they respond to a seemingly innocent suggestion by Berish that they perform an impromptu *Din-Toïre*, a trial. But this will be an unusual trial, a trial "Against the Master of the Universe. Against the Supreme Judge" (p. 55). Berish has one stipulation: he is to be the prosecutor. "I want to understand why He is giving strength to the killers and nothing but tears and the shame of helplessness to the victims" (p. 43). So there must be a trial:

> Let one killer kill for His glory, and He is guilty. Every man who suffers or causes suffering, every woman who is raped, every child who is tormented implicates Him. What, you need more? A hundred or a thousand? Listen: either He is respon-

sible or He is not. If He is, let's judge Him; if He is not, let Him stop judging us. (p. 54)

There is an added pressure. Events are building up to another pogrom: with two Jews still alive, who can sleep safely at night? A priest keeps bursting in with warnings to flee, or hide, or come under "the protection of the cross," which means, less elliptically, to convert. The Jews decline all offers.

A snag develops in preparing for the trial: there is no defense attorney. When one of the minstrels asks, rhetorically, "Is there no one in the whole universe who would take the case of the Almighty God?" a Stranger, who has entered just a few moments earlier, steps forward: "Yes. There is someone . . . I will" (p. 109).

The Stranger refuses to identify himself. He does divulge that his name is Sam, and everybody has a recollection of having seen him some place or other. Maria, the serving girl at the inn, who screams at his entrance, tells them that he seduced her and then, having achieved his intentions, slapped her and called her "a common harlot." But the others are charmed by the debonair Sam, who has a real way with words. If a case can be made for God Almighty, Sam is surely the one who can make it.

The presumption is correct. Sam is a brilliant attorney. Urbane, witty, intelligent, he counters Berish's every argument with deft parries.

To the initial angry charge that God is guilty of "hostility, cruelty and indifference. Either He dislikes His chosen people or He doesn't care about them" (p. 125), Sam responds that in a court case anger cannot go bail for evidence.

So it is facts the court wants? Berish provides details of the pogrom: three houses of study pillaged, the main synagogue burned down, the sacred scrolls profaned, over a hundred Jewish families slaughtered . . .

Sam acknowledges that these are indisputable but irrelevant facts. It is God who is on trial, and God did not do these things: "Men and women and children were massacred by other men. Why involve, why implicate their Father in Heaven?" (p. 128).

Berish speaks for the victims: "Let their premature unjust

deaths turn into an outcry so forceful that it will make the universe tremble with fear and remorse!" (p. 130).

But by what right, Sam rejoins, can the prosecutor speak for the dead? They could just as well be rejoicing that they have been allowed "to leave this ugly planet behind them and enter a world of eternal peace and truth" (p. 130).

After some further exchanges, Sam starts playing trumps: "If God chooses not to answer, He must have His reasons. God is God, and His will is independent from ours—as is His reasoning" (p. 132). All we can do is "Endure. Accept. And say Amen" (p. 132). The angel in *Ani Maamin* has found a new mouthpiece.

Berish, like the patriarchs in the poem, rejects the advice: "Never! If he wants my life, let Him take it! But He has taken other lives. Don't tell me they were happy to submit to His will . . ." (p. 132). He is unyielding: "Let Him kill me, let Him kill us all, I shall shout and shout that it's His fault. I'll use my last energy to make my protest known. Whether I live or die, I submit to Him no longer" (p. 133).

Sam has another card up his sleeve. What about all the Jews who suffered in the past and died with God's name on their lips, repeating that "God's ways are just"? Who is Berish to complain when others affirmed? Berish responds, "I'll speak for them, too. For them, too, I'll demand justice" (p. 134).

The priest breaks in once more. The crowd is on its way to the inn. Another pogrom is in the making. There is no time to hide, but there is still time to accept the protection of the cross. This time the priest coaxes them: They'll play a trick on the mob. Accept the cross with the Purim masks on, and then be able to repudiate the promise when the present danger has passed and the masks have been removed. His humanity has finally outstripped his office.

Berish, the accuser of God, does not waste time weighing the offer: "Well, the answer is no. My sons and my fathers perished without betraying their faith; I can do no less" (p. 154).

As soon as the priest leaves, Sam seizes the advantage:

I take note of the important fact that the prosecutor opted for God against the enemy of God; he did so at the sacrifice of his life. Does it mean that the case is to be dismissed?

No, Berish insists, "I have not opted for God. I'm against His enemies, that's all." The trial must go on.

I lived as a Jew and it is as a Jew that I shall die—and it is as a Jew that, with my last breath, I shall shout my protest to God. And because the end is near, I shall shout louder! Because the end is near, I'll tell Him that He's more guilty than ever!

Sam, by contrast, breathes serenity and piety:

I'm His servant. He created the world and me without asking for my opinion; He may do with both whatever He wishes. Our task is to glorify Him, to praise Him, to love Him—in spite of ourselves. (p. 157)

The court is impressed. It would like very much to know who Sam really is—a saint? a penitent? a prophet? a rabbi? a miracle worker? an emissary? a mystical dreamer? Who else could evince such a powerful faith in face of impending death? Surely he can intercede on their behalf and save them all!

The howling mob can be heard outside. Pitifully inadequate defense barricades are erected in the inn. A final gesture: since it is Purim they will die with their masks on, masks created for celebration.

The judges put on theirs. So does Sam.

It is not for nothing that Wiesel calls him "Sam," rather than "Samu-el." His mask is the face of Satan.

When I was first told this tale by its author, shortly before its publication, I was rendered numb and speechless, initially unable to absorb the devastating implications of the denouement. Had all the earlier painful groping toward affirmation now been negated? Only much later could I begin to see the play as an affirmation that is strangely strengthened by its powerful negation.

The powerful negation is the unremitting rejection of "consolatory theism." Never mind, the argument goes, some day it will be all right; every price will have been worth paying. Such arguments have been around ever since the book of Job,

and longer, though not always so persuasively stated. They
have been staples of every attempt to justify God in the face
of evil, the ultimate refuge of every theological orthodoxy. If
less than fully convincing, they have taken some of the sting
away from the "problem of evil" by suggesting that we are not
left in total darkness.

The play insists that arguments justifying God in the face of
evil are not only inadequate, they are diabolical. In attempting
"to justify the ways of God to man," we do the devil's work,
making a pact with deception. No arguments can justify one
dead child with a look of terror frozen on his or her face. If
they "explain" that terror, they are blasphemous.

But out of Berish's powerful negation comes affirmation.
He is a strange affirmer, this Berish. Loud, angry, impetuous,
single-minded, a Job who refuses consolation and continues to
accuse and defy, to the very end. But—a Job whose very accusation acknowledges the reality of the One accused, whose
human words of protest testify to an Eternal Word against
which they are set, who will die rather than renounce the
tortured faith that remains his, despite all attempts to dislodge
it. The very strength of his denial is witness to the depth of his
affirmation. Sam is wrong; Berish's willingness to die rather
than renounce does not negate his complaint against God, but
strengthens and intensifies it. "Only the Jew knows that he
may oppose God as long as he does so in defense of His
creation." Elie Wiesel's teacher taught his student well.

Wiesel describes the circumstances of the play's inception
in an introduction to the volume: "Inside the kingdom of
night, I witnessed a strange trial. Three rabbis—all erudite and
pious men—decided one winter evening to indict God for
allowing His children to be massacred."

What the introduction does not say is even more awesome:
after the trial, at which God was found guilty as charged, one
of the rabbis looked at the watch he had somehow been able
to preserve in the kingdom of night, and said: "Oy! It's time
for prayers." And the three rabbis—"all erudite and pious
men"—bowed their heads and prayed.

On speaking of God by speaking of humanity

The quarrel with God continues, sometimes throbbing and sad, often strident and angry. The argument will not disappear. But neither will prayer and devotion, whether in the kingdom or night or the kingdom of day. We will go on contending with God.

If we find it difficult to speak of God, we still find it necessary to speak of humanity. We discovered earlier that the two modes of speech are interrelated, and that in the dialogue between human beings, God is present. We further discovered that when Wiesel speaks of humanity, he finds himself also speaking of God. Perhaps that description can become an intention—the clearest way to speak of God is by speaking of humanity. That would enable human speech to point toward divine activity without claiming sure knowledge about the inner workings of the divine mind. A more modest form of speech, it might prove more trustworthy.

At a pivotal point in the progression of his novels—the conclusion of *The Town Beyond the Wall*—Wiesel inserts a "legend" about a dialogue between man and God, in which, at man's instigation, they change places "for only one second." God becomes a man and then God is duped. For man uses his one second of omnipotence to refuse "to revert to his former state," while God is trapped, impotently, in humanity. After "centuries, perhaps eternities," it is clear that the arrangement is not working, and the ancient dialogue is renewed. It is a dialogue "charged with hatred, with remorse, and most of all—with infinite yearning" (*Town*, p. 190).

There could be no clearer signal, nor a more haunting one, of the shared matrix within which humanity and God are bound to one another. Each is a pointer to the other; each, in however ineffable a fashion, shares in the plight and the possibilities of the other. To speak of either is to speak of both.

If we accept the presupposition of the legend, we can engage in an imaginative exercise based on categories drawn from Wiesel's first four books, which describe various postures that human beings adopt when dealing with monstrous evil—victim, executioner, spectator, participant. To take the legend seriously is to acknowledge that in speaking of humanity's

response to monstrous evil we are also speaking analogously
of God's response. We can learn some things from such a
transfer.

1. God as *victim.* The notion not that there never was a God,
but rather that the God who once was now no longer is, was
given currency by Friedrich Nietzsche, who not only announced the death of God but identified the perpetrators of
the crime, "it is we who have killed him." Whatever justification there might have been for such a verdict in the nineteenth
century has been augmented in the twentieth century by the
Holocaust. Appraisers like Richard Rubenstein believe the
death camps destroyed not only Jews but the God of the Jews
as well. Any God affirmed during and after Auschwitz could
only be a moral monster. When the polarities of God and
Auschwitz confront one another, it is God who is destroyed
and Auschwitz that is triumphant. If before Auschwitz there
was a God, after Auschwitz there is not.[1] God is the victim
destroyed by the camps, destroyed by those who ran the
camps, destroyed by all who were complicit in the camps
devastating efficiency. So Nietzsche is right on both scores: not
only is God "dead," but "it is we who have killed him."

No one should be allowed to escape easily from the thrust
of the charge. The burden of proof is on those who affirm God
in a post-Auschwitz world. For significant numbers of morally
sensitive people, when God and monstrous evil clash, the victim is God.

2. It is sad, even terrifying, to think of God as victim. But
there is something worse: God as *executioner.* Some religions
posit powerful, implacable, and malevolent deities, so en-
dowed with the righteous fury of judgment that their followers
unashamedly claim them as executioners. But every religion
that affirms a God either omnipotent or omniscient, or both,
is perilously close to proclaiming a God who is ultimately
executioner. Protestant and Catholic orthodoxies have a difficult time escaping the charge. If God is truly in control, all that
happens, not only for good but also for ill, is finally traceable
back to God.

The usual way of dealing with this conclusion is to assert
that human beings, in distorted exercises of their freedom, are
responsible for the massive suffering the Holocaust embodied.

But the assertion does not exculpate God, since God made the original decision to grant the freedom and presumably knew what the consequences of such a decision would be. Theological statements that such freedom was worth the cost in human misery, are morally repugnant after reading even the most restrained descriptions of the death camps. Fine theological distinctions between God "ordaining" evil directly and only "permitting" it indirectly are small consolation to the victims of evil, and only postpone the assignment of ultimate responsibility to God.

So even though they seek to avoid the implications of their position, traditional orthodoxies are perilously close to affirming God as executioner.

3. Partly in an effort to soften the harshness of such a position, deism reduced God's role to that of *spectator*. Flourishing in the rationalistic Britain of the eighteenth and nineteenth centuries, the deists viewed the cosmos as analogous to an intricate watch, whose existence posited a watchmaker, but a watchmaker who, having created the watch and set it in motion, could relinquish control and let the watch run by itself without further interference. Similarly, God, having created the world and set it in motion, could leave it to run on momentum provided at creation. Such a God is distant and disengaged, a spectator to the whole process, removed from immediate involvement or responsibility.

The analogy, seeking to relieve God of any direct responsibility, fails to do so. When a watch turns out to be defective, the watchmaker can be held accountable. If the watch gets dust in it and refuses to run correctly, the watchmaker should be able to clean it. So, by analogy, when creation becomes a grotesque distortion of what it was meant to be, God the creator can be called to account, either for defective workmanship or for failure to repair damage done by others. The divine spectator escapes culpability no more surely than does the human counterpart. In both cases, the spectator is finally siding with the executioners.

4. What about the fourth possibility? Could we conceive of God as *participant*? In the human analogue, Wiesel has Pedro, Michael, Gavriel, and a host of others enter into situations of those in trouble, share their vulnerability, and, by such active

identification with the other, offer the means of beginning to cope with the evil. While there are no sure victories for the human participants, there is the possibility of engaging in ongoing struggles against the forces of evil.

Is it audacious to think that such a role could also describe God's struggle with evil? If so, Wiesel is audacious in pointing to the possibility, and he does so, however guardedly, in the conclusion of *Ani Maamin.* We left the plot in abeyance at the point when the patriarchs decide that their importunities will continue to be ignored at the divine throne. They conclude that they must return to earth and inform Jews that they should no longer count on God. As they prepare to leave, the Chorus invokes blessing upon them. If God remains silent, Jews who have revered God's name will not.

Each of the patriarchs, as he withdraws from the heavenly throne, recounts a tale in which, in the face of insurmountable odds and a silent heaven, a Jew nevertheless affirms. In one instance, a child expresses belief in the one who is carrying her, futilely, away from the Nazi machine guns. In another, a Jew in a doomed village suddenly "sings/ Of his ancient and lost faith" (p. 95), proclaiming that he still believes in the coming of the Messiah, even though he is late, even though God be unwilling. In a third, a Jew in a death camp on the first night of Passover, unable to celebrate the meal, nevertheless says,

> Still, I recite the Haggadah
> As though I believe in it.
> And I await the prophet Elijah,
> As I did long ago,
>
> [p. 101]

ending with the affirmation:

> I shall wait for you.
> And even if you disappoint me
> I shall go on waiting.
>
> [p. 101]

"Auschwitz," he declares, "has killed Jews/ But not their expectations" (p. 103).

After each of these recitals of an indomitable willingness to go on waiting, to refuse to succumb to despair, the Narrator informs us that God is being moved. The first time God permits "a tear to cloud his eyes," then "a tear streams down God's somber countenance," and finally, "God, surprised by his people, weeps for the third time—and this time without restraint, and with—yes—love" (pp. 93, 97, 103). The weeping is veiled from the sight of Abraham, Isaac, and Jacob. But their faith has moved God deeply. Moved God, indeed, in the most literal sense of the word, for as Abraham, Isaac, and Jacob go away, the Narrator informs us that although they do not know it, "They are no longer alone: God accompanies them, weeping, smiling, whispering" (p. 105).

So finally God does speak, and "The word of God continues to be heard. So does the silence of his dead children" (p. 105).

This is no *deus ex machina* ending in which a divine being comes on stage to set everything right. God is not brandishing thunderbolts or edicts of judgment. God's presence is a veiled presence. The protagonists in the drama are not even aware of it; on God's part there is only "weeping, smiling, whispering." But there is participation, there is "—yes—love." There is assurance that the burdens will no longer be borne alone, that a divine presence—however veiled—is beginning to share that task.

About none of Wiesel's works have there been more varied critical estimates than about the ending of this drama. Many Jewish critics find it weak and unconvincing.[2] A weeping God, who needs him? And anyhow he comes too late. Better no God than such a one.

Christian critics (who are always tempted to read things into Jewish statements that do not belong there) tend to be more affirmative. I find the ending strong on three scores: (1) It does not try to dispose of past or present suffering; if, as Wiesel writes, "The word of God continues to be heard," he acknowledges in the very next line, "So does the silence of his dead children." (2) The ending counters the charge of aloofness in the heart of the divine. The change may come too late—six million deaths too late—but the God at the end of the drama is a God who listens and is changed by the pleas of the children of earth, a God who is moved to tears, a God who follows the patriarchs back to earth to participate in their suffering. The dialogue cited in the legend at the end of *The Town Beyond the Wall* continues, and the earlier "hatred" and "remorse" are being supplanted by "infinite yearning." (3) Another strength can be affirmed by those who have difficulty with the above. This is the hope that Abraham, Isaac, and Jacob have in their children, in the ongoing life of the Jewish community. Before the machine guns, a child expresses faith; in the village, a Jew continues to believe; in the death camp, an inmate affirms that, even there, he will wait for the Messiah to come. Even though the divine presence is veiled, such acts of human presence are not.

It is out of affirmations of a presence and a hope, both veiled and unveiled, that the story of God's people continues to be written.

Wiesel not only writes about hope for a future that lies in Israel's children, he places himself within that circle of hope by dedicating the book to his child:

> For Shlomo-Elisha
> Son of Eliezer,
> Son of Shlomo,
> Son of Eliezer. . .

They are the first words one reads after the title page. They cannot really be read until after one has read the final page. Then they become a smile through tears.

On starting all over again

Let us grant Wiesel his point. He is not a theologian and he is not trying to create a system of thought. He is a teller of tales and he is trying to evoke response. If he wanted to communicate through systematic reflection, he would write systematic reflections. The cruelest betrayal an interpreter could inflict on a teller of tales would be to reduce the tales to a series of abstract statements, prefaced by the words, "Now this is what he *really* meant," thereby transforming the teller of tales, against his will, into a theologian.

To be sure, there is an *implicit* theology in any story, any drama, any poem, that is dealing with the human spirit and the way the human spirit responds to challenge. But if it is not the task of the teller of tales to make the implicit explicit, neither is it the task of the interpreter to do so in his stead. The task of the interpreter is to force the reader back into repeated engagement with the story, each time on a deeper level. So our present concern is not to draw out the implicit theology in Wiesel's writings (though we shall see what he says to our own theologies in the next chapter). It is rather to show how after the Holocaust any theology, implicit or explicit, needs a new starting point from which to retell the tale and keep the story alive.

Wiesel helps us in ways that are devastating, perplexing, and energizing.

1. The most *devastating statement* of the need for a new starting point comes toward the end of *The Accident* (pp. 89–104), Wiesel's third book. He has told us the story of Sarah, the twelve-year-old girl who was the sport of the German officers in the camp, a chattel, a piece of shared property, who was so dehumanized that a life of prostitution was her only possible mode of survival after the war.

What is history for one who enters Sarah's world? "A source of malediction," in the hands of a God who "tortures twelve-year-old children" (pp. 96–97). What is the scene of our human activity? "The immense brothel we call the universe," whose doorkeeper is God (p. 98). And Sarah, "sent to a special barracks for the camp officers' pleasure," who is she? Sarah is "a saint" (p. 100). Who is the God of such a world? After hearing Sarah's story, the narrator knows why God and death have been allied in human minds ("whoever sees God must die"). Savagely he writes, "Why should He want to kill a man who succeeded in seeing Him? Now everything became clear. God was ashamed. God likes to sleep with twelve-year-old girls. And doesn't want us to know" (p. 98). Conclusion:

> Whoever listens to Sarah and doesn't change, whoever enters Sarah's world and doesn't invent new gods and new religions, deserves death and destruction. (*Accident,* p. 96)

The indictment comes in an early book, followed by twenty more, and Wiesel does not precisely follow the instructions of his narrator to "invent new gods and new religions," since he

painfully and slowly finds his way back toward the Hasidic faith
of his childhood. But he has radically challenged old gods and
old religons, and made it impossible for his readers to relapse
into comfortable orthodoxies.

2. Perhaps he has done more than that. The difficulty of
gauging his achievement can be measured by his most *perplexing statement* of the need for a new starting point. Toward the
end of *The Gates of the Forest,* the rebbe and Gregor begin a stern
exchange that escalates to passionate intensity. The rebbe remarks that nothing has changed since Auschwitz. Not even
God has changed. This hits its mark.

> Gregor was angry. "After what happened to us, how can you
> believe in God?"
>
> With an understanding smile on his lips the Rebbe an-
> swered, "How can you *not* believe in God after what has hap-
> pened?" (p. 192)

The rebbe's "answer"—which is in the form of a question
(naturally)—is no momentary mood or slip of the pen. It is
repeated as an affirmation by the Chorus in *Ani Maamin,* written nine years later:

> Ani maamin [I believe], Abraham,
> Despite Treblinka.
> Ani maamin, Isaac,
> Because of Belsen.
> Ani maamin, Jacob,
> Because of and in spite of Majdanek.
>
> [p. 105]

It is not hard to identify with Gregor's question, "After what
happened to us, how can you believe in God?" By a tremendous act of faith, we may even be able to identify with the
Chorus's affirmation, "I believe despite Treblinka . . . and in
spite of Majdanek." Wiesel has reminded us that no death-of-
God theology originated in the camps. Desperate challenges
to faith, yes; destroyers of faith, no.

But the rebbe's question leaves us aghast, the more so since
it is asked with an "understanding smile on his lips": "How can
you *not* believe in God after what happened?" Auschwitz as a
reason for faith? And the Chorus staggers us: "[I believe] Because of Belsen. . . . Because of . . . Majdanek."

What is going on here? Who could possibly talk this way? Actually, what is going on is that we are seeking too analytically to dissect the mood Wiesel is creating. For his whole point is that the two types of statement *can never stand alone.* Either by itself is false. The rebbe's "answer" by itself is blasphemy, but as a counterpoise to Gregor's question is is essential. Similarly, the affirmations of the Chorus will never "work" with ellipses. The affirmations must be inclusive, "Because of *and* in spite of Majdanek."

Wiesel is denying us the privilege of either easy denial or easy belief. When one says, in the light of Auschwitz, "There are no longer reasons to believe," that becomes too simple; another must immediately say, "There are still reasons to believe, now more than ever." When one says, in the light of Auschwitz, "There are still reasons to believe," that becomes too simple; another must immediately say, "There are reasons not to believe, now more than ever." And such a dialogue is finally not an external dialogue between two persons; it is an interior dialogue within every person.

If faith must encompass denial, denial must also encompass faith. No easy faith, but no easy denial either. The Chorus is finally right; the only faith worth having is faith "because of and in spite of . . ."

Perhaps Wiesel has given us "new gods and new religions" after all.

3. Along with a devastating and a perplexing statement of the need for a new starting point, goes an *energizing statement,* present in many forms and many places.

Simplest version: the advice of Rebbe Pinhas of Koretz, "You want to serve God? Start with serving His children" (*Masters,* p. 16).

Most audacious version: "It is given to man to transform divine injustice into human justice and compassion" (*Messengers,* p. 235).

Most demanding version: the remark of the "Kotzer" to a disciple who thought he could have improved on how God created the world, "You could have done better? . . . Then what are you waiting for? You don't have a minute to waste, go ahead, start working!" (*Messengers,* p. 36).

These are all ways of stating that no theological reflection

may preoccupy us so much that we turn aside from the needs
of human beings. Faith after the Holocaust will always have
more modest proportions than the faith that preceded it, a
faith struggling toward articulation in one of Wiesel's prayers:

> I no longer ask You for either happiness or paradise; all I ask
> of You is to listen and let me be aware of Your listening.
> I no longer ask You to resolve my questions, only to receive
> them and make them part of You.
> I no longer ask You for either rest or wisdom, I only ask You
> not to close me to gratitude, be it of the most trivial kind, or
> to surprise and friendship. Love? Love is not Yours to give.
> As for my enemies, I do not ask You to punish them or even
> to enlighten them; I only ask You not to lend them Your mask
> and Your powers. If You must relinquish one or the other, give
> them Your powers. But not Your countenance. (*Generation*, p.
> 189)

Belief or unbelief?

Theological concepts, philosophical formulations, lines of
distinction between intellectual affirmation and intellectual
denial, finally pale to insignificance in the face of immediate
human realities and human decisions. In the end, it is not the
word that matters but the deed. The deed may define the
unspoken word and deny the spoken one.

What does it mean to affirm God? What does it mean to
deny God?

The killers affirmed God in church, in their children's bed-
rooms, in the carols they sang at Christmas, and the hymns
they sang at Easter—and they denied God by humiliating,
torturing, and destroying a special group of God's children.

As for the victims . . . How do we talk about their affirmation
or denial? With stories, of course. But stories that leave us with
enigmas rather than resolutions. Of course.

> Facing the inmates assembled on the *Appel Platz*, the two
> men seem to be acting out an unreal scene.
> "Deny your faith and you will eat for an entire week," the
> officer is yelling.
> "No," says the Jew quietly.

"Curse your God, wretch! Curse Him and you will have an easy job!"

"No," says the Jew quietly.

"Repudiate Him and I will protect you."

"Never," says the Jew quietly.

"Never? What does that mean? A minute? In a minute you will die. So then, you dog, will you finally obey me?"

The inmates hold their breath. Some watch the officer; others have eyes only for their comrade.

"God means more to you than life? More than I? You asked for it, you fool!"

He draws his gun, raises his hand, takes aim. And shoots. The bullet enters the inmate's shoulder. He sways, and his comrades in the first row see his face twist. And they hear him whisper the ancient call of the martyrs of the faith: " *'Adoshem hu haelokim, adoshem hu haelokim.* God is God, God alone is God."

"You swine, you dirty Jew," screams the officer. "Can't you see I am more powerful than your God! Your life is in my hands, not in His! You need me more than Him! Choose me and you'll go to the hospital and you'll recover, and you'll eat, and you'll be happy!"

"Never," says the Jew, gasping.

The officer examines him at length. He suddenly seems fearful. Then he shoots a second bullet into the man's other shoulder. And a third. And a fourth. And the Jew goes on whispering, "God is God, God is . . ." The last bullet strikes him in the mouth.

"I was there," his son tells me. "I was there, and the scene seems unbelievable to me. You see, my father . . . my father was a hero . . . But he was not a believer." (*A Jew Today*, p. 130)

Not a believer?
The last word is Rebbe Naphtali's:

A visitor, a friend of his father, turned to him one day: "Naphtali . . . if you tell me where God can be found, I'll give you a gold coin."—Answered the child: "And I'll give you two if you tell me where He can *not* be found." (*Masters*, p. 108)

CHAPTER 6

Birkenau and Golgotha
(challenges to a Christian journey)

With every approaching Easter, the Jews tremble.
— *The Oath*, p. 204

You think you are suffering for my sake and for my brothers', yet we are the ones who will be made to suffer for you, because of you.
— Shlomo, to Jesus on the cross, *A Beggar in Jerusalem*, p. 68

If the victims are my problem, the killers are yours.
— Elie Wiesel, to Christians, *"Freedom of Conscience—A Jewish Commentary,"* p. 642.

One can do without solutions. Only the questions matter. We may share them or turn away from them.
— *A Beggar in Jerusalem*, p. 16

Once upon a time there had not been a Holocaust. It had not entered into the mind of humanity to conceive of Birkenau, Chelmno, Sobibor, Treblinka, Majdanek, or Auschwitz. But even then, anti-Semitism had left a legacy of hatred over generations and centuries, often fueled and fanned by the Christian church. This meant that a young Jewish boy could grow up in the Carpathian mountains and know what it meant to fear Christians—fear them enough so that he could later put in the mouth of one of his characters the statement, "With every approaching Easter, the Jews tremble" (*The Oath*, p. 204).

> As a child I was afraid of the church to the point of changing sidewalks. In my town, the fear was justified. Not only because of what I inherited—our collective memory—but also because of the simple fact that twice a year, at Easter and Christmas, Jewish schoolchildren would be beaten up by their Christian neighbors. Yes, as a child I lived in fear. A symbol of compassion and love to Christians, the cross has become an instrument of torment and terror to be used against Jews. I say this with neither hate nor anger. I say this because it is true. Born in suffering, Christianity became a source and pretext of suffering to others. ("Art and Culture after the Holocaust," p. 406)

In Sighet, the rule of Jewish survival was clear: have as little contact as possible with Christians. The young Elie followed the rule faithfully: don't speak to Christians at school, play only with Jews during recess, avoid letting Christians snatch your yarmulka. "My dream back then? To live in a world completely Jewish, a world where Christians would have scarcely any access" ("Recalling Swallowed-up Worlds," p. 610).

He says he felt no animosity; indeed, he interpreted Christian hostility as a kind of envy—Jews, after all, had the true God. That being so, he likewise felt no curiosity; he had no awareness of the content of a Christian catechism, or the nature of a Christian ritual, and felt no deprivation. His attitude toward Christianity was nurtured solely by ignorance: "I had no idea that Judaism and Christianity claimed the same roots. Nor did I know that Christians who believe in the eternity and in the divinity of Christ also believe in those of God, *our* God. . . . All I knew of Christianity was its hate for my people" (*A Jew Today*, p. 5).

A revision of the Jewish agenda: the inevitability of contact

The first significant contact with Christians did not come until after the war, when Wiesel, then a newspaper correspondent in Paris, interviewed the Roman Catholic author, François Mauriac.[1]

Rather than talking about the Jewish politician Mendès-France, who was supposed to be the topic of the interview, Mauriac talked about other Jews, and in particular the Jew Jesus, "who, unable to save Israel, ended up saving mankind" (*A Jew Today*, p. 17). Every comment somehow led back to him.

Wiesel, first fascinated, then irritated, and ultimately angry, finally interrupted:

> Sir . . . you speak of Christ. Christians love to speak of him. The passion of Christ, the agony of Christ, the death of Christ. In your religion, that is all you speak of. Well, I want you to know that ten years ago, not very far from here, I knew Jewish children every one of whom suffered a thousand times more, six million times more, than Christ on the cross. And we don't speak about them. Can you understand that, sir? We don't speak about them. (*A Jew Today*, p. 18)

Mauriac slumped. Wiesel got up and left, without even a handshake. While he was waiting for the elevator, the old man caught up with him and humbly asked him to return. And wept.

The dialogue continued, Mauriac insisting that it was wrong for survivors not to speak about what had happened in the kingdom of night. They had an obligation to testify.

This insistence by Mauriac helped Wiesel break his vow of silence: "One year later I sent him the manuscript of *Night*, written under the seal of memory and silence" (*A Jew Today*, p. 19). Two years after the publication of *Night*, *Dawn* appeared. It was dedicated "to François Mauriac."

Mauriac records the devastating impact of witnessing what he felt to be the worst horror for a believer: "the death of God in the soul of a child who suddenly discovers absolute evil" (Foreword to *Night*, p. 9). And he also records how he, experienced Catholic apologist that he was, could find no words to speak—no ability to articulate the conviction, as he later put it, that "the stumbling block of his faith was the cornerstone of mine," or that "if the Eternal is the Eternal, the last word for each of us belongs to Him." No, Mauriac reports, exhibiting a reticence worthy of more frequent emulation by Christians in dealing with Jews, "I could only embrace him, weeping" (p. 11).

There were other meetings with Mauriac. Issues concerning Judaism and Christianity were openly, sometimes hotly, debated. ("There are Christians," Wiesel said on one occasion, "who like Jews only on the Cross.") Wiesel has promised that one day the notes he took after those conversations will be published. Even without them, it is clear that the friendship with Mauriac permanently altered Wiesel's boyhood agenda of having as little as possible to do with Christians.

"Christianity . . . died in Auschwitz"

The altering of that agenda was no necessary boon. To have grown up with the legacy of anti-Semitism, much of it Christian in origin, was one thing, and Jews have had a lot of experience dealing with it. But to deal with that in a post-Holocaust world was of a new and unexplored order of magnitude. Wiesel's first fictional grappling with Christianity, expressed in the "reverse" passion play in *The Gates of the Forest,* led to the conclusion that if Judas was the executioner in the first century, the descendents of Judas (and Jesus) have ever since been the victims, and that if Christ was the victim in the first century, the spiritual descendents of Christ have ever since been the executioners.

Wiesel occasionally comments on those intervening centuries. The narrator in the short story, "Testament of a Jew from Saragossa," states:

> The period of the Inquisition had exercised a particular appeal to my imagination. I found fascinating those enigmatic priests who, in the name of love and for the sacred glory of a young Jew from Galilee, had tortured and subjected to slow death those who preferred the Father to the Son. (*Legends,* p. 94)

Sometimes "enigmatic priests" did the torturing. More often, they simply announced Jewish apostasy and let matters take their course. As tension is building up to a fresh pogrom in Shamgorod in 1649, Wiesel exposes the heretofore hidden anti-Semitism of the Orthodox priest. The priest states flatly that since the Jews rejected Christ, God has given up on the

Jews and entrusted the carrying out of the divine mission to
Christians. Mendel, a Jew, responds with biting words:

> That you are God's whip, that is quite possible. But don't be
> so proud of it! God is closer to the Just struck by the whip than
> to the whip. God may punish the Just whom He loves, but
> despise the instrument of punishment. He throws it in the
> garbage, whereas the Just will find his way to the sanctuary.
> (*Trial,* p. 98)

The priest, incensed, responds that God has disowned the
Jews. Mendel, again:

> Are you certain of that? How can you be so sure? Because we
> suffer? Between the man who suffers and the one who makes
> him suffer, whom do you think God prefers? Between those
> who kill in His name and those who die for Him, who, in your
> judgment, is closer to Him? (*Trial,* p. 98)

There is similar irony in David's comment in *A Beggar in
Jerusalem* when the very survival of Israel hangs in the balance;
he summarizes the advice Jewish leaders are getting:

> Message from Paris: above all, do not fire the first bullet. Re-
> quest from Washington: above all, be patient, keep us in-
> formed. Warning from Moscow: the enemies of our friends are
> our enemies or will become so. The Vatican, faithful to its
> principles, kept silent. (*Beggar,* p. 133)

Jews and Christians share a problem in relation to the Holocaust. It is the problem of *belief:* how can one affirm God in a
world where the Holocaust has taken place? We examined
Wiesel's response to this problem in the preceding chapter,
and will begin a Christian response later in the present one.
There is another problem, however, which Christians alone
have to face, and that is the problem of *complicity,* the problem
of why so many Christians laid the historical groundwork for
the anti-Semitism that flowered under Hitler, and were either
active proponents of Hitler's policies, or stayed on the sidelines playing the role of spectator.

The historical record, when related directly to the Holocaust, is a baleful one.

> If you study the history of Christianity you will see that it is full
> of anti-Semitism. More than that—there would have been no

Auschwitz if the way had not been prepared by Christian
theology. Among the first to dehumanize the Jew was the Christian. . . . Yes, absolutely, there is anti-Semitism in the Church.
. . . (*Victory*, p. 20)

On another occasion, looking at the long history, Wiesel
comes to the same conclusion:

We have to say it: All these hatreds culminated in the Holocaust. If it were not for the education of some Christian books,
in some villages and in some towns, I don't think that the
Holocaust could have taken place. There would have been an
upsurge of conscience in the killers. And the killers did not have
an upsurge of conscience. ("Freedom of Conscience—A Jewish
Commentary," p. 642)

For Wiesel as a Jew, the problem is the victims: why did they
submit to death, again and again, often silently? It is a problem
with which he continuously struggles. However, (and he calls
it "cruel" but necessary to say so) "as surely as the victims are
a problem for the Jews, *the killers are a problem for the Christians*"
(*A Jew Today*, p. 12, italics added; see also "Freedom of Conscience," p. 642, and *Dimensions*, p. 17).

The problem is agonizing: Why did Pius XII never condemn the death camps? Why were so many members of the
S.S. also members of Christian churches? How could there
have been killers who went to confession between massacres?
How could so many of them have received education in the
church and in Christian institutions? The questions are Wiesel's (see *A Jew Today*, p. 11); Christians must make them their
own, including the most poignant of all questions: "How do
you explain that a person could be a Christian and a killer of
children?" ("Freedom of Conscience," p. 642).

Wiesel has said elsewhere about the Holocaust, "If not all
victims were Jews, all Jews were victims." Christians are called
upon to say in addition, "If not all Christians were killers, all
killers were Christians." "Bad Christians," surely, as Wiesel
conceded in an address at Northwestern University, "but
Christians" (*Dimensions*, p. 17).

It suggests a frightening conclusion: "The sincere Christian
knows that what died in Auschwitz was not the Jewish people
but Christianity" (*Responses*, p. 152).

The betrayal of Jesus

The point of greatest similarity between Jews and Christians is that they share a common hope—at the appointed time, God will send a Messiah ("the anointed one") to fulfill the divine purpose and draw all of humanity together.

The point of greatest division between Jews and Christians is that they disagree about "the appointed time." For Jews, that time has not not yet come; for Christians it has already come, in the life, death, and resurrection of a certain Jew, Jesus of Nazareth, whom Christians call "Christ," a title which is simply the Greek equivalent of the Hebrew word "Messiah."

The estimate one makes of the Jew Jesus, and how that estimate is expressed, is thus crucial to the way Jews and Christians understand and deal with one another. Clarity and forthrightness count for everything here, and Wiesel has an important contribution to make on both scores.

When Michael is thrown into prison in Szerencseváros, the cellmate from whom he receives help is Menachem, a believing Jew from Wiesel's home town of Sighet. His name, as we have noted, can mean either "comforter" or "Messiah," and it is striking that this figure, representing the initial recovery of the Jewish heritage in Wiesel's novels, is initially described as having "the moving face of a Byzantine Christ" (*Town*, p. 144). Later, Wiesel refers to Menachem's "handsome, Christlike face," that "radiated compassion" (p. 175).

The fact that Wiesel can make such references suggests that for him the basic problem is not Jesus as such. Who could fault an individual who, no matter under what name, "radiated compassion" in a prison cell? Who could be scornful of someone whom Shlomo, one of the "beggars" in Jerusalem, describes as "the innocent preacher who had only one word on his lips: love" (*Beggar*, p. 67)? No, the basic problem is not Jesus, it is what Jesus' followers have done with him. Indeed, if Jesus is to be faulted, it would be primarily for not having seen clearly enough that his life and death would be distorted by his followers in ways inimical to his own understanding of his mission.

Take the tale that Shlomo tells in *A Beggar in Jerusalem*. Shlomo claims to have been there at the crucifixion and to have had a conversation with the crucified one. He tells Jesus, who up to that point has been serene in the midst of pain and death, that his followers will betray him. In Jesus' name, Shlomo asserts, his disciples will persecute and crush those who disagree with them. Jesus bursts into tears of despair at the prediction that his suffering will increase rather than alleviate the suffering of others—a prediction the reader knows to be an accurate one. The great tragedy of the cross, therefore, is that Jesus realized too late that his teaching and example would be turned into something inhuman. Too late, for his action, once undertaken, could not be undone. Shlomo is so overcome by the poignancy of this misplaced trust that he too ends up weeping, not only for those who will be slaughtered in Jesus' name, but for Jesus as well (*Beggar*, pp. 67–68).

Subsequent history, vindicating the accuracy of Shlomo's insight, leads Wiesel to remark that "the Christians betrayed the Christ more than the Jews did" (*Conversation*, p. 48), which could stand as an accurate gloss on Jesus' own tortured question to his followers, "Why do you call me 'Lord, Lord', and not do what I tell you?" (Luke 6:46). The indictment can be pushed even farther, and Wiesel does so, in commenting on the violence against Gregor by the townspeople in *The Gates of the Forest*:

> Whether [Jesus] was the Christ is a matter for Christians to decide. As far as the Jews are concerned, he may be retroactively guilty for all the murders and massacres that were done in his name. (*Conversation*, pp. 47–48)

What is certainly clear is that Christians have failed to embody the vision of their leader. They have condoned, enacted, and even glorified violence in the name of the one who came to put a stop to just such things. Such a record is sufficiently negative to raise serious questions about the accuracy of the claim that in Jesus of Nazareth the Messianic hope of all the ages has been fulfilled. We can formulate one version of this question out of our consideration of *Ani Maamin:* if the Messiah has actually come, why is the world still so unredeemed? The problem may be even deeper, however. Not only is the world unredeemed, but those who announce that redemption has occurred belie that claim by their actions. Wiesel probes

the deeper problem in many places, never more succinctly
than in *The Oath:* "Any messiah in whose name men are tortured can only be a false messiah" (*The Oath*, p. 138).

Wiesel has another problem when the Messianic claim is
attached to the name of Jesus: not only has the claim about
Jesus' Messiahship been used to justify torture and persecution, it has also been used to glorify death. The centrality of
the crucifixion as a norm for human (and divine) behavior
suggests that passive acceptance of death is a good and redemptive thing, and that it is ennobling to accept such a fate
instead of struggling against it. Every Jewish bone in Wiesel's
body cries out against this:

> For the Jew, all truth must spring from life, never from death.
> To us, crucifixion represents not a step forward but a step
> backward. (*Messengers,* p. 76)

To affirm life means always to struggle against death, never to
affirm it, never to give in to it, never to make it—somehow—
good. Any religion that makes dying a redemptive act carries
the danger of encouraging people to acquiesce in the face of
death, especially the death of others, thus weakening the will
to struggle against oppression and persecution.

Wiesel feels that the biblical story of Abraham and Isaac on
Mount Moriah, with all of its difficulties, is infinitely preferable
to the theological transformation it has undergone at the
hands of Christians, who have seen it as prefiguring the crucifixion, in which the Son dies in submission to the will of the
Father. No, Wiesel counters, "On Mount Moriah the act was
not consummated: the father did *not* abandon his son. Such is
the distance between Moriah and Golgotha" (*Messengers,* p.
76).

What finally happened on Moriah, Wiesel insists, was
mercy. "The living remains alive, thus marking the end of an
era of ritual murder" (p. 76). The sacrifice of the son was not
exacted, and the justification of slaughter was henceforth
abrogated, whereas—and who can fault the descriptive truth
of the comparison Wiesel proceeds to make?—"from the beginning Golgotha has served as pretext for countless massacres of sons and fathers cut down together by sword and fire

in the name of a word that considered itself synonymous with love" (p. 76).

Wiesel has at least one other quarrel with Christian Messianism. A character in *The Oath* comments in the midst of a political discussion, "You want to know what communism is? Simple. It is messianism without God, just as Christianity is messianism without man" (p. 62). You want to know what *that* is? Simple. God insists that we cooperate with him. Not even the Messiah can come without our help. To claim that the Messiah isn't as dependent on us as we are on him is to deny that God asks us to share in the holy work of redemption.

A revision of the Christian agenda: the shape of a response

The indictment is stinging. It is also true. And while truth is a weapon that may need to be wielded sternly, it is a weapon finally wielded in the interest of healing. Wiesel is clear-sighted here. Astonishingly, he writes about Christian complicity without hatred. Pain always, anger frequently, bitterness occasionally, hatred never. "What I am about to say," he writes on one occasion, "will surely hurt my Christian friends" (*A Jew Today*, p. 11), and on another occasion, "But still the truth must be said. And I certainly do not say it with hate . . . and not even with resentment. I really say it to bring us together, to share and to be open" ("Freedom of Conscience," pp. 73–74).

In the midst of a justifiable indictment, Wiesel still hopes for new openings, new ways, from within the Christian tradition, to begin again. We have already heard him say, "Yes, absolutely, there is anti-Semitism in the church." But that is not all he says. He goes on:

> And the person who understood it best was Pope John XXIII. He understood that he had to change the course and outlook of the Church. . . . He understood that anti-Semitism was a disease which afflicted the Church, and he felt that the time had come to redirect and reroute the Church's destiny by curing the disease. (*Victory*, p. 21)

Wiesel here charts the nature of a Christian response. He does not ask Christians to leave the church, or hate it, or only denounce it; he asks them to acknowledge that anti-Semitism is a disease that has afflicted the church, and recognize that the task is "to redirect and reroute the Church's destiny by curing the disease."

How do Christians "cure the disease"? At the very least, by confessing its reality, rethinking faith in the light of it, and engaging in deeds that seek to cancel out its power.

The reality of complicity. The record of Christian complicity in the death of six million Jews is scarcely debatable. Christians are a link in the chain of attitudes toward Jews that Raul Hilberg describes as conversion, exile, and extermination:

> The missionaries of Christianity had said in effect: You have no right to live among us as Jews. The secular rulers who followed had proclaimed: You have no right to live among us. The German Nazis at last decreed: You have no right to live.[2]

Christian anti-Semitism was present not only among the early church fathers but also among the Protestant reformers, especially Luther, who in their turn had been tutored in the subject by medieval Catholicism. There were centuries of fertile Christian soil in which Hitler could plant and cultivate his anti-Semitic program. He encountered no significant Christian opposition to his policies. The Confessing Church, in saying "no" to Hitler, gave some attention to the plight of Jews, but the attention was chiefly on behalf of Jews who had converted to Christianity and were being denied ecclesiastical rights by the state. Catholics and Protestants alike were part of the thundering silence that assured Hitler that he could continue his assault against Jews with impunity. After a painstaking review of the evidence, John F. Morley comes to a sober assessment:

> It must be concluded that Vatican diplomacy failed the Jews during the Holocaust by not doing all that was possible for it to do on their behalf. It also failed itself because in neglecting the needs of the Jews, and pursuing a goal of reserve rather than humanitarian concern, it betrayed the ideals that it had set

for itself. The nuncios, the secretary of state, and, most of all, the Pope share the responsibility for this dual failure.[3]

In the face of all this, a natural Christian reaction is to respond that the record of the church was not all bad. Indeed, there were a few individuals who were sensitive not only to the demonic nature of Nazism, but to the specific anti-Semitism that was so central to it. As early as 1933, Dietrich Bonhoeffer had said to his fellow Christians, "Only he who cries out for the Jews has the right to sing Gregorian chant," and Bishop Lichtenberg openly prayed for Jews during the mass in defiance of a Nazi directive. Others, quiet and unsung heroes and heroines, like the residents of the town of Le Chambon in France, hid Jews in their homes, provided false papers for them, helped them escape to neutral territory. There were hundreds of "righteous Gentiles" who risked their lives and sometimes lost them, to save Jews from Hitler's slaughterers. Yad Vashem, the Holocaust memorial in Jerusalem, honors them prominently in an avenue of trees that will one day encircle the memorial, and Jews everywhere express gratitude that there were a few who helped redeem the name humanity.

But there were so few. The "righteous Gentiles" were the tiny exception, and their genuine courage and compassion cannot go bail for the overwhelming number of Christians who played the role of spectator, standing at the window, against whom the only possible verdict is "guilty."

What does one do with guilt? Acknowledged too glibly and easily, confession of guilt becomes an example of what Bonhoeffer called "cheap grace." Dwelt on too oppressively and morbidly, it generates immobility and despair. If confession sounds easy (if not quite, in Bonhoeffer's terms, "cheap") it is nevertheless, when sincere, very hard. But it is indispensible if the ground is to be cleared for subsequent action. And there are hints that it is beginning to take place.

During the war, Bonhoeffer wrote, with direct reference to the Jews:

> [The church] confesses her timidity, her evasiveness, her dangerous concessions. . . . She was silent when she should have cried out because the blood of the innocent was crying aloud

to heaven. She has failed to speak the right word in the right way and at the right time.[4]

At the end of the war, Martin Niemoeller, a Lutheran pastor who spent seven years in concentration camps, joined with other German church leaders in the Stuttgart Declaration of 1945, in which they confessed:

> We are not only conscious of oneness with our nation in a great community of suffering, but also in a solidarity of guilt. With great pain we say: Unending suffering has been brought by us to many peoples and countries. . . . We accuse ourselves that we did not witness more courageously, pray more faithfully, believe more joyously, love more ardently.[5]

And in 1965, at the end of the Second Vatican Council, the Roman Catholic Church also formally confessed to sins from its institutional past against the Jewish people:

> The Church repudiates all persecutions against any man. More-over, mindful of her common patrimony with the Jews, and motivated by the gospel's spiritual love and by no political considerations, she deplores the hatred, persecutions, and displays of anti-Semitism directed against the Jews at any time and from any source.[6]

By far the most significant response has come from the Synod of the Protestant Church of the Rhineland, issued on January 11, 1980, out of a need on the part of the signatories "to achieve a new relationship between the Church and the Jewish people." The motivations for seeking this new rapport are:

> (1) Recognition of Christian co-responsibility and guilt in the Holocaust: the defamation, persecution and murder of the Jews in the Third Reich.
>
> (2) New biblical insights regarding the enduring significance of Israel in redemption history (e.g. Rom. 9–11) which were obtained as a result of the Church Struggle.
>
> (3) The insight that the continuing existence of the Jewish people, its return to the land of promise and the creation of the State of Israel are signs of God's faithfulness to his people.
>
> (4) The willingness of Jews to meet, engage in joint study and work in spite of the Holocaust.

As a result of such recognitions, the Synod goes on to declare: "We confess with sorrow the co-responsibility and guilt of Christianity in Germany with respect to the Holocaust. . . . We believe in the continuing election of the Jewish people as the people of God and recognize that through Jesus Christ, the Church has been included in the covenant of God with his people. . . . [We] reject the view that the people of Israel is rejected of God or displaced by the church. . . ."

There are many other emphases in this remarkable document, but the above are examples of the new acknowledgment that Judaism is the root out of which Christianity came, and that the church must remind its members in new and compelling ways that "you do not support the root, the root supports you" (Rom. 11:18).

One could wish that Bonhoeffer's confession had been shared by the whole church, that the Stuttgart Declaration had made explicit reference to the Jews, that the Vatican Council Declaration had (as John Sheerin put it) contained more pain and anguish. But such acts of confession were at least the *beginning* of a long, hard road toward moral recovery, and the synodical statement of the Protestant Church of the Rhineland shows how much ground has been covered.

The challenge to belief. If complicity is a particular problem for Christians, the challenge to belief is a problem for both Jews and Christians. In the light of the unremitting evil of the Holocaust, words like "victory," the triumph of "justice," the power of "love," all founder—on Jewish and Christian lips alike—and claims that God's will is fulfilled have the ring of blasphemy. *This* is the fulfillment of God's will?

Irving Greenberg's searing "working principle" for the post-Holocaust world towers over everything that can be said: "No statement, theological or otherwise, should be made that would not be credible in the presence of burning children."[7] That, on one level, is a mandate to muteness: who could dare accept its challenge? And yet, since we *must* speak, the stricture can induce a measure of modesty about our claims that has seldom been a characteristic of Christian theology.

Wiesel's stress on questions rather than answers is particularly important for Christians. Henceforth, no faith claim can

be exempt from ongoing scrutiny; no assertion about God can
be called self-evident; no victory communiqué can remain un-
challenged; no proclamation ending with an exclamation point
can be exempt from being transformed into a question mark.
(God is love! God is love? Can you be sure? Can you say that
in the presence of burning children?)

The affirmations Christians make must be rethought and
restated in the light of the Holocaust. The task of doing so is
book-length, and all that can be attempted here is an indication of beginnings, and a charting of tasks.

Much theology continues to be written as though the Holocaust had never happened. But there are exceptions worth
noting. Jürgen Moltmann acknowledges that "there would be
no 'theology after Auschwitz' in retrospective sorrow and the
recognition of guilt, had there been no 'theology in Auschwitz'." By the latter he means a recognition that even there the
Shema Yisroel continued to be said. That God's name was invoked in the camps makes it possible for those who were not
in the camps to reflect on the meaning of that fact.[8]

The Roman Catholic theologian Hans Küng, in *On Being a
Christian,* after asserting (perhaps a little too simplistically) that
"Nazi anti-Judaism was the work of godless anti-Christian
criminals," immediately concedes that they could not have
succeeded without almost two thousand years of Christian
anti-Judaism to build on, and ends his discussion by declaring
forthrightly that "after Auschwitz there can be no more ex-
cuses. Christendom cannot avoid a clear admission of its
guilt."[9] Küng also criticizes the Vatican Council statement on
the Jews as being too weak. But it would be too much to say
that Küng's book *as a whole* is significantly influenced by the
Holocaust.

The most significant response by a German theologian has
been that of Johannes B. Metz, another Roman Catholic. In an
essay, "Christians and Jews after Auschwitz,"[10] Metz clearly
acknowledges that Christians can no longer do theology alone.
"It is possible only together with the victims of Auschwitz.
This, in my eyes, is the root of Jewish-Christian ecumenism"
(p. 19). Auschwitz can never be "understood," and Christians
must "forgo the temptation to interpret the suffering of the
Jewish people from our standpoint, in terms of [salvation]

history" (p. 19). Auschwitz really is a new starting point for Metz:

> Faced with Auschwitz, I consider as blasphemy every Christian theodicy . . . and all language about "meaning" when these are initiated outside this catastrophe or on some level above it. (p. 19)

He scores Christianity for having had "an excess of answers and a corresponding lack of agonized questions" (p. 23), for "a dangerous triumphalism" (p. 24), for having had within its history "a drastic deficit in regard to political resistance and a corresponding excess of political conformity" (p. 25), and for concealing "the practical core of its message" (p. 27). Metz submits that Christians concerned about the dead of Auschwitz and subsequent relations with Jews must resolve "never again to do theology in such a way that its construction remains unaffected, or could remain unaffected, by Auschwitz" (p. 28).

The most substantive Christian attempt to do what Metz is pointing toward is Paul Van Buren's *Discerning the Way* (Seabury, 1980), the first of a projected series of four volumes that gives every promise of living up to its subtitle, *A Theology of the Jewish-Christian Reality.* Van Buren is genuinely beginning the Christian theological task all over again, influenced not only by the Holocaust but by the whole Jewish-Christian relationship over two thousand years, which has been so badly misconceived from the Christian side.[11]

What areas of Christian thought need drastic rethinking? All areas, among which the following are only examples:

Christians sing a hymn, "How Firm A Foundation," that celebrates *the providential care of God.* In one verse, God speaks as follows:

> When through fiery trials thy pathway shall lie,
> My grace all-sufficient shall be thy supply.
> The flame shall not hurt thee, I only design
> Thy dross to consume, and thy gold to refine.

Auschwitz symbolizes six million negations of the divine promise that in the face of "fiery trials" the flames will not "hurt." There was no "all-sufficient grace" for the one million

Jewish children who died, many of whom were burned alive. It is blasphemy to affirm that the "fiery trials" of Auschwitz were God's "design," to consume the dross and refine the gold of human existence.

The words are a scriptural paraphrase by Isaac Watts, but they come from the Hebrew scriptures, reminding us that the Biblical promise was originally made *to the Jews:*

> Fear not, O Israel . . . when you walk through fire you shall not be burned, and the flame shall not consume you. . . . Fear not, for I am with you. . . . Behold, I have refined you, but not like silver. I have tried you in the furnace of affliction. (Isaiah 43:2, 42:5, 48:10)

That only compounds the problem.

Who can still affirm in the face of Auschwitz that God is a caring and powerful God in whose hands our destiny is safe? It is no longer sufficient to exhort, as Katharina von Schlegel does in another well-known hymn,

> Be still my soul, the Lord is on thy side;
> Bear patiently the cross of grief or pain;
> Leave to thy God to order and provide,
> In every change He faithful will remain.

That didn't work at Auschwitz, and it doesn't work after Auschwitz.

Ironically, earlier Christian estimates of *human nature* survive less damaged than affirmations about God, though that is no particular consolation, considering the nature of the estimates. For it has always been a long suit of Christian, and particularly Protestant, theology, to stress the deep-rooted and all-pervasive nature of human sin. The doctrine of original sin, scoffed at and disbelieved by the culture that gave us Auschwitz, is given grim and relentless empirical vindication by Auschwitz itself, an unyielding reminder that people are basically self-centered, willing to destroy others for their own survival, bent on domination and exploitation.

There is, of course, another side to Christian teaching, affirming that human beings are created in the image of God, a claim that appears almost nonexistent in a holocaust world, save for those rare acts of nobility and dignity that were occasionally practiced, even by the guards. The Holocaust makes clear that demonic impulses in human life are not limited to those already definable as moral monsters, but continue to surface in ordinary, decent people. People like us.

Doctrines of *redemption,* affirming that the evil human situation can be transformed into a situation of hope and new life and fresh beginnings, no longer work in or after Auschwitz. Such views conjure up a faith that has been destroyed and is irretrievable, in this world at least.

In another world? Here is either the greatest deception or the greatest hope. Christians assert more readily than Jews that the suffering, pain, and defeats of this life will be overthrown in another life, and that since God is Lord of life and death, not even death can finally thwart the divine will to draw all into eternal fellowship. It is clear that six million hopes for fulfillment in this life were negated by Auschwitz. The difficulty many sensitive people have with asserting a fulfillment in another life is that such a conviction makes it too easy to accept the anomalies and defeats of this life without protest, and to acquiesce in the ongoing human suffering, usually of others, that is thereby condoned—a worthy protest against easy answers, a necessary reminder of the need to struggle unremittingly against pain imposed on any creature.

And yet must there not be an affirmation that the last word to children is not a bonfire prepared to destroy them, in a world in which (as the child-poet of Theriesenstadt put it) there are no more butterflies?

Forgiveness has always been affirmed by Christians as a strong virtue, best exemplified in Jesus' utterance on the cross about the forgiveness of his enemies at precisely the moment his enemies were doing him in. But the Holocaust raises the possibility that forgiveness is a weak virtue that encourages repetition of wrongdoing rather than amendment of life.

When the President's Commission on the Holocaust visited the memorial to the Warsaw Ghetto uprising, one of the survivors gave a powerful and moving speech on the theme, "Never Forget—Never Forgive." Never *forget,* he said, what the Nazis did to Jews on this spot, and never *forgive* what they did either, lest future tyrants be tempted to think they could repeat such deeds with impunity. The first half of the exhortation poses no problem for Christians. But Christians need to struggle with the second half. What is to be the attitude of Christians toward the perpetrators of the Nazi crimes?

Recall the scene in Auschwitz: the gas chambers are malfunctioning, and to meet the daily quota of deaths, children are lined up and thrown on the open flames, those in the back of the line knowing that the fate of those in the front of the line is also in store for them. Does God forgive such deeds? Can human beings do so? Would there not be a deadly flaw in the moral fabric of any universe in which people could do such things and escape punishment? Is there any length of time, any series of eternities, in which perpetrators could undergo punishment commensurate with such evil? Could it be anything but an indulgent morality that assured the doers of such deeds that the final word is "There, there, you are forgiven, all is well again"?

And yet if there is not a resource of forgiveness, of mercy, of grace—human or divine, human and divine—we are caught in a web of guilt that finally destroys us all. Nevertheless, with events as monstrous as these, forgiveness must not too quickly be offered as a healing balm, since it could be construed as license to sin yet again against God and the human family, or to legitimate a universe lacking a sustainable moral fabric.

One could continue in similar fashion through every Christian affirmation, raising further questions that call for new ways of thinking and being. We have already seen, for example, that belief in *the church* as "the body of Christ," commissioned to do the ongoing work of healing and redemption in the world, is drastically challenged by the degree to which church members have been faithless to the example of their leader. The scriptural observation that "judgment begins at the house of God" (1 Peter 4:17) will have to inform all subsequent re-evaluation.

Instead of continuing an exhaustive journey through the whole of Christian theology, however, we will conclude with more detailed attention to two areas of Christian conviction that are particularly tested by the Holocaust.

The first of these concerns Christian convictions about *Christ*, convictions that are subject to an incredible irony: if Jesus had been in Auschwitz, he would not have been found among the Christians, who were the executioners; he would have been found among the Jews, who were victims. He would not have been above the gas chamber dropping the pellets of Zyklon B through the roof, he would have been inside the gas chamber inhaling the poison. He would not have been a commandant with epaulets affixed to his shoulder, he would have been a criminal with a number tattooed on his forearm. And this, not because of a free decision to align himself with the victims; this, simply because . . . he was a Jew.

Christians are called to undertake a new appraisal of who Jesus is, and the starting point will not be a figure sitting on the right hand of God, Alpha and Omega; the starting point will be one Jeshua bar Josef—a first century Jew with the dust and grime of the road upon him, getting tired, hungry, and discouraged, a worker who cast his lot with the poor of the land (the *am-ha'aretz*), who made all sorts of outrageous demands on rich young rulers and those who ignored the prisoners and the starving and the children—a Jew, in other words, who would have been with the Jews in Auschwitz even if he had not been forced to be there. It will also be a Jesus possessed of a wild dream, a dream that justice and love and liberation and compassion could be real in the here and now, and need not be relegated only to another world or another life.

Jews and Christians could share that much, at least, of the dream and walk such a road together, seeking to embody the dream in deeds. A time would come, of course, when the road forked and Christians and Jews would go in different directions, separated even then not so much by differing estimates of the worth of the dream, as by differing estimates of the dreamer. And since Christian estimates of the dreamer tend to escalate over the centuries in ways that threaten his real humanity, the one thing that must not be lost is that full sharing in humanity. Christians must never forget that their faith stands or falls on the claim that it was *in a first century Jew* that the one they affirm as God incarnate is present.

And as the Christian estimates of Jesus do escalate, from rabbi to long-expected Messiah to incarnate deity, the whole Messianic question is refocused in the light of the Holocaust. We noted earlier the Messianic dilemma that Wiesel and all Jews share: *the world is so evil, why does the Messiah not come?* For them, the dilemma can be even more cruel: even if the Messiah should come, would it not be too late? Six million deaths too late?

It has been a staple of Christian apologetics for two millenia that the yearning cry, "Why does the Messiah not come?" has been answered with the claim, "In Jesus of Nazareth the Messiah *has* come, our world has been redeemed, the power of evil has been broken, rejoice!"

But to the one who has truly heard Wiesel in the light of the Holocaust that answer may seem too glib, too cheap. The world does not appear so redeemed, the power of evil seems stronger than ever, the injunction to rejoice sounds hollow if not blasphemous. What is offered as an "answer" may only provide a deepening of the dilemma. It is the reverse of the Jewish dilemma, and it goes: *the Messiah has come, why is the world so evil?* A world like the present one, *without* a Messiah, may be abominable, but there is no particular reason why it should be different than it is; whereas a world like the present one, *with* a Messiah, carries a fairly convincing message that the redemption effort failed, and that rather than God conquering evil, evil appears to have conquered God.

If the dilemma seems unreal, we may appeal to the burning children to inform us.

What does the penitence and theological modesty we have been describing mean for *the relationship between Christians and Jews?* It means a sharp reversal at the very heart of the Christian enterprise. It means: no more proselytizing of Jews by Christians, no more attempts to "convert." This will come as a surprise, if not a shock, to many Christians, but there are both theological and historical reasons for making it.

The theological reason proposes that the relationship between Christianity and Judaism is a unique one—different from the relationship between Christianity and all other world religions, and that injunctions to seek converts that might apply in those other relationships do not apply in this one.

Long ago, God made a covenant with the Jews: God would be their God, they would be God's people. The promise was made to Abraham and Sarah and all of their descendents. A Jew becomes a child of the covenant simply by being born.

But the privilege of the covenant is extended to non-Jews

as well. They enter the covenant not by birth but by choice, by deciding to affirm as their own the God of the covenant. It is through Jesus of Nazareth that the God of the Jews reaches out to the non-Jews, and Christianity, comprised of the followers of Jesus, becomes, so to speak, the missionary arm of the God of the Jews, the means by which Gentiles are brought close to the God of Abraham, Isaac, and Jacob. One is born a Jew, one becomes a Christian.

Both Jews and Christians, therefore, worship the same God. By virtue of having been born into the covenant people, Jews already know the God whom Christians come to know through Jesus. So Jews and Christians are called to witness, each in their own way, to that one God they both acknowledge.

The historical reason for disavowing a Christian mission to the Jews has been illustrated on almost every page of this book. The history of the Christian church is so baleful in relation to the Jews that there is an arrogance and insensitivity almost beyond comprehension in the Christian assumption that somehow Jews "need" to be part of that community, or would even feel welcome or fulfilled in the body that has destroyed so many tens of thousands of Jews in the past. To Christians, the cross is a symbol of divine love for all people, whereas to Jews it is a symbol of Christian hatred for Jewish people, a symbol Christians have upended and brandished as a sword of terror and destruction. If a Jew wishes to become a Christian, that is, of course, a decision he or she must be free to make, and the Christian community is graced by such presence, but the initiative belongs with the Jew rather than the Christian.

The doing of deeds. In the light of all that we have been examining, what are Christians to do? Surely, first of all, listen and believe what is said.

"Grandfather says," young Toli reports before the pogrom at Kolvillàg, "that when a Jew says he is suffering, one must believe him, and when he is afraid, one must assume his fear is justified. In neither case does one have the right to doubt his word" (*The Oath*, p. 214). Listen and believe.

There is a second thing as well. One can push the grandfather's insight even further: when a Jew, or anyone, not only says "I am suffering . . ." but goes on to say, ". . . and *you* are the cause of my suffering," then the one addressed is under double obligation, not only to listen and believe, but also to act in such a way that there will be no further need to make the statement. That will not set right the past—it is not within our power to raise the dead—but it may mean that there will be no more dead for whom the listener must bear responsibility.

To press the matter. Even the most extravagant Christian statements about the new era inaugurated by the coming of Messiah stop short of claiming that the fullness of the Messianic age has dawned. That first coming must be brought to fulfillment by a "second coming," by an action of God who "will wipe away every tear from their eyes, neither shall there be mourning nor crying nor pain any more" (Revelation 21:4).

Those who affirm such a hope are not permitted to sit down and wait for it. They are exhorted to live now in ways comformable to the vision of what is yet to be. Jesus' words, already quoted, "Why do you call me 'Lord, Lord', and do not the things that I say?" are appropriate once more. He reminds his hearers that the mark of true belief is not theological orthodoxy (saying "Lord, Lord"), but "doing" the things that he said (struggling for justice, loosing the bonds of oppression, setting at liberty those who are oppressed). What is important is not enunciating dogmas, but energizing lives. The demand is not for Messianic affirmation but for Messianic deeds, deeds that define the nature of the Messianic kingdom. In fact, it is the doing of Messianic deeds that is the true Messianic affirmation (cf. Matt. 25:31–46).

And here is where Jews and Christians can work together. For while they will disagree about the content of the Messianic affirmation, they can agree about the importance of Messianic deeds, and engage together in the doing of such deeds. Gregor to Clara, near the end of *The Gates of the Forest:*

> Whether or not the Messiah comes doesn't matter. We'll manage without him. . . . We shall be honest and humble and strong, and then he will come, he will come every day, thousands of times every day. He will have no face, because he will have a thousand faces. The Messiah isn't one man, Clara, he's

all men. As long as there are men, there will be a Messiah.
. . . (p. 223)

We will presume to improve even on Gregor, and say, "As long as there are those *who do Messianic deeds* there will be a Messiah." For people can be dishonest and arrogant and strong, as well as "honest and humble and strong." But whenever deeds are done that embody the Messianic vision, we can say that the Messiah is present, whether or not his name is expressly invoked in their doing.

Birkenau and Golgotha

To be faithful to the spirit of Elie Wiesel, such a chapter should end with a story. In this case, the story is a true one. It takes place on the roof of one of the crematoria at Birkenau, the death camp of Auschwitz, on a gray, cheerless day in the summer of 1979.[12]

A group of us are standing on ruins the Germans tried (unsuccessfully) to obliterate, to hide evidence that six million Jews had been shot and gassed and burned in such places, solely because they were Jews.

I reflect: if Golgotha revealed the sense of God-forsakenness of one Jew, Birkenau multiplies that anguish at least three and a half million times. For the rest of my life, this crematorium will represent the most powerful case against God, the spot where one could—with justice—denounce, deny, or (worst of all) ignore God, the God who was silent.

Of what use are words at such a time? So many cried out to God at this spot and were not heard. Human silence today seems the only appropriate response to divine silence yesterday.

We remain silent. Our silence is deafening.

And then it comes—first from the lips of one man, Elie Wiesel (standing in the camp where thirty-five years earlier his life and family and faith were destroyed), and then in a mounting chorus from others, mostly Jews, the great affirmation: *Shema Yisroel, Adonai Elohenu, Adonai echod,* Hear, O Israel, the Lord our God, the Lord is One.

At the place where the name of God could have been ago-nizingly denied, the name of God is agonizingly affirmed—by those with most reason to deny. I shake in the tension between my impulse to deny and their decision to affirm.

Because of having stood *at Birkenau,* it is now impossible for me to affirm God in the ways I did before.

Because of having stood at Birkenau *with them,* it is now possible for me to affirm God in ways I never did before.

CHAPTER 7

The Ongoing Struggle of Light Against Darkness: Or, "What Is There Left for Us To Do?"
(a human journey)

"So be it!" he shouted. "[God is] guilty; do you think I don't know it? That I have no eyes to see, no ears to hear? That my heart doesn't revolt? That I have no desire to beat my head against the wall and shout like a madman, to give rein to my sorrow and disappointment? Yes, he is guilty. He has become the ally of evil, of death, of murder, but the problem is still not solved. I ask you a question and dare you answer: 'What is there left for us to do?' "
—the Rebbe in *The Gates of the Forest*, p. 197, emphasis added.

Thanks to [Job], we know that it is given to man to transform divine injustice into human justice and compassion.
—Wiesel in *Messengers of God*, p. 235

So you hope to defeat evil? Fine. Begin by helping your fellow-man. Triumph over death? Excellent. Begin by saving your brother.
—Azriel in *The Oath*, p. 14

The imagery of light and darkness has been central for

Wiesel from the beginning: the light of Sighet was eclipsed by
the darkness of Auschwitz. Irrevocably, it seemed. And then,
from the kingdom of night there was a long journey that en-
compassed a false dawn and a false day before the beginnings
of a true dawn and a true day began to penetrate the darkness
. . . of a prison cell. That the recipient of the faintest slivers
of light was imprisoned and (as far as we know) may have died
there is a symbol of the frailty of the victory being described.
But beyond that cell, in other books and other characters,
fresh hints of new beginnings are sketched—a broken marriage begins to be rebuilt, a broken city begins to be reclaimed,
a broken oath begins to be redemptive.

At every moment the darkness threatens to engulf the tiny
islands of light that have appeared in a sea of darkness—the
marriage may founder, the city may fall, the pogrom may be
repeated. All the victories are fragile, all the withdrawals of
darkness are tentative. Nevertheless, Wiesel seeks to enlist us
in the ongoing struggle of light against darkness, of memory
against indifference.

He offers no guarantee that cosmic support can be enlisted
in the struggle. Indeed, the weight of the evidence suggests
the opposite, as the three quotations at the beginning of the
chapter intimate. Let us review them:

Assume the very worst, as the rebbe does: against all human
desire, all human hope, God stands against us. An occasion for
revolt, sorrow, disappointment. But not for giving up. Face all
that unflinchingly, and there is still a question before us:
"What is there left for us to do?" How do we still beat back
a darkness that continually threatens the light?

Assume the very worst, as Wiesel does in response to Job:
God acts unjustly. An occasion, likewise, for revolt, sorrow,
disappointment. But not for giving up. For, in the most moving, challenging—and audacious—line Wiesel has ever written, there is still a task before us: "It is given to man to
transform divine injustice into human justice and compassion."

Assume something less than the worst, as Azriel does: that
whether there is cosmic support or not, we desire to defeat evil
and triumph over death. An occasion for seeking resources
and asking for aid, and then questioning, with a kind of gasp,

our own temerity. But there are some clear marching orders: enrichment for such cosmic endeavors is rooted in the deep soil of humanity. We are to help our fellow-man and save our brother and sister.

These are signposts along a human journey on which Wiesel is embarked with us. There are other signposts, including God's engagement on the journey with us, and Jews and Christians will continue to decipher such pointers with Wiesel's ongoing help. For many others, such signposts do not command allegiance. But no matter what we believe about God (sustaining friend? implacable foe? terrifying presence? disturbing absence?) we are all confronted with the rebbe's relentless question, "What is there left for us to do?"

From Jewish particularity to human universality . . . in that order.

The starting point of our journey seems unpromising. The proposal to include us all begins with a case of special pleading: we want to widen our circle to include the whole human family, and the first marching order calls on us to narrow it to a tiny segment of that family—the Jews.

All our instincts cry out against it: let us think in universal terms, we respond, so that no one is excluded; then, once we have established that wide reality, we can focus more narrowly. Anything preferential can only sabotage our will to be inclusive.

Wiesel argues that such instincts are wrong: the true order of knowing and doing does not move from universal to particular, but just the reverse. He feels this initially in his vocation as a writer. As he has said repeatedly, should he try to write simply as a "human being" to other human beings, his words would fall flat. But when he writes *as a Jew*, out of his own particularity, he not only speaks to Jews, he speaks to all. The order is from Jewish particularity to human universality.

Does this seem arbitrary? Consider: we no longer ask women to deny that their view of the world is influenced by feminist concerns; we ask them to contribute their distinctive concerns to our overall understanding, so that our own per-

spective can be enlarged. We no longer ask blacks to deny that
their view of the world is influenced by the history of oppression of blacks by whites; we ask them to contribute their distinctive concerns to our overall understanding so that our own
perspective can be enlarged. We no longer ask white males to
deny that their view of the world is influenced by mainline
masculine concerns; we ask them to contribute their distinctive
concerns to our overall understanding, so that our perspective
can be enlarged. The point is that *a "universal perspective" is a
fiction.* There is no such thing, except perhaps for God. There
is only a perspective informed by particularist assumptions,
trying to see as widely as possible. The temptation is to assume
that our own stance is the truly universalistic one. Confident
in the latter belief we then seek subtly (or not so subtly) to
impose it on others. It is the seedbed of every fanaticism.

The more one speaks out of his or her particularity, the
more chance there is that the words will dislodge others from
thinking they speak universally, and thus draw everyone closer
to a universal stance than any of us can obtain by ourselves.
Conclusion: start with the particularities.

> It was Unamuno who said, "When a Spaniard speaks of being
> in love, he speaks about all people being in love." And when
> I speak of persecuted Jews, I also mean persecuted human
> beings everywhere. ("A Personal Response," p. 37)

So it is not only legitimate, but necessary, for Wiesel to start
uncompromisingly with the fact of his Jewishness and urge
other Jews to do likewise.

> A Jew cannot attain the fulfillment of his human condition if he
> sets himself outside his community. If he decides to save man-
> kind by cutting himself off from the Jewish people, he is betray-
> ing both. The Jew can help mankind by helping Jews or
> mankind but only as a Jew. (*Victory*, p. 17)

As Wiesel reflects on the historical emancipation of Jews in
the nineteenth century, he observes that as Jews tried to "as-
similate," not only was their Jewishness diluted but also their
humanness. Trying to be universalistic by the denial of their
particularity was a disaster for them and also for those around
them. Writing to "A Young Jew Today," Wiesel counsels:

Remember: the Jew influences his environment, though he resists assimilation. Others will benefit from his experience to the degree that it is and remains unique. *Only by accepting his Jewishness can he attain universality.* . . . By working for his own people a Jew does not renounce his loyalty to mankind; on the contrary, he thereby makes his most valuable contribution. (*Generation*, pp. 172–3, italics added: see also *A Jew Today*, pp. 109 ff.)

Wiesel goes on to offer examples of how Jewish concern for Jews redounds to the benefit of all:

By struggling on behalf of Russian, Arab or Polish Jews, I fight for human rights everywhere. By calling for peace in the Middle East, I take a stand against every aggression, every war. By protesting the fanatical exhortations to "holy wars" against my people, I protest against the stifling of freedom in Prague. By striving to keep alive the memory of the holocaust, I denounce the massacres in Biafra and the nuclear menace. Only by drawing on his unique Jewish experience can the Jew help others. A Jew fulfills his role as man only from inside his Jewishness.

That is why, in my writings, the Jewish theme predominates. It helps me approach and probe the theme of man. (*Generation*, p. 173)

Particularity as a starting point is by no means a concluding point. It does not lock the Jew into exclusively Jewish concerns. On the contrary, it frees the Jew for universal human concerns. Corroboration is furnished by the subject matter of the book to which Wiesel gives his most "particularistic" title, *A Jew Today*. While the essays have their share of specifically Jewish concerns, they spill over such presumed boundaries on almost every page, expressing moral concern about human indignities in Biafra, South Africa, Bangladesh, the Sahel, Vietnam, and even reach out to initiate a dialogue with Palestinian Arabs.

An episode in Wiesel's own life speaks volumes about how particularistic Jewish concerns reach out to encompass universal human concerns. His first public action as chairman of the President's Commission on the Holocaust was not to stress the special needs or concerns of Jewish people, but to call public attention, through an open letter to the American people, to the plight of the Vietnamese "boat people," refugees being denied access to their own land and refused entrance to all other lands. This contemporary concern grew out of a specific Jewish memory—the experience in 1938 of Jewish "boat people," who left Hamburg in search of asylum in any other country than Germany, were denied entrance by all countries in the north Atlantic, and finally had to return to Germany, where most of them were sent to Theriesenstadt. The particularity of that Jewish episode sensitized those who remembered it to a wider non-Jewish episode.

To begin with the particular is to be moved to a concern for all. "[The Jews'] mission," Wiesel writes, "was never to make the world Jewish, but, rather, to make it more human" (*A Jew Today*, p. 13).

No wonder that Wiesel's "favorite prayer" is the one by Rebbe Israel: "Master of the Universe, know that the children of Israel are suffering too much; they deserve redemption, they need it. But if, for reasons unknown to me, You are not willing, not yet, then redeem all the other nations, but do it soon!" (*Souls*, p. 133).

So particularity has universal implications, not only for Jews but everyone; the feminist, black, and white male particularities previously cited also share in this truth. Feminists seek liberation for men as well as women; blacks argue that freedom for whites is bound up with freedom for blacks; white males acknowledge that their claims to normative perspective need to be cut down to size.

If such statements seem overly optimistic, that itself is a reminder that we have not yet learned the lesson Elie Wiesel is trying to teach us.

There is another way in which Jewish concerns become universal concerns. "Whatever happens to us," Wiesel remarks, "may happen to everybody" (*Dimensions*, p. 17).

We have already noted the frightening foreshadowing of this in the pogrom at Kolvillàg: when members of the mob have sated their fury against all available Jews, they turn on one another and continue a senseless slaughter, culminating in the incineration of a building in which Christians are locked, as a result of which the whole village goes up in flames. The narrator's horror focuses on the fact that in that episode he sees the future.

That is a fictional presentation of a historical truth. Here is an actual episode:

> *Stories about indifference towards Jews can warn against indifference toward other people as well.* When the Warsaw Ghetto was burning in April 1943, Polish boys and girls would go to watch Jewish fighters jump into the flames. It was their entertainment.
>
> One year later, the city staged an uprising and the whole of Warsaw was on fire; it was then the turn of the Russian army to stand watching the same city burning with the same indifference. For the Poles indifference was no longer a sin but a punishment. As it turned out, whoever was indifferent to the ghetto was ultimately indifferent to his/her own fate. ("A Personal Response," p. 37, italics added)

The burning of the Warsaw *ghetto* was an anticipation of the burning of *Warsaw*. Jews tell about the ghetto not only out of concern for Jews but for all humanity. The consequences of the Holocaust are consequences for all.

> If there is a lesson to be found in Auschwitz, it is for the world to learn, not for us. We are still engaged in telling the tale. The world should learn its own lesson on its own level for its own good, namely: *when people do things of this nature to Jews, tomorrow they will do them to themselves.* This, perhaps, may be our mission to the world: we are to save it from self-destruction.
>
> Our mission involves other peoples. Jews do not live alone. As a result of what the world has done to us, it may find a way to save itself. By now it must admit that we do have in our possession a key to survival. We have not survived centuries of atrocities for nothing. ("Jewish Values in the Post-Holocaust Future," p. 299, italics added)

As the last two quotations illustrate, we are always led back to the Holocaust. In the light of that fact, we must explore one of the most sensitive issues in holocaust discussion: should we emphasize the particularity of Jewish suffering in the Holocaust, and if so, why?

The U.S. Holocaust Memorial Council, of which Wiesel is chairperson, has probably devoted more attention to this question than to any other. During a visit to Poland and Russia by members of the Council (of whom the author was one), no matter was raised more insistently by Poles and Russians. Whenever it appeared that members of the Council had a special concern about Jews, there was vehement opposition. The response went: we want the Holocaust to unite us in opposition to atrocities. We do not want to single out Poles or Russians or Georgians or Jews or anyone else in ways that might divide us. Six million Jews died at the hands of the Nazis? What about twenty million Russians? Jewish inhabitants lost their lives in the Warsaw Ghetto? What about Polish inhabitants who lost their lives in the sack of Warsaw? Why single out the Jews for special attention?

Sometimes the arguments had the ring of moral conviction, sometimes they were clothed in barely-concealed anti-Semitism.

To all of which, three types of response are appropriate:

1. If there is a post-Auschwitz priority for remembering Jewish victims, it is because there was a pre-Auschwitz priority for creating Jewish victims. It is a fact that the initial and main German extermination target was the Jews. There were other targets—gypsies and homosexuals, for example (though gypsies were killed in Poland but not in Hungary or Romania). And had the Nazis succeeded not only in exterminating all the Jews, but in winning the war itself, it is reasonable to assume (Nazi logic being what it was) that similar genocidal impulses would have been implemented against other groups, perhaps starting with the Slavs. But it was in fact against Jews that the policy was initiated, attained its clearest focus, and came perilously close to fulfillment. That alone legitimates a decision to give special attention to those victims who were the special target of Nazi annihilation, as a starting point for concern about other victims as well.

2. A conviction that the Jewish role in the Holocaust is unique is further legitimated because there was a unique motivation in singling out the Jews as victims. Other victims of the Nazis were killed for *what they did*—they were military opponents of the Third Reich, advocates of an ideology contrary to Nazism, citizens of countries formally at war with Germany, or whatever. Jews might or might not have been one or all of those things; that did not matter. Jews were killed not because of what they did but simply because of *who they were*. The distinction is basic. A Jew did not need to *act*, in order to be subject to extermination, a Jew needed only to *be*. In a defini-

tion frequently cited in previous pages, the Jewish "crime" was having the wrong grandparents. Such a "crime" sufficed to put *any* Jew on the list for Auschwitz or Treblinka. In the ultimate refinement of this logic, Jewish children were gassed or burned alive, not because they were plotting treason or engaging in espionage or throwing grenades or refuting Nazi philosophy; Jewish children were gassed or burned alive because they were . . . Jewish children.

If there is anything that should establish a dimension of uniqueness, and therefore a sense of priority, to the Jewish victims of the Holocaust, it is this fact: Jews were exterminated not for what they did but solely for who they were. *All Jews were victims.*

3. But those who are persuaded by the above discussion may still be uneasy: doesn't this lead to exclusivism? Isn't it unfair to remember Jews at the expense of others?

The assumption behind the question is invalid: to remember Jews is *not* to forget others. It has not been the case that a stress on the uniqueness of Jewish victimization has led to a forgetfulness of the victimization of the others. "If all Jews were victims," as Wiesel has said many times, *"not all victims were Jews."* Rather than being divisive, the acknowledgment of the uniqueness of the Jewish victimization is unifying, pointing beyond itself to the suffering of all. As Wiesel commented when receiving the Joseph Award of the Anti-Defamation League for his contribution to "human rights" (not "Jewish rights"):

> We aspire to endow our words with a force that unites people from as many horizons as possible. We believe that even the Holocaust must bring together Jews and Jews, Jews and Christians, believers and non-believers. ("A Personal Response," p. 35)

The fact that Jews died forces us to face, rather than ignore, that Poles died, Russians died, political prisoners died, homosexuals died, and—yes, Germans died as well. All must be remembered. All must be mourned. All must be honored. If we begin with Jewish particularity, we can only end with human universality.

Why single out the Jews? In a letter to President Carter, on the occasion of presenting the report of the President's Commission on the Holocaust, Wiesel responded:

> Our Commission believes because they were the principal target of Hitler's Final Solution that we must remember the six million Jews and, *through them and beyond them but not without them,* rescue from oblivion all the men, women and children who perished in those years in the camps and forests of the kingdom of night.

From repudiation of hatred to affirmation of anger

Wiesel has struggled with the intensity of hatred any Jew must have had after the war for any German.

Hatred of Germans, he reports, was not a reality within the camps. "We didn't hate the Germans, and the Germans didn't hate us. It was worse. You can hate only a human being" ("Talking and Writing and Keeping Silent," p. 272). Neither Germans nor Jews considered their counterparts true human beings: "You do not hate the stone that crushes you, or the animal that devours you. Only man inspires hate, and only man suffers it" (*Legends,* p. 177).

But after the war, when Germans could be seen as human beings, then there was festering and devouring hatred. For seventeen years Wiesel deliberately avoided contact with Germans. Only then did he finally return to Germany, a place he had once left "forever." He found himself talking to Germans, smiling, answering questions, engaging in "civilized behavior."

And he was shocked. He had lost his taste for hating others, and he began to hate himself for losing it. Disturbed, even ashamed, at having let hatred escape him, he cut his visit short.

Later, reflecting on the experience, Wiesel wrote:

> There is a time to love and a time to hate; whoever does not hate when he should does not deserve to love when he should, does not deserve to love when he is able. . . . Today, even having been deserted by my hate during that fleeting visit to Germany, I cry out with all my heart against silence. Every Jew, somewhere in his being, should set apart a zone of hate— healthy, virile hate—for what the German personifies and for

what persists in the German. To do otherwise would be a betrayal of the dead. (*Legends,* p. 177–178)

Three things are notable in this reflection: first, the initial
hatred is gone, but there was a time when it was appropriate;
second, the thing to fear in the demise of hatred is not sentimentality or cheap forgiveness, but indifference, described as
"silence"; third, a certain kind of hatred should persist, should
even be cultivated—hatred not for the individual German so
much as for "what the German personifies," hatred not for all
things German so much as for "what persists in the German,"
which in the context means those traits that created the Holocaust.

But such a position, understandable and even possessed of
an inflamed moral passion, was not a resting point for Wiesel.
In the same volume of essays from which the above reflections
are taken, he has moved to a repudiation of hatred. Reflecting
on the widespread indifference to what was happening to Jews:
"I repeat: hatred is no solution. There would be too many
targets. . . . Were hatred a solution, the survivors, when they
came out of the camps, would have had to burn down the
whole world" (*Legends,* p. 233).

In a still later essay, "To a Young German of the New Left,"
he writes:

> There was a time when I thought I too could, and must, hate
> your fathers. I was against the cheap liberalism that requires
> one to forget and forgive—and absolve—for the sake of politi-
> cal or religious expediency. Whoever loves his executioner, I
> thought, creates a dangerously false vision of love and a dan-
> gerously unreal image of man. (*Generation,* p. 157–158)

But he discovered that it was impossible to keep the flames
of hatred well stoked. Even the flames of love turned out to be
vulnerable.

> With the passing years one learns that feelings, like persons,
> escape us. In time, the most vital sources run dry. Even love,
> even hate. Reviving the one is no less disappointing than plung-
> ing back into the other. We thought we carried within ourselves
> dormant volcanoes; they are burned out. Who knows? Perhaps
> "to hate" like "to love" may be conjugated only in the present
> tense. (*Generation,* p. 158)

New events inspire new emotions. And as Wiesel grappled with members of the new German left who were siding with the Arabs and against Israel, he saw them "carrying on the work planned and undertaken by your fathers" (*Generation,* p. 162). This did not lead to a resurgence of hatred on Wiesel's part. But (if we recall the exchanges between Michael and the spectator in *The Town Beyond the Wall*) it led to something even more devastating. The letter concludes:

> Even if you perpetuate the evil spread by your fathers, I shall not hate you. I shall denounce, unmask and fight you with all my power. But your hate will not contaminate me. No, I shall never hate you. Not for yesterday and not even for today. It is something else: for yesterday you have my pity; for today, my contempt. (p. 162)

Contempt. In the novel, it was reserved for what is less than human. In desperate extremities, it may be all that is left.

Is there anywhere else to go with hatred? In a number of places Wiesel suggests that there is: the project is to transmute hatred into anger, and turn anger to creative ends. This is the positive achievement that Wiesel sees as having taken place, almost through grace, among his contemporaries. After recalling all the killings, the deaths, the tragedies, he asks, "What do we do with these questions, these memories? What do we do with the anger?" And he responds, "The great miracle of my generation is that somehow the anger was channeled to humanistic purposes" ("A Personal Response," p. 36).

A beautiful remedy. But how does one channel anger "to humanistic purposes"? There are some possibilities. They are initiated by remembering that anger is not a solitary emotion. It implies community, humanity. Wiesel's portrait of Rebbe Barukh of Medzebozh embodies this truth: "He was angry? Naturally he was. *He was angry because he cared,* because he was concerned, because he was present to anyone in need of human presence" (*Masters,* p. 60, italics added).

If anger proceeds from caring, from concern, from impulses that are communal in origin, then anger at injustice, anger at indifference, "anger channeled to humanistic purposes," must be cultivated in community as well. Rebbe Barukh proposed a community of creative anger to one of his students:

> I know there are questions that have no answers; there is a
> suffering that has no name; there is injustice in God's creation
> —and there are reasons enough for man to explode with rage.
> I know there are reasons for you to be angry. Good. Let us be
> angry. Together. (*Masters,* p. 60)

The repudiation of silence, the necessity of outrage—such
things when shared together are capable of serving creative
ends.

"Love and anger are compatible," Wiesel learns from
Rebbe Barukh, "provided they are motivated by *Ahavat-Israel,*
by concern for Israel" (*Masters,* p. 59). Good news. For we have
already learned from Wiesel that concern for Israel and concern for the whole human family are also compatible.

Wiesel has embodied the steps from hatred, through contempt, to creative anger. The culmination of that journey is
portrayed in his collection of essays, *A Jew Today.* They are by
turns tender, bitter, reminiscent, forward-looking, compassionate . . . and angry. They exemplify almost every emotion
of which the human heart is capable, save one.

There is no hatred.

From immoral order to a moral society

Without a commitment to human universality, affirmed out
of our own particularities, without a repudiation of hatred and
a channeling of anger "for humanistic purposes," we will have
either destructive chaos or demonic order. Sometimes the two
appear indistinguishable. Which was Germany in the period
1933–1945? If there appeared to be a certain "chaos" in the
camps, it was nevertheless a highly controlled chaos in which
even capriciousness ("you shall die immediately . . . *you* shall
live a little longer") served the ends of order, order defined
immorally.

Against all that, is it futile to delineate the characteristics of
a moral society? In one sense, Wiesel has never explicitly
addressed the problem, but in another sense he never addresses anything else. Surely his overriding concerns are: How
are we to live together? How are we to fashion a counterpart

to the kingdom of night? How are we to have a world that is safe for children? How are we to create a moral society?

Out of the *corpus* of Wiesel's writings we can distill a vision of a moral society as *a society that takes full account of the personhood of all its members, particularly its children.* As simple and as complicated as that. As minimal and all-inclusive as that.

An immoral society will be the opposite—a society in which certain members are deemed superior, and in which the rest are deemed inferior, unimportant, or expendable, particularly its children. The latter describes Nazi Germany of course, but it also describes large portions of the world today. The issue is not of historical interest only; we live in an immoral society.

What flesh can we put upon such bones, to describe more fully "a society that takes full account of the personhood of all its members, particularly its children"? Were we being fully faithful to Elie Wiesel, we would respond to the question by telling stories. Failing in that skill, we will delineate half a dozen characteristics that can be distilled from his writings.

One characteristic is stated explicitly by Wiesel: "in a moral society, *falsehood never takes on the mask of truth.*" Even if we cannot fully attain it, the quest for truth will be the measure of our integrity: "Man is not measured by his success in attaining truth, but by his efforts to attain it." A high calling, often betrayed, not least in our own time, making the vocation to truth even more important: "if millions preach falsehood, there must be at least one voice, however lonely and weak, to call it falsehood" ("A Personal Response," p. 36). That may be the task of the lonely company of the prophets (whose vocation we will examine in the next section). But it is also the task of anyone seeking to live responsibly in society. It means not only not labeling gas chambers as "shower rooms," but also shouting that the "shower rooms" are in fact gas chambers. It means no longer saying, "We know what is good for you," when we really mean, "We are going to manipulate you for our own ends and make you think we are doing you a favor." It means not saying, "The Holocaust was a hoax, the Jews didn't really suffer, and only a million of them died," and it also means saying, "Any view of the present that fails to acknowledge that there was a Holocaust in the past, threatens the future."

Second, a moral society will be *compassionate rather than vindictive*. There may be times, in the face of great evil, when outrage and struggle must predominate, but they will never be normative; they will only be provisional expedients seeking to establish conditions that *can* be normative. Wiesel has explored the cul-de-sac of vindictiveness in the story of Joshua, the one whose "life was filled with dark, implacable violence in the service of God, whose name is—peace" (*Portraits*, p. 5). The book of Joshua is full of battles, bloodshed, vindictiveness, retribution. It is "difficult to feel empathy for anyone whose life was as marked by violence as it was untouched by poetry" (*Portraits*, p. 9).

At first Wiesel was disturbed by the lack of poetry in the book of Joshua, but then he realized that it was fitting to keep poetry out of a book about wars and bloodshed.

> The Book of Joshua . . . is full of bloodshed and violence, and it does lack poetry. But its very lack of literary beauty can be seen as a virtue. Joshua won many battles but the Bible does not boast about them. That is true of all Jewish wars. The prophets refused to sanctify them, the poets declined to romanticize them. Songs were written to celebrate miracles, not wars. (*Portraits*, p. 27)

We may sometimes have to fight, even to kill, Wiesel concedes, but we may never exult in our killing even for a noble cause, never glorify our battles, never make holy crusades out of acts of destruction. Vindictiveness is not a characteristic of the moral society. It tends to destroy not only persons but the very concept of personhood; one's enemies are reduced to the status of things, to be disposed of, in anger or revenge. There must be compassion (on occasion, to be sure, a tough-minded compassion), if we are to honor personhood in the other as well as in ourselves. And if we do not honor it in them, we will debase it in ourselves; in *Dawn*, Elisha's murder of John Dawson brought about not only the physical destruction of John Dawson but the moral destruction of Elisha.

Third, a moral society will express *special concern for the powerless*. An increasing gap is developing in our world between the few with massive power and the many with ever-decreasing power or no power at all. A society will be moral to the degree that those within it are ceaselessly concerned about those who lack power, those who will therefore be the oppressed and the victimized, those about whom Wiesel writes particularly in *A Jew Today*—not only Jews, but the oppressed in Cambodia, South Africa, or wherever. Our social structures are not going to bend very much in the direction of the powerless. So it is the more important that individuals or small groups take it upon themselves, in working toward a moral society, to be concerned with the powerless, to establish places where the voiceless are enabled to speak on their own behalf, to have a part, perhaps for the first time, in the creation of their own destinies.

Fourth, a moral society will be a society of *participants rather than spectators.* The terms evoke a flood of episodes from Wiesel's novels. One thing that happens in the progression of the writings is that individuals, cut off from each other and unable to make the most elemental acts of trust in other human beings, gradually become empowered to leave the shell of self-imposed isolation, participate in the destiny of others, realize how risky it is, and nevertheless embrace the risk. The narrator in *The Oath* finally says, "Every truth that shuts you in, that does not lead to others, is inhuman" (*The Oath,* p. 73). Michael, in prison, realizes that unless he can draw the mad inmate across from him into relationship, there will soon be two madmen in the cell. Wiesel tells us that personhood is never achieved in isolation; it is always a matter of relationship. For there to be an "I" there must also be an "Other", a "Thou." At the end of *The Town Beyond the Wall,* Michael is looking into the eyes of another human being, a relationship is being established, and Michael can offer the other his own name.

The opposite of participation is not only isolation; the non-participant becomes a spectator, the role so chillingly embodied in the observer at the window in *The Town Beyond the Wall* who feels "nothing" as Jews are taken to the camps, and who by doing nothing sides with the executioners rather than the victims. His is the most complicit role, worse even than the executioner. The withdrawal from participation is an abdication of personhood.

Fifth, a moral society will *cling to hope rather than succumbing to despair*. It may sometimes cling despairingly, but cling it must, or it will nurture the seeds of its own destruction.

Today, it would be hard to speak for hope and against despair without witnesses like Elie Wiesel. Those who can talk convincingly about hope, and "against despair," will be those who have tasted the bitterness of despair in ways unimaginable to the rest of us, and yet have not succumbed to it. Such hope will always be hope "in spite of"—in spite of everything that seeks to destroy it. Perhaps hope is too strong a word, but at least there must be a commitment "never to give up—never to yield to despair" (*A Jew Today*, p. 164).

That, says Wiesel, is the essence of being Jewish. When Jews in Russia dance defiantly in the streets on Simchat Torah, that is an instance in which "Jews are able to draw new reasons for hope from their despair" (p. 165). He concludes his essay "Against Despair" with the words:

> We owe it to our past not to lose hope. Say what you will, despair is not the solution. Not for us. Quite the contrary. We must show our children that in spite of everything, we keep our faith—in ourselves and even in mankind, though mankind may not be worthy of such faith. We must persuade our children and theirs that three thousand years of history must not be permitted to end with an act of despair on our part. To despair now would be a blasphemy—a profanation. (*A Jew Today*, p. 167)

Finally, a moral society will be *perpetually unfinished*. A moral society will not be one in which all questions have been answered but one in which all questions continue to be asked. It will be characterized by ongoing challenges to complacency, ongoing pleas for defiance, ongoing refusals to accept things as they are.

The German culture, because it has produced Goethe and Schiller, is safeguarded against perpetuating injustice? Think again. The United States, not having used nuclear weapons since 1945, will not use them in the future? Think again. Christians, trying to come to terms with the anti-Semitism in their tradition, have exorcised it once and for all? Think again.

No victories in history are ever so securely nailed down that they could not come unstuck. At no time can we affirm that the moral society has arrived, or that the path to it goes straight up a gentle slope. Around the next bend may be new horrors. In the wake of every achievement come fresh ambiguities. Each rise can be the prelude to a greater fall. A Holocaust, forgotten, could happen again.

Here I propose a risky image, as we seek to draw out of the evil of the past safeguards against the repetition of such evil in the future. I see the fires of the Holocaust as a gruesome beacon, fires that so penetrate our contemporary landscape that *all* the dark corners of it are illuminated by that ghastly torch. Little pockets of evil that might otherwise escape attention are exposed when we look at them in the light of the Holocaust. That event of unique magnitude can point us toward other events of lesser magnitude, which we can see more readily and more promptly in its light, and thus be enabled to stamp them out before they get out of control and render us helpless when we confront them, too late.

About no society that has ever existed or ever will exist can we afford complacency. Society will be moral to the extent that we see it in constant need of challenge, renewal, reconstruction. Society will be immoral to the extent that the leaders can say, "Trust us to do what is good for you. We know best, and one day you'll thank us. And if you don't trust us, we will have to get you out of the way because you are interfering with the master plan."

To which need be added only, *"Sieg heil!"*

A moral society will be perpetually unfinished.

What quality do we need in the persons who create such a society?—moral madness.

From immoral sanity to moral madness

Mad people stalk the pages of Wiesel's writings. To him they are normal, even normative, parts of human existence. To us they are strange, even frightening, intrusions. We may wonder about Wiesel's preoccupation and virtual obsession with them.

And then we discover that the mad people challenge the assumptions of the lucid, and that the mad people communicate the real truth about the human situation.

This is unsettling. No one wants a tidy universe messed up. No one wants to be told, "You've got it wrong. Things must at least be turned upside down and backwards." So we put such people out of sight and out of hearing. Or we dispose of them by calling them mad.

This is what happened to the Hebrew prophets. Hosea reports: "The days of punishment have come, the days of recompense have come; Israel shall know it. The prophet is a fool, the man of the spirit is mad" (Hosea 9:7, RSV). Elisha is referred to as "this mad fellow" (2 Kings 9:11, RSV). Stern measures are proposed for Jeremiah: "Every madman who prophesies" is to be put "in the stocks and collar" (Jeremiah 29:26, RSV; cf. *Portraits*, p. 109).

The prophets see life from a different perspective than their contemporaries, and insist on calling attention to the discrepancy. As a result, they do "crazy" things: they call kings to account for injustice, they excoriate religious leaders for being co-opted, they announce the fulfillment of God's will through pagan leaders, they even rail against the God in whose name they presume to speak. In Abraham Heschel's phrase, they exhibit "moral madness."

But there is an important difference, Heschel goes on, between the prophet and the psychotic. The latter crosses the threshhold into another world and finds it difficult, if not impossible, to return, whereas the prophet, confronted by a vision drawn from elsewhere, feels compelled to share the vision: "The ideas he brings back to reality become a source of illumination of supreme significance to all other human beings."[1]

Wiesel makes a similar distinction in different terminology. In response to a query, "Why are you not mad?" he replied:

> Maybe I am and I don't know it. If I am, I try to know it. When I see the world, the way it is; when I watch the events, the way they unfold; when I think of what is going to happen to our generation, then I have the feeling that I am haunted by that madness—that we all are. Then in order to save myself from *that* madness, I go back to another madness—a holy madness—the one that became a victim, the one that kept us alive for so many centuries, for thousands of years.

He elaborates:

> When I speak of madness I mean a mystical madness. I am against insanity, generally speaking. I think man should not be insane—man should fight insanity. But from time to time, when there are choices and options to be made and taken, then madness—mystical madness—is important. One has to be mad today, in this time and age, to say certain things and believe that they could make a difference. (*Conversation,* pp. 2–3)

Wiesel's "mystical madness" is close to the "moral madness" of the prophets.

We assume that there is a way of looking at reality which can be called "sane," and another way of looking at reality which can be called "mad," and we further assume that the distinction is determined by majority consensus. Sanity is the way the world appears to most of us; madness is the way it appears to a few "others," who see things so differently that we put them beyond the pale of sanity.

And the disturbing question throughout Wiesel's novels is: *what if we have things reversed?* What if the minority viewpoint is in fact the true one? What if the ones we call "mad" are really sane? What if the rest of us are the ones who fail to see the world as it truly is?

We have already met some of Wiesel's madmen. There is Moché in *Night,* who reports in 1944 that Germans are gassing and burning Jews. But the Jews of Sighet know that Germans don't gas and burn Jews; theirs is the culture of Goethe, Schiller, and Beethoven. Conclusion: Moché is mad, he sees what is not there, he has lost touch with reality.

There is Madame Schächter, locked in the cattle car with other Jews being deported, who screams about "the fire" she sees coming out of great chimneys. There is, of course, no fire; they are locked inside a cattle car. Conclusion: Madame Schächter is mad, she sees what is not there, she has lost touch with reality.

But of course Moché was right: the Nazis *were* gassing and burning Jews. And Madame Schächter was right: there *were* fires, the fires of the crematoria. Drastically revised conclusion: if Moché and Madame Schächter are "mad," it is a case of "moral madness," or "mystical madness," for they see what *is* there, they are the only ones in touch with reality.

At the Eichmann trial, years later, Wiesel was staggered by the ease with which the court was able to certify Eichmann as "sane," and therefore able to stand trial.

> It occurred to me that if he were sane, I should choose madness. It was he or I. For me, there could be no common ground with him. We could not inhabit the same universe or be governed by the same laws. (*Generation*, p. 6)

Who was mad and who was sane in the time of Eichmann? The "sane" people in charge of things were burning babies alive in the camps. "Reality" dictated that Jews be exterminated and that all means of achieving such extermination were permissible. To challenge either assumption was to embrace an unacceptable view of reality, i.e. to be mad.

Under the circumstances, is not madness preferable to sanity?

The "mad" persons in Wiesel's writings, then, are those who see things in a way radically different from other persons, and have the effrontery to speak out, no matter what the cost. The cost is likely to be high, for others cannot cope with such people.

Consider Dan, one of the mad beggars in *A Beggar in Jerusalem*. He goes off to a far country and decides not to return, even though statesmen and presidents plead with him to do so, for they think him brilliant and indispensable. But Dan refuses.

> In the past, you see, man could escape danger, inhumanity, by fleeing to another city, another state or continent. Today there is no place left to go, no place to hide. . . . Not all your scientists put together could guarantee the serenity of a single human being, yet they could easily destroy the last man's last breath on our planet. And still you seriously think that deliberately, of my own free will, I would return to your powder keg? You're all rushing into collective suicide, and you'd like to have me there with you as an accomplice? (pp. 52–53)

How does one cope with such an accusation? The president, on the receiving end of the above communication, and unable to understand such logic mutters, "He is mad, absolutely, incurably mad."

To which one of his ministers responds, "What a brilliant idea."

So they deal with Dan's message not by responding to its substance, but by discrediting its source: Dan is mad, we can ignore his message. A new variation on an old theme: Moché is mad, we can ignore his message; Madame Schächter is mad, we can ignore her message.

Another episode in *A Beggar in Jerusalem* offers further refinement. A mass killing is being carried out by the Nazis. One of the victims refuses to die. Bullets go through him but he is still uninjured. The executioner finally runs out of bullets, and says to the Jew:

> You're humiliating me, you're taking your revenge. One day you'll regret it. You'll speak, but your words will fall on deaf ears. Some will laugh at you, others will try to redeem themselves through you. You'll try to reveal what should remain hidden, you'll try to incite people to learn from the past and rebel, but they will refuse to believe you. They will not listen to you. In the end you'll curse me for having spared you. You'll curse me, because you'll possess the truth, you already do; but it's the truth of a madman. (pp. 94–95)

The passage is as tragic prospectively as it is retrospectively. For not only did Nazis kill Jews in the past; attempts are now being made to deny that Nazis killed Jews in the past, to assert that the Holocaust never happened. In the face of that new development, one must (in the ironically prophetic words of the Nazi executioner) "incite people to learn from the past and rebel," even though "they will refuse to believe you," though "they will not listen to you."

The soldier knows that the Jew will be disbelieved not because he is wrong, *he will be disbelieved because he is right.* He does "possess the truth," but it is a truth so unpalatable that extensive attempts will be made to discredit it because "it's the truth of a madman." Wiesel put the episode on paper in 1967; fifteen years later its prospective relevance is frightening.

A further question: what if the truth of the madman comes from God? "If man be the messenger of man," Wiesel queries, "why should a madman not be the messenger of God?" (*Beggar,* p. 47). An unpleasant suggestion: it would imply that God, too, is mad. Perhaps God is the source of truths too difficult to bear. Wiesel's play *Zalmen, or The Madness of God* raises such a possibility. It is not, ostensibly, a play about God but about Jewish persecution in Russia. Zalmen, the beadle, tries to goad a timid rabbi into protesting the persecutions. The rabbi must do a "mad" thing—speak out against the injustices, even though it means putting himself and his congregation in jeopardy. Zalmen speaks:

> We are the imagination and madness of the world—we are imagination gone mad. One has to be mad today to believe in God and in man—one has to be mad to believe. One has to be mad to want to stay human. Be mad, Rabbi, be mad! (p. 79)

The rabbi finally gives in. With foreign visitors present he speaks out so they can carry the message elsewhere. He has accepted Zalmen's challenge. And, as we have seen earlier, all for naught, it appears. For the state Inspector cleverly decides to ignore the whole episode. "As far as we're concerned—as far as the outside world is concerned—you have done nothing. Your dream was the dream of a madman. Why should we make you into a martyr?" (p. 170).

The play is not subtitled "the madness of Zalmen," or "the madness of the rabbi," but "the madness of God." Perhaps the madness of God is the decision of God to be found among the weak—with those who always seem to be put down (the Jews, to take a not-so-random example), with those whose viewpoint will always be dismissed by the rest as mad (the prophets, to take another not-so-random example), to exhibit the divine presence where least expected and most easily discounted (among madmen, to take the least random example of all). What Nazi bureaucrat, what Soviet inspector, would entertain the notion that his clearly invincible power was subject to the weakness of a God who took part in the suffering of the Jews? Madness.

The atheist Inspector inadvertently puts his finger on a clue: "You're forgetting your God, Rabbi—let Him dream your dreams" (p. 94). The juxtaposition of impossible dream, madness, and God is significant. Perhaps God does "dream the dream," implants it in the hearts of the mad, and calls upon them to share it, using madmen to give an accounting to the world, an accounting appropriately called "the madness of God." If it is mad to believe in persons in a world like ours, it is doubly mad to believe in God in a world like ours. Perhaps only prophets can encourage others to do so.

The category of madness as used by Wiesel comes close again to the biblical concept of prophecy with which we began. What can be said about the vocation of the prophet in the light of this discussion?

1. Since the viewpoint of the prophet and the viewpoint of society are in conflict, the prophet's speech will involve *denunciation*. The temptation of the prophet is always to avoid this: Isaiah was urged by the people to "prophecy to us smooth things," which translates, "Tell us that things are fine," which translates "Don't upset us," which translates, "Don't call upon us to change." Wiesel, and his characters, refuse to comply. Madness.

2. It is not enough just to denounce. Along with denunciation must go *annunciation* (to borrow the category of another prophet of our time, Paulo Freire). There must be annunciation of new hopes and possibilities, the presentation of positive alternatives. If despair must be denounced, then something like hope must be announced. And annunciation is even more devastating than denunciation, for it not only proclaims an alternative but insists that hearers embody the alternative: opt for justice, love your enemy, act compassionately. Madness.

3. Prophetic madness, however, is not sheer caprice; there is a prophetic *tradition*. There are precedents to which to appeal, a certain consistency to the prophetic message in biblical and postbiblical times. Since their contemporaries thought the Old Testament prophets mad, it should not be surprising if modern-day prophets are similarly described. Nor can Christians escape by assuming that this is an exclusive concern of the Hebrew Scriptures. Jesus' own family thought him mad; "beside himself," they said, as they went to rescue him from public embarrassment (Mark 3: 20–21). They had just cause: he was talking about loving enemies in first-century Palestine, turning the other cheek to Roman soldiers, going to Jerusalem when the politicians were out to eliminate troublemakers. Madness.

4. Prophetic madness is consciously aligned with the madness of God. (Paul, a gentler firebrand, merely called it "the foolishness of God," which he then characterized as "wiser than the wisdom of men.") The prophets are characterized by *a special sense of relationship to God;* their alternative vision of reality is not their own creation. They have the effrontery, the dementia, to claim to speak in God's name, legitimating their words with the prefatory formula, "Thus says the Lord . . ." Madness.

They also have the effrontery, the dementia, to contend with God. The Biblical prophets did not gladly accept a word from on high. They were not easy and malleable instruments of the divine fashioning. They challenged God. They asked questions. They were rude. They demanded an accounting.

And who are we to question God? Our little minds were never meant . . . Madness.

And yet, it is those who wrestle, challenge, argue, fight, and sometimes despair, whose affirmations, so hardly won, earn them the right to be heard, whose "word from the Lord" will have a ring of authenticity denied to those who easily and glibly have the divine intention clearly catalogued and itemized. It is this part of the prophetic vocation, the necessity of contention with God, that Wiesel embodies in the entire *corpus* of his writing.

What we need today are those like Elie Wiesel who will not let us rest content with tiny cenceptual schemes, finished systems of thought, political structures that enhance the continuation of an inhuman *status quo,* values that debase persons and exalt products. Only the prophets, the madmen, can wrench us loose, force us to look in new directions; propound the crazy notion that in a presumably materialistic universe we are not just hope turned to dust but also dust turned to hope; insist that to be a Jew, or a Christian, or a Chilean, or a Greek, is not to look at the world exclusively for the benefits that can be garnered for the Jew or the Christian or the Chilean or the Greek, but for all the human family; force us to look at the way we waste and squander and destroy our universe, and then suggest that more important than any private gains we make is the question of how we will bequeath to our children a world that not only has breathable air, but can allow them to breathe that air without terror of the fire or the firing squad, or the simple denial of bread.

No prophetic annunciation in Wiesel is announced simplistically by pat formulas. It receives no vindication by assurances or proofs. Its survival will always be in spite of massive evidence to the contrary. To believe in others will remain an act of madness in a world like ours. To believe in God will compound the madness.

But it may be the only road toward true sanity.

CHAPTER 8

"And Yet, And Yet . . .":
A Small Measure of Victory
(an unlikely journey)

> *There were many periods in our past when we had*
> *every right in the world to turn to God and say,*
> *"Enough. Since You seem to approve of all these*
> *persecutions, all these outrages, have it Your way: let*
> *Your world go on without Jews. Either You are our*
> *partner in history, or You are not. If you are, do Your*
> *share; if You are not, we consider ourselves free of past*
> *commitments. Since You choose to break the Cove-*
> *nant, so be it."*
>
> *And yet, and yet . . . We went on believing, hoping,*
> *invoking His name. . . . We did not give up on Him.*
> *. . . For this is the essence of being Jewish: never to*
> *give up—never to yield to despair.*
> *—A Jew Today, p. 164*

It happens frequently in Wiesel's writings: a story is told, a line of argument is developed, and there is only one possible conclusion. We wait for the verdict to be delivered, curious not as to its content but only as to how it will be stated.

And then, two words intrude, usually repeated: "And yet, and yet . . ." *Et pourtant, et pourtant . . .*

They are less a formula than a signal. They may be Wiesel's most important words. For they signal that conclusions do not have to follow from premises, that directions can be reversed, that there are new possibilities beyond what we anticipated, that we are not locked into ineluctable patterns.

Occasionally the words signal a letdown. We had been hoping for a creative conclusion, and it is denied us. At the end of *Four Hasidic Masters,* Wiesel glowingly describes how the Masters drew people together in community, helped them celebrate, created an atmosphere where dreams could be moulded. Surely, we reason to ourselves, such men must have lived at the pinnacle of celebratory life, full of gladness, secure in friendship. We wait for such a summation. A summation comes, but it is not what we had expected: "And yet, and yet . . . all these Masters who moved others to joy, to new heights of ecstasy, seemed to struggle with melancholy and at times even with despair" (*Masters,* p. 122).

Usually, however, the shift is the other way. We confront situations whose logic would suggest an outcome of melancholy or despair, and yet, and yet, the outcome gives little-used words fresh currency because their value has not been debased by overuse—words like hope, faith, celebration, joy, victory. Defeat is defied, fate frustrated, negation negated.

Like this: having just talked at length about persecutions, pogroms, slaughter, desecration, child-burnings, Wiesel concludes:

> Our people has lost many of its children. We are alone, terribly alone. And sad, terribly sad. We are entering ever more difficult times. The era ahead of us will be critical.
>
> And yet, and yet . . . We owe it to our past not to lose hope. Say what you will, despair is not the solution. Not for us. Quite the contrary. We must show our children that in spite of everything, we keep our faith—in ourselves and even in mankind, though mankind may not be worthy of such faith. We must persuade our children and theirs that three thousand years of history must not be permitted to end with an act of despair on our part. To despair now would be a blasphemy—a profanation. (*A Jew Today,* pp. 166–167)

The point is secure with either illustration: we are not so locked into either sorrow or joy that outcomes stemming from either of them are inevitable. We are freed to expect the unexpected.

But the point is most frequently illustrated when the direction is from negation toward affirmation. When despair is beckoning, hope responds; when anguish is summoned, joy emerges; when mourning is appropriate, celebration intrudes.

How can this be so? Why does the weight of all the evidence not crush the spirit of the messenger, however dauntless he tries to be?

Before proceeding, a caveat: As we claim this unexpected gift and are nurtured by it, let us never claim it in a way that appears to deny the anguish, the pain, the sorrow, that preceded it and within which it nevertheless lifts its voice. *Nothing that preceded it is denied.* No one is entitled to say "And yet, and yet . . ." early in the discussion. It is legitimate only at the end, only in the light of, and in spite of, what came before. To affirm, apart from the strength of the denials, is too cheap. Indeed, it borders on blasphemy, because the pain it discounts is likely to be the pain of others. There is nothing cheap in Wiesel's affirmations; they are paid for with blood and shattered memories. Each preceding page is documentation.

Footnote to the caveat: the caveat is particularly important for Christians, who are usually too eager to move to premature victory statements. Nor must Christians read more into Jewish statements than the statements will bear on their own terms. Example: the last words of Menachem-Mendl, the "Kotzer," were, "At last I shall see Him face to face." To a Christian, the phrase bespeaks serenity, the consummation of a life of devotion, a Pauline victory after seeing only "through a glass darkly." But to the Kotzer, and to Wiesel in interpreting the Kotzer, something different is communicated: "We don't know—nor will we ever know—whether these words expressed an ancient fear or a renewed defiance" (*Souls,* p. 254). No serenity here; the true possibilities were fear . . . or defiance. Let the tension between that and serenity stand as an ecumenical warning.

How then, in the light of all the anguish that precedes it, can there be an unexpected yet affirmative "And yet, and yet . . ."?

First of all, remembering Wiesel's acknowledgment that whatever he has, he has received, we note that the trait is characteristically Hasidic. The *zaddikim* counseled joy for others, whether they attained it themselves or not. It is not in-

consequential that the French title of Wiesel's initial collection
of Hasidic tales is *Célébration hassidique.* The Hasidic message of
celebration is strongly communal, but even if a Jew is isolated,
the affirmation rings true. Wiesel reminds such a one:

> Your experience is not meaningless, it is part of an entity
> that takes it into account. Know that eternity is present in every
> moment; that every table may become altar and every man high
> priest. Know that there is more than one path leading to God,
> but that the surest goes through joy and not through tears.
> Know that God does not like suffering and sadness and least of
> all those that you deliberately inflict upon yourself. God is not
> that complicated; He is not jealous of your happiness nor of the
> kindness that you show to others. On the contrary: the road to
> God goes through man. (*Souls,* p. 208)

Since the call to celebration is Hasidic, it is Jewish also.
"Judaism," Wiesel writes, "teaches us to turn every experience
into a dynamic force. . . . Our strength is in our freedom.
. . . We also have many reasons not to despair. . . . When all
hope is gone, Jews invent new hopes. Even in the midst of
despair, we attempt to justify hope" (*A Jew Today,* pp. 165–
166).

The phrases sing. This is a faith that goes back to the Scriptures themselves and to the Messianic faith with which they are
permeated. Strange faith, this faith in a Messiah who keeps
failing to put in an appearance, and yet (and yet) a persistent
faith, full of hope. Azriel, sole survivor of the pogrom in Kollvillàg, muses toward the end of his life:

> As a child I believed that the Messiah would deliver us from
> all solitude. . . . I was convinced that at the end of night there
> lay redemption. But Satan interfered and man stood by idly.
> Man is strange; he is waiting for the Messiah, yet it is Satan he
> follows.
>
> And yet, and yet. I, an old man with one foot in the grave,
> persist in believing, in proclaiming that the world needs the
> Messiah, that men cannot survive without the hope that one day
> he will come to judge and free them. (*The Oath,* pp. 67–68)

Cause for rejoicing. It is not inconsequential that the French
title of Wiesel's initial collection of biblical tales is *Célébration
biblique.*

The Hasidic and Jewish thrust toward affirmation contains both defiance and creation.

Defiance. Another characteristic phrase used often by Wiesel is the phrase, "in spite of . . ." There is evidence only to sustain despair? We will repudiate despair *in spite of* the evidence. History shows only a record of destructiveness? We will affirm creativity *in spite of* history. Pogroms, you say? We will continue to affirm our destiny *in spite of* pogroms. Death? Even here, we will affirm life *in spite of* death. *Lochaim!*

Ani Maamin, as we saw, offers the most insistent orchestration of the theme. Evidence is mounted with pitiless cumulative force before the very throne of God, a catalogue of cruelties piled on cruelties, with divine indifference to compound the anguish. Sufficient cause, surely, for rebellion and repudiation. But, in spite of all, the poem tells us, Jews continue to affirm, if not God, then their own Jewishness. Seder will continue to be celebrated, belief in one another will be reaffirmed, the Messiah will be awaited in faith, even though he tarry, even should he eventually come . . . too late. So powerful is the "in spite of" that even God, unmoved by everything that has been said, is finally moved by creatures who refuse to be pawns of fate, and instead defy, defy.

No wonder (or, perhaps, amazing wonder) that out of such a heritage Wiesel can say, "I still believe in words. I still believe in language. I still believe in ideas, and in spite of everything I still believe in man. In spite of man, I still believe" ("Directions," TV script, November 14, 1976).

Defiance, but also *creation,* for the point is made positively as well. One does not just defy, believing in spite of everything, one is also *for* joy, *for* hope, *for* celebration. We lack indication that such things abide? In that case let us create them. No hope? Let us invent it. No joy? Let us will its existence. No reason to celebrate? Let us establish occasions to do so.

Again, how Jewish: "We must not forget that during the war, in the ghettos, they were still having weddings, children, circumcisions. They had romances, courtships, celebrations . . ." (*Conversation,* p. 111). The ghettos as such could furnish no reasons for affirmation. But Jews in the ghettos could. And did. If there was no beauty, they created it. If there was no joy, they invented it.

Wiesel saw this spirit exemplified during his first trip to Russia; the episode has become almost normative for him. The oppressive experiences of the centuries were being recapitulated in twentieth-century Soviet society: discrimination, persecution, arrest, execution. But even so, in 1965 during Succot, the rabbi in Leningrad *commanded* the Jews to rejoice. It was an order. They were not to succumb to their oppressive environment. They were not to let someone else determine when they could be glad and when they should be sad. Acknowledging Wiesel's presence as a guest from elsewhere, the rabbi exhorted:

> We must not submit, I tell you! I order you to rejoice, I command you to create a disturbance! . . . A song of gladness for your guest, let him tell of the gladness in our hearts! Do you hear? I tell you . . ."

It is not easy to command people to rejoice; Wiesel reports, "The sentence unfinished, his head fell forward on his chest and he sobbed like a child" (*Silence,* p. 39).

But the celebration took place. It was affirmation. It was defiance. It was creation. Creation of a new thing.

Hasidic, Jewish, but an affirmation as well of the nature of the human spirit, even if not necessarily an affirmation of the nature of the universe in which the human spirit dwells. "In a world of absurdity," Wiesel insists, "we must invent reason; we must create beauty out of nothingness" ("Jewish Values in the Post-Holocaust Future," p. 299). Perhaps there are shattered fragments of beauty that we can reassemble, the "divine sparks" of which earlier *hasidim* spoke, but if not, beauty must be created by us anyhow. "We must show that although there is no hope, we must invent hope" (*Conversation,* p. 111).

There is a strain of Albert Camus in all this, and Wiesel acknowledges the debt:

> [The Jew's] is a Messianic dimension; he can save the world from a new Auschwitz. As Camus would say: one must create happiness to protest against a universe of unhappiness. But— one must *create* it. ("Jewish Values in the Post-Holocaust Future," p. 291)

We recall Pedro, in *The Town Beyond the Wall,* pressing the same theme:

> To say "I suffer, therefore I am" is to become the enemy of man. What you must say is "I suffer, therefore you are." Camus wrote somewhere that to protest against a universe of unhappiness you had to create happiness. That's an arrow pointing the way: it leads to another human being. And not via absurdity. (*Town,* p. 127)

But Wiesel goes beyond Camus. For Camus had to make up a whole universe for himself. Wiesel is the inheritor of a universe, and he stands consciously in a long heritage. For thousands of years, Jews have stood where he now stands, and defined new possibilities as he now does. What is at stake is not only defiance (rolling the same Sisyphean stone interminably up the same mountain) or creation (claiming happiness in so doing); what is at stake is, however modestly proportioned, victory, "a small measure of victory."

> When you live on the edge of the mountain, you see very far. You see the abyss, but you also see very far. And so, because never in human history have people had more reasons to despair, and to give up on man, and God, and themselves, hope is now stronger than ever before. It's irrational; it's absurd, of course. But it may be a way of achieving a certain victory. Not absolute victory. A small measure of victory. (*Victory,* p. 5)

Byron Sherwin, speculating in good Jewish fashion on the mystical meaning of numbers, points out that Wiesel's Auschwitz number, 7713, adds up to 18, and that the number 18 equals *Hai.* Life![1]

How does one get from 7713 to 18? From death to life?

Laughter is a bridge between the two. There is frequent laughter in Wiesel's novels. Much of it is the laughter of madmen. Often it is the laughter of despair acknowledging that all doors are closed. But sometimes it is the laughter of anticipation that new doors are opening. Laughter can negate and laughter can affirm. It is a bridge that joins two worlds.

In discussing Rabbi Nahman of Bratzlav, who laughed a lot, Wiesel creates a catalogue of varieties of laughter. What kind of laughter might Rabbi Nahman's have been? There are many possibilities:

Laughter that springs from lucid and desperate awareness, a mirthless laughter, laughter of protest against the absurdities of existence, a laughter of revolt against a universe where man, whatever he may do, is condemned in advance. A laughter of compassion, for man who cannot escape the ambiguity of his condition and of his faith. To blindly submit to God, without questioning the meaning of this submission, would be to diminish Him. To want to understand Him would be to reduce His intentions, His vision to the level of ours. How then can man take himself seriously? Revolt is not a solution, neither is submission. Remains laughter, metaphysical laughter. (*Souls,* pp. 198–199)

Metaphysical laughter . . . Not an item to be captured by a definition. Perhaps a quality to be illustrated by a story, the *akedah.* We have examined it in a previous chapter, so let us now hear the story behind the story—the story of how the story came to exercise such power over Wiesel. It will get as close as we can get to understanding "metaphysical laughter."

When I say laughter I don't mean comedy. Laughter as defiance. I'll give you an example in Abraham, Isaac, and Jacob, our ancestors, our forefathers. Isaac in Hebrew means Itzhak, he who will laugh. And I was always wondering, why did he get such a silly name? Why would he laugh? And I worked on it very, very hard. The whole holocaust, the binding of Isaac, was always mystifying to me and terrorizing to me. I worked on it many months to write an essay on that, and I came to a very poetic conclusion that in this word, in this name, in this episode could be contained our history. Isaac, the most tragic figure of our history. He has seen his father almost become a killer. He has seen his God who ordered his father to betray him. He has seen the knife. He was the first survivor, after all. So of course he will always be traumatized by that experience, but yet he will be able to laugh.

So laughter becomes a defiance. A defiance and a victory. The only way to be victorious over God is to laugh, not at Him, but with Him. (*Responses,* pp. 155–156)

Laughter *at* God will get us nowhere. But laughter *with* God . . . Where might that take us? Could it, to build on the Isaac episode, help us explore the mystery of suffering? It could at least help us explore suffering in a new fashion. Suffering can never be "justified"—a thousand theodicies to the contrary notwithstanding. Nor, apparently, can suffering be ended, as a thousand experiences confirm. However, by remaining defiant in the face of suffering, seeking to limit it, refusing to accept it as a justifiable end or a necessary means, we can still deal with it. Hear the modern Itzhak, who has laughed with God, as he writes to a young Palestinian Arab:

> Suffering confers neither privileges nor rights; it all depends on how one uses it. If you use it to increase the anguish of others, you are degrading, even betraying it. . . . And yet the day will come—I hope soon—when we shall all understand that suffering can elevate man as well as diminish him. Neither end nor means, it can bring him closer to his truth and his humanity. In the final analysis, it is not given to us to bring suffering to an end—that frequently is beyond us—but we can humanize it. (*A Jew Today*, pp. 105–106)

We have come to the end of a long journey. The last lap of the journey has indeed been "unlikely." There is massive evidence to justify giving way to despair and concluding our journey with a dirge or a requiem. And yet, and yet . . . the messenger urges us to sing a song of joy. There is no absolute victory, he has already told us, but there can be "a small measure of victory." In spite of everything.

Let the messenger himself conclude. He tells us tales about the "holy Seer of Lublin," and how during his lifetime Lublin became a "center for Messianic dreams." Surely, in this holy spot, God's people, caught up in the fervor of Messianic hope, would have a glorious future.

Came the Holocaust. And Lublin, Lublin during the era of the kingdom of night? Listen:

> Lublin, during the darkest hours, became a center for torment and death. Lublin, an ingathering place for condemned Jews, led to nearby Belzec. Lublin meant Majdanek, Lublin meant the great fall not of one man, nor of one people, but of mankind. (*Masters*, p. 95)

So the hopes of the Seer, rather than being realized, were negated. Not only negated. Reduced to zero, trampled upon, ground down, transformed into bitterness and ashes. A tragic conclusion to what had looked like a hopeful tale. Our conclusion.

But we have not heard all. The messenger's conclusion:

> And yet, and yet . . .
>
> What do we learn from all this? We learn that the tale of Lublin survives Lublin, that the beauty of Lublin is mightier than Lublin. . . . The Master may come close to despair, his followers may not. Hasidism is a movement out of despair, away from despair—a movement against despair. Only Hasidism? Judaism too. Who is a Jew? A Jew is he—or she—whose song cannot be muted, nor can his or her joy be killed by the enemy . . . ever. (*Masters,* p. 95)

To which one can only add:

God grant that in that sense, at least, we can all be Jews—those whose songs cannot be muted, nor can our joy be killed by the enemy.

Ever.

Notes

Introduction

1. Cited in Langer, *The Holocaust and the Literary Imagination,* p. 23.

2. Wiesel's third book, *The Accident,* is entitled *Le Jour* (Day) in the original French.

3. David Rousset's phrase in *The Other Kingdom.* I will frequently use the French phrase as a further reminder of the incommensurability between that world and ours.

4. Des Pres, *The Survivors,* p. vi.

5. In addition to indirect autobiography in his fiction, Wiesel is often directly autobiographical elsewhere. This is true of *Night,* his experience in the death camps, and *The Jews of Silence,* the account of his first trip to Russia. The three books of essays contain illuminating autobiographical material. Almost the whole of *Legends of our Time* is so ordered. See also the following essays in *One Generation After:* "Journey's Beginning," "The Watch," "The Violin," "First Royalties," "The Death of my Teacher," "Russian Sketches," and "Excerpts from a Diary"; and the following in *A Jew Today:* "To be a Jew," "An Interview Unlike Any Other," "A Quest for Jerusalem," all nine "Excerpts from a Diary," and "Dodye Feig."

1. Becoming a Messenger

1. Visiting Babi Yar later in the day, Wiesel was forced to point out that the monument, for all its elegant splendor, made no reference to the fact that 85,000 Jews were slaughtered there between Rosh Hashanah and Yom Kippur. They had died in anonymity; they are remembered in anonymity even today.

2. From the Greek, *holo-,* meaning "whole" or "entire," used in the formation of compound words, and *kaustikos,* meaning "burning," so

227

holo-caust, "a complete devastation or destruction, especially by fire, a sacrifice or burnt offering."

3. The two that help the most, complementing one another by their different perspectives, are Raul Hilberg, *The Destruction of the European Jews,* and Lucy Dawidowicz, *The War Against the Jews: 1933–1945.* The Event took place: they speak of it.

4. In Rosenfeld and Greenberg, eds., *Confronting the Holocaust,* p. 51.

5. Steiner, *Language and Silence,* pp. 53–54; cited in Des Pres, *The Survivors,* p. 171.

6. Quoted in Rosenfeld and Greenberg, eds., *Confronting the Holocaust,* p. 163.

7. Ibid.

8. Langer, *The Holocaust and the Literary Imagination,* p. 91.

9. Berenbaum, *The Vision of the Void,* pp. 92, 100.

10. See *Messengers of God* and *Five Biblical Portraits.*

11. These aspects of the vocation of the messenger will be examined in chapter 5, "The Silence of God and the Necessity of Contention."

12. Greenberg, "Polarity and Perfection," *Face to Face,* pp. 12, 14.

2. Darkness that Eclipses Light

1. During the same period *Legends of our Time* (1966), *The Jews of Silence* (1966), and *Zalmen, or The Madness of God* (1968) were also published. Dates are those of the original French versions.

2. The point is even clearer in the French; Wiesel uses *la nuit* explicitly, where the English translation reads "darkness." See *L'Aube,* p. 141.

3. Camus, *Neither Victims nor Executioners,* p. 24.

4. Ibid., p. 25.

5. The English title, although spoiling the progression of the titles *(Night, Dawn, Day),* compounds the irony. Not only is *Day* not really day, but we know that *The Accident* was not really an accident.

6. Buber, *I and Thou,* p. 68.

3. Light that Penetrates Darkness

1. Camus, "The Artist at Work," *Exile and the Kingdom,* pp. 110–158.

2. The Camus quotation: "Man must exalt justice in order to fight against eternal injustice, create happiness in order to protest against the universe of unhappiness." (Camus, *Resistance, Rebellion, and Death,* p. 28.)

3. In the French, Wiesel here uses *l'aurore,* instead of *l'aube,* which he used in his earlier writing. A new reality demands a new vocabulary.

4. Halperin, *Messengers from the Dead,* p. 71.

4. From Auschwitz to Mt. Moriah

1. The books that illustrate this journey are, respectively, many of the essays; *Souls on Fire, Four Hasidic Masters, Somewhere a Master; Ani Maamin;* and *Messengers of God, Five Biblical Portraits,* and *Images from the Bible.*

2. Other Hasidic tales retold in this volume are found on pp. 33, 41.

3. In Rosenfeld and Greenberg, eds., *Confronting the Holocaust,* p. 117. The present discussion is much indebted to Sherwin's essay.

4. For a fuller examination of this point, see Berenbaum, *The Vision of the Void,* pp. 109–117, which is critical of Wiesel, and my more affirmative comments in chapter 5 below.

5. See the further discussion of this theme in chapter 5.

6. Russia assumes increasing importance in Wiesel's later writings. In addition to *The Jews of Silence,* the journalistic account of his first visit, see *Legends of our Time,* pp. 179–197; *One Generation After,* pp. 176–181; and *A Jew Today,* pp. 24–25, 47–51, 114–121. Both of the plays, *Zalman, or The Madness of God* and *The Trial of God,* are situated in Russia. The most recent novel, *The Testament,* is the story of Jews in Russia over a span of half a century.

7. See the further development of this theme in chapter 7 below.

8. This material was set in type before the Israeli actions in Lebanon in the summer and fall of 1982. Since then, Wiesel has joined fellow Jews and others in anguished cries about the nature of Israel's military policy.

5. The Silence of God

1. Rubenstein, *After Auschwitz,* especially chs. 1–4, 13–14.

2. For a careful appraisal, see Berenbaum, *The Vision of the Void,* pp. 110–117.

6. Birkenau and Golgatha

1. We possess accounts of this meeting by both Mauriac and Wiesel. See the "Foreword" by Mauriac in *Night,* pp. 7–11, and *A Jew Today,* pp. 16–20.

2. Hilberg, *The Destruction of the European Jews,* pp. 3–4.

3. Morley, *Vatican Diplomacy and the Jews during the Holocaust, 1939–1943,* p. 209.

4. Bonhoeffer, *Ethics,* p. 113.

5. Cited in Littell, *The German Phoenix,* p. 189.

6. *Declaration on the Relationship of the Church to Non-Christian Religions,* 4. *The Documents of Vatican II,* pp. 666–667.

7. In Fleischner, ed., *Auschwitz; Beginning of a New Era?,* p. 23.

8. Moltmann, *The Crucified God,* p. 278. I have indicated in my preface to their otherwise illuminating volume, *Long Night's Journey into Day,* that I do not share the strictures of Alice and Roy Eckardt against Moltmann's effort.

9. Küng, *On Being a Christian,* p. 169.

10. Metz, *The Emergent Church,* pp. 17–33.

11. There has been a whole literature of Christian response too vast to be documented here. Writers who have made notable contributions are, among many others: Gregory Baum, Harry James Cargas, Alice and Roy Eckardt, Thomas Idinopulos, Franklin Littell, John Pawlikowski, John Roth, Rosemary Ruether, Michael Ryan, J. Coert Rylersdaam, Krister Stendhal, Leonard Swidler, and Robert Willis.

12. Reported in my *Creative Dislocation—The Movement of Grace,* pp. 28–29.

7. The Struggle of Light Against Darkness

1. Heschel, *The Prophets,* p. 408.

8. "And Yet, and Yet. . ."

1. In Cargas, ed., *Responses to Elie Wiesel,* p. 146.

Bibliography

The basic bibliography for Wiesel's work through 1974 is Molly Abramowitz, *Elie Wiesel: A Bibliography*, Metuchen, NJ: The Scarecrow Press, 1974. A helpful "selected bibliography" can be found in Alvin H. Rosenfeld and Irving Greenberg, eds., *Confronting the Holocaust: The Impact of Elie Wiesel*, Bloomington, IN; Indiana University Press, 1978, pp. 207–212.

Books by Wiesel in English

Most of Wiesel's books have been published in a number of hardcover and paperback editions. The writings after *Night* fall into four major categories: fiction, historical exploration, drama, and essays. (In the references below, the initial date indicates the year of publication in French or English, and the data following indicates the edition from which quoted material is cited.)

Night (*La Nuit*, 1958), New York, NY; Avon Books, 1969, is Wiesel's account of his own experience in Birkenau, Auschwitz, Buna, and Buchenwald. It is the basic resource out of which all the subsequent writings are drawn. It should be read first.

Fiction: The novels should be read in chronological order so that the reader may accompany Wiesel, at however distant a remove, through his journey from the reality of nihilism toward the possibility of affirmation.

Dawn (*L'Aube*, 1960), New York, NY; Avon Books, 1970, is the story of Elisha, a post-Holocaust Jew who joins the guerilla

231

forces, goes to Palestine, and exchanges the role of victim for that of executioner.

The Accident (*Le Jour*, 1961), New York, NY; Avon Books, 1970. Eliezer, a post-Holocaust Jew now living in New York, employs various strategies of flight, including a suicide attempt, in trying to cope with his destructive past.

The Town Beyond the Wall (*La Ville de la chance*, 1962), New York, NY; Avon Books, 1969. The possibilities of human engagement and participation appear for the first time, following explorations of madness and the role of the spectator.

The Gates of the Forest (*Les Portes de la Foret*, 1964), New York, NY; Avon Books, 1967. The reality of communion between two persons is extended toward community with others—and with God.

A Beggar in Jerusalem (*Le Mendiant de Jérusalem*, 1968), New York, NY: Avon Books, 1971. A fictionalized treatment of the Six Day War that sweeps back and forth across the whole span of Jewish history.

The Oath (*Le Serment de Kolvillàg*, 1973), New York, NY: Random House, 1973. The story of a pogrom in middle Europe in the 1920s that raises the agonizing question of whether silence might be a more appropriate response to human evil than speech.

The Testament (*Le Testament d'un Poete Juif Assassine*, 1980), New York, NY: Summit Books, 1981. Surveys half a century of European history in recounting the story of a Russian Jew torn between loyalty to Judaism and communism.

Historical exploration: As the contemporary Jews in Wiesel's novels struggle with the question, "What does it mean to be a Jew in the present?" they are increasingly forced to ask, "What did it mean to be a Jew in the past?" Wiesel's own recovery of his Hasidic heritage is developed in *Souls on Fire* (*Celebration hassidique*, 1972), New York, NY; Random House, 1972; *Four Hasidic Masters and Their Struggle Against Melancholy*, Notre Dame, IN: University of Notre Dame Press, 1978, and in *Somewhere a Master*, New York, NY: Summit Books, 1982. His explorations of the Biblical material are found in *Messengers of God* (*Celebration biblique*, 1975), New York, NY: Random House, 1976, *Five Biblical Portraits*, Notre Dame, IN: University of

Notre Dame Press, 1981, both of which contain extensive material from the midrash, and *Images from the Bible,* Woodstock, NY: The Overlook Press, 1980, which contains many reproductions of the paintings of Shalom of Safed. (Another instance of the use of midrashic material is *Ani Maamin,* referred to below.)

Drama: Zalmen, or The Madness of God (Zalmen ou La Folie de Dieu, 1968), New York, NY: Random House, 1974, is a play about persecuted Jews in Russia, and deals with pressures on a rabbi to speak out in the presence of foreigners, and the resultant action on the part of the state. *Ani Maamin: A Song Lost and Found Again,* New York, NY: Random House, bilingual edition, 1974, is the libretto for a cantata set to music by Darius Milhaud, and describes the encounter between the patriarchs and the inhabitant of the Divine Throne over the plight of Jews during the Holocaust. *The Trial of God (Le Procès de Shamgorod,* 1978), New York, NY: Random House, 1979, details the aftermath of a pogrom in Russia in 1649, in which God is put on trial by Berish, one of the two survivors, for crimes against humanity.

Essays: Legends of our Time (Chants des Morts, 1966), New York, NY: Avon Books, 1970, deals with a variety of topics including considerable autobiographical material both pre- and post-Auschwitz. *The Jews of Silence* (1966, originally a series of articles written in Hebrew for *Yediot Aharanot)* New York, NY: Signet Books, 1967, is an extended account of Wiesel's first visit to Soviet Jewry. *One Generation After (Entre Deux Soleils,* 1970), New York, NY: Random House, 1970, contains essays centering around the quarter-century "anniversary" of the world's discovery of Auschwitz. *A Jew Today (Un Juif Aujourd'hui,* 1978), New York, NY: Random House, 1978, offers Wiesel's reflections on a variety of themes (South Africa, Vietnam, the Sahel, Bangladesh) from his uniquely Jewish perspective.

Other Writings, Interviews, and Talks by Wiesel Cited in the Text

"Jewish Values in the Post-Holocaust Future: A Symposium." *Judaism* 16 (1967), pp. 266–299.

A Small Measure of Victory. An interview with Elie Wiesel by Gene Koppell and Henry Kaufman. Pamphlet, University of Arizona, 1974.

"Talking and Writing and Keeping Silent." In *The German Church Struggle and the Holocaust,* edited by Franklin H. Littell and Hubert G. Locke, pp. 269–277. Detroit: Wayne State University Press, 1974.

Harry James Cargas in Conversation with Elie Wiesel. New York: Paulist Press, 1976.

"Art and Culture after the Holocaust." In *Auschwitz: Beginning of a New Era? Reflections on the Holocaust,* edited by Eva Fleischner, pp. 403–416. New York: KTAV Publishing House, 1977.

"Freedom of Conscience—A Jewish Commentary." *Journal of Ecumenical Studies* 14 (1977), pp. 638–649.

Dimensions of the Holocaust. Evanston: Northwestern University Press, 1978. Wiesel's contribution is on pp. 5–17.

Responses to Elie Wiesel, edited by Harry James Cargas. Interviews with Wiesel on pp. 9–12 and 150–157. New York: Persea Books, 1978.

"Why I Write." In *Confronting the Holocaust: The Impact of Elie Wiesel,* edited by Alvin H. Rosenfeld and Irving Greenberg, pp. 200–206. Bloomington: Indiana University Press, 1978.

"Then and Now: The Experience of a Teacher." *Social Education* 42 (1978), pp. 266–271.

"A Personal Response." *Face to Face: An Interreligious Bulletin* 6 (1979), pp. 35–37.

Days of Remembrance. Pamphlet, National Civic Holocaust Commemoration Ceremony, April 24, 1979. Wiesel's contribution is on pp. 13–18.

Fine, Ellen. "Dialogue with Elie Wiesel." *Counterpoint* 4:1 (Fall 1980) pp. 19–25.

"Recalling Swallowed-up Worlds." *Christian Century* 98 (May 27, 1981), pp. 609–612.

Other Works Cited in the Text

Abbott, Walter M., S.J., ed. *The Documents of Vatican II.* New York: Association Press, 1966.

Berenbaum, Michael. *The Vision of the Void: Theological Reflections on the Works of Elie Wiesel.* Middletown, CT: Wesleyan University Press, 1979.

Bonhoeffer, Dietrich. *Ethics.* London: SCM Press, 1955.

Brown, Robert McAfee. *Creative Dislocation—The Movement of Grace.* Nashville: Abingdon, 1980.

Buber, Martin. *I and Thou.* New York: Charles Scribner's Sons, 1970.

Camus, Albert. *Exile and the Kingdom.* New York: Knopf, 1958.

———. *Neither Victims Nor Executioners.* Chicago: World Without War Publications, 1972.

———. *Resistance, Rebellion, and Death.* New York: Knopf, 1961.

Dawidowicz, Lucy. *The War Against the Jews 1933–1945.* New York: Holt, Rinehart, and Winston, 1975.

Des Pres, Terence. *The Survivors.* New York: Oxford University Press, 1976.

Eckardt, Alice and Roy Eckardt. *Long Night's Journey Into Day.* Detroit: Wayne State University Press, 1982.

Fleischner, Eva, ed. *Auschwitz—Beginning of a New Era? Reflections on the Holocaust.* New York: KTAV Publishing House, 1977.

Halperin, Irving. *Messengers from the Dead.* Philadelphia: Westminster Press, 1970.

Heschel, Abraham. *The Prophets.* New York: Jewish Publication Society, 1962.

Hilberg, Raul. *The Destruction of the European Jews.* New York: Harper and Row, 1961.

Küng, Hans. *On Being A Christian.* New York: Doubleday, 1976.

Langer, Lawrence L. *The Holocaust and the Literary Imagination.* New Haven: Yale University Press, 1975.

Littell, Franklin H. *The German Phoenix.* New York: Doubleday, 1960.

Metz, Johannes B. *The Emergent Church.* New York: The Crossroad Publishing Company, 1981.

Moltmann, Jürgen. *The Crucified God.* New York: Harper and Row, 1974.

Morley, John F. *Vatican Diplomacy and the Jews During the Holocaust, 1939–1943.* New York: KTAV Publishing House, 1980.

Rosenfeld, Alvin H., and Irving Greenberg, eds. *Confronting the Holocaust: The Impact of Elie Wiesel.* Bloomington: Indiana University Press, 1978.

Rousset, David. *The Other Kingdom.* New York: Reynal and Hitchcock, 1947.

Roth, John K. *A Consuming Fire: Encounters with Elie Wiesel and the Holocaust.* Atlanta: John Knox Press, 1979.

Rubenstein, Richard. *After Auschwitz.* Indianapolis: Bobbs-Merrill, 1966.

Van Buren, Paul M. *Discerning the Way: A Theology of the Jewish-Christian Reality.* New York: Seabury Press, 1980.

General Index

237

Index of Names

241

Writings by Wiesel